Steam Yachts at War

STEAM YACHTS AT WAR

The Naval Deployment of British & American Armed Yachts 1898–1918

Steve R Dunn

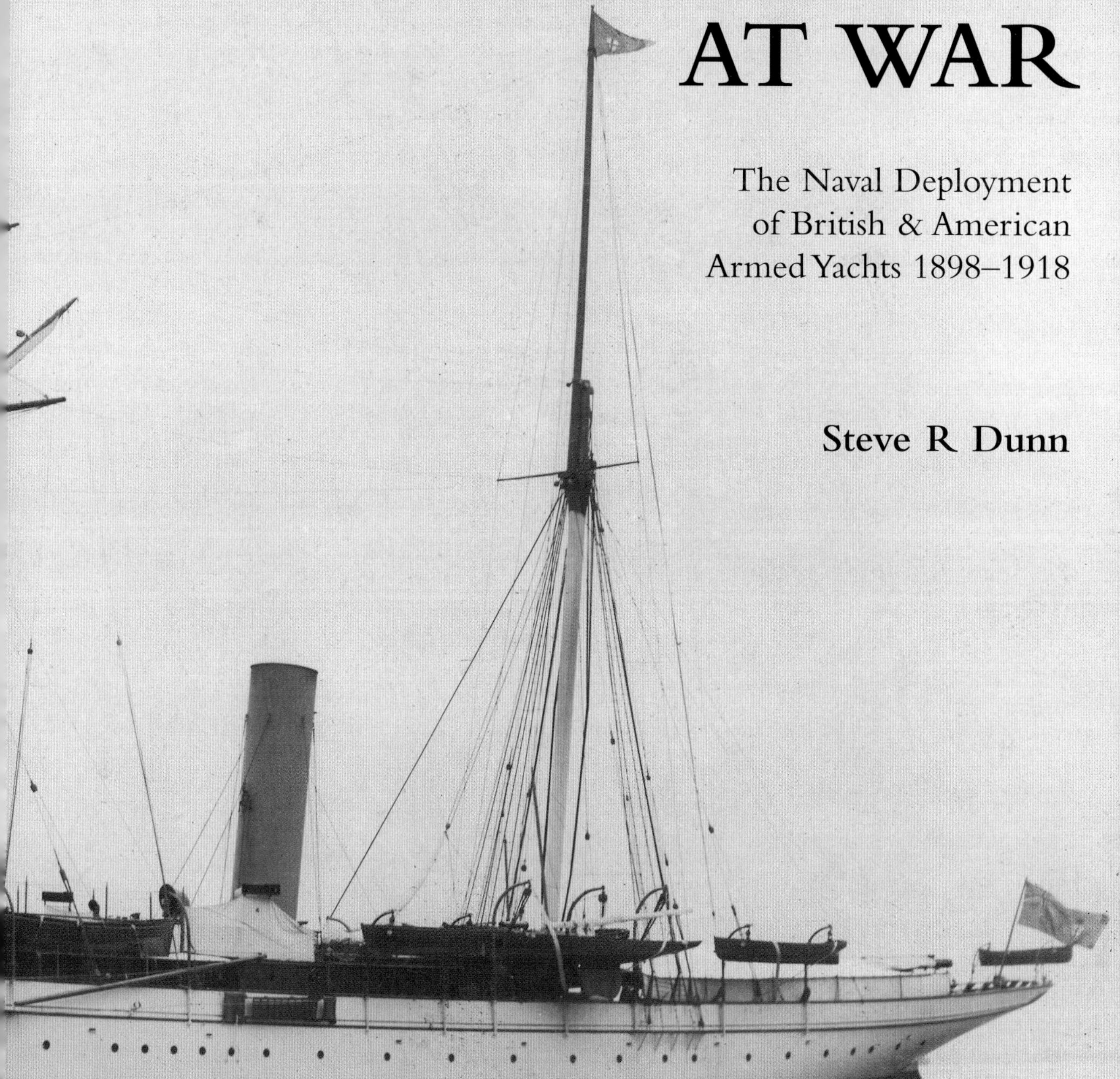

Seaforth
PUBLISHING

Title pages: A photograph by Debenham of Cowes of SY *Rona*, which later became HMY *Gossia*. The various launches and yachts that she carried can be seen in her davits. *(Alice Wood Collection)*

By the same author

The Petrol Navy: British, American and Other Naval Motor Boats at War, 1914–1920
The Harwich Striking Force: The Royal Navy's Front Line in the North Sea, 1914–1918
British Naval Trawlers and Drifters in Two World Wars
The Power and the Glory: Royal Navy Fleet Reviews from Earliest Times to 2005
Battle in the Baltic: The Royal Navy and the Fight to Save Estonia and Latvia, 1918–1920
Southern Thunder: The Royal Navy and the Scandinavian Trade in World War One
Bayly's War: The Battle for the Western Approaches in World War One
Securing the Narrow Sea: The Dover Patrol, 1914–1918
Blockade: Cruiser Warfare and the Starvation of Germany
Formidable: A True Story of Disaster and Courage
The Coward? The Rise and Fall of the Silver King
The Scapegoat: The Life and Tragedy of a Fighting Admiral and Churchill's role in his death

www.steverdunn.com

First published in Great Britain in 2024 by
Seaforth Publishing,
A division of Pen & Sword Books Ltd,
George House, Beevor Street, Barnsley S71 1HN
www.seaforthpublishing.com

British Library Cataloguing in Publication Data
A catalogue record for this book is available from the British Library

ISBN 978 1 3990 5972 5 (hardback)
ISBN 978 1 3990 5973 2 (epub)
ISBN 978 1 3990 5974 9 (kindle)

Pen & Sword Books Limited incorporates the imprints of Atlas, Archaeology, Aviation, Discovery, Family History, Fiction, History, Maritime, Military, Military Classics, Politics, Select, Transport, True Crime, Air World, Frontline Publishing, Leo Cooper, Remember When, Seaforth Publishing, The Praetorian Press, Wharncliffe Local History, Wharncliffe Transport, Wharncliffe True Crime and White Owl

Typeset and designed by Stephen Dent

Printed and bound in India by Replika Press Pvt Ltd

FSC www.fsc.org MIX Paper | Supporting responsible forestry FSC™ C016779

CONTENTS

Dedication

For Eve and Joseph Clark: may they sail through life.

'Anyone who has to ask about the annual upkeep of a yacht can't afford one.'

J P Morgan, attr in Chaneles S, *The New Civility*, p.123

'My yachts were, I suppose, outstanding status symbols.'

J Paul Getty

'I want a fine little steam yacht
Just yours and mine little steam yacht
Sailing over the Summer seas with gladsome song.
We'll have a captain and crew dear, Then you'll have nothing to do dear,
Nothing to do but love me all day long.'

Refrain from *I Want a Fine Little Steam Yacht*,
song by Paul West and Herman Avery Wade (1908)

'Don't you think it would be splendid to do something for one's country? Normally, alas, I'm an idle man on the whole I fear, but this is a chance of useful action.'

Yachtsman and author Erskine Childers to his sister Dulcibella
(quoted in Ring, *Erskine Childers*, p.58)

ABBREVIATIONS

AA anti-aircraft

A/S anti-submarine

HMY His Majesty's Yacht

HP horse power. One horse power equals 33,000 foot-pounds per minute.

- NHP nominal horse power was an early nineteenth-century rule of thumb used to estimate the power of steam engines. It assumed a steam pressure of 7 psi.
- BHP brake horsepower is the power measured using a brake (load) dynamometer at a specified location, such as the crankshaft or output shaft of the transmission.
- IHP indicated horse power is the theoretical power produced in a reciprocating engine if it is completely frictionless in converting the expanding gas energy in the cylinders.

GRT Gross Register Tons (a measure of capacity)

Knots Nautical Miles per Hour. A nautical mile is 1,852m, 6,076ft or 1.151 miles.

MMR Mercantile Marine Reserve

QF Quick firer

RN Royal Navy

RNR Royal Naval Reserve

RNVR Royal Naval Volunteer Reserve

RYS Royal Yacht Squadron, a prestigious sailing club based at Cowes, Isle of Wight.

SNO Senior Naval Officer

SY Steam Yacht

T-124 mercantile terms of engagement into the Royal Navy that protected some rights previously held but made the seafarer subject to naval discipline.

TM Thames Measurement (an old tonnage measurement for race handicapping purposes and port dues)

USN United States Navy

USNRF United States Naval Reserve Force

USS United States Ship

PREFACE

THIS IS THE STORY of how rich men's playthings became weapons of war. Steam yachts were the peacock tail-feathered, must have, luxury item of the late nineteenth and early twentieth century. But when wars came, in 1898 and 1914, they suddenly transformed into warships and often their crews became warriors, not servants.

Steam yachts became possible because of a concatenation of three factors. Firstly, the development of a relatively small, reliable and powerful marine steam engine as a result of the invention of the triple-expansion system. Secondly, the growth of yachting and the yacht club as places of status and display, much favoured and patronised by British and European royalty. And finally, the very considerable wealth of a small number of landed aristocrats and *nouveau riche* businessmen, especially in the United States of America.

They were the epitome of wealth and the symbol of standing, the Learjets of their day. Hugely expensive to build and run, fitted out like waterborne palaces, they gave their owners privacy, the ability to travel wherever they pleased without let or hindrance, and membership of an exclusive stratum of society.

But when wars came – for America in 1898 and 1917, for Britain in 1914 – steam yachts became a stopgap navy, filling in for neglected investment in small craft or for dubious strategic assumptions. Their wonderful fitments were ripped out, antiquated guns and sometimes depth charges were fitted, and their crews signed into the naval reserves. Around the coasts of the USA, Britain and France, in the Mediterranean and elsewhere they fought an often unseen enemy; and men lived and died on them in ways never dreamed of when they were constructed.

But the First World War, in which many yachts served, also terminated their brief efflorescence of existence. Post-war, labour costs, construction prices and the eventual proliferation of commercial aviation, ended their pomp with only few exceptions. Rolls-Royce motor cars, private aeroplanes and luxury, fast, cruise liners took their place.

This book tells the story of the use of private steam yachts in war, the Spanish-American War of 1898 and the global conflict of 1914–18. It examines the peacetime origins of the yachts and their owners and designers before considering the use, success and loss of the now navalised steam yacht in maritime conflict. They were beautiful craft and this volume is richly illustrated with pictures and plans of them, in war and at peace.

The narrative is not necessarily in chronological order but rather ordered by topic. Naval ranks are given as at the time of the action described. The twenty-four-hour clock is used throughout for clarity; where ante or post meridian was given in the original documents, the time has been converted. Confusingly, many yachts went under several names during their lives, or the same name was used on several successive yachts, and certain appellations such as *Venetia* or *Sapphire* seem to have been very popular. Hopefully, the text makes clear which vessel is being referred to. A date in brackets after the name of a ship is the year in which it was launched.

Finally, a note on size. Warships were measured in displacement tonnage, cargo vessels in gross register tons (grt) and yachts in one of two ways; gross register tons or Thames Measurement (TM). The latter was an arcane system, originally used for handicapping purposes in yacht racing, but common at the time. I have chosen to use grt wherever possible, for reasons of simplicity.

CHAPTER ONE

THE RISE OF THE STEAM YACHT

YACHTING AND YACHTS reached the acme of their popularity, and gained the imprimatur of European royalty to become the 'sport of kings', during the 'long nineteenth century', say 1800 to 1914.

It was King Charles II who first popularised the yacht in the seventeenth century. While in exile in Holland, the king had become enamoured of the Dutch vessel known as a *jacht*. Charles' early experience of Dutch *jachts* led him to desire similar vessels for himself. His return to the English throne was celebrated by the city of Amsterdam, which presented him with a luxurious 60ft yacht, including a crew of twenty, named the *Mary*. The first English-built yacht was the *Katherine*, of 49ft length at the keel and 19ft beam. By 1685 there were twenty yachts in the royal squadron (there would be twenty-five over the two reigns of Charles and his brother James), including one specially built and launched in 1670 for Queen Henrietta, named *Saudadoes* ('greetings to you' in Portuguese), although only seven were truly royal and assigned to the immediate service of the king and his family.

Soon the first organised regatta took place, a forty-mile race on the Thames in 1661 between *Katherine* and *Anne*, James, Duke of York's new yacht. The king himself was at the helm of *Katherine* – and unsurprisingly won. A new sport was born.

After that, the association between royalty and yachts continued down the ages. George III enjoyed his yachts, William IV had been a Royal Navy officer and liked to sail, Queen Victoria loved her maritime excursions and particularly Cowes week. Edward VII, as prince of Wales and king, was an ever present at Cowes and relished the racing, as did his son, George V. Yachting and sailing had royal endorsement.

With the rise of sailing came the yacht club. By the 1800s yachting had grown to include the world's wealthiest men. Yacht clubs began to form in

The ensign and burgee of the Royal Yacht Squadron.

William IV, who put the 'squadron' into the RYS name, painted by Sir Martin Archer Shee, *circa* 1800. *(Author's collection)*

the eighteenth century to accommodate the new interest shown, and to codify and establish races and rules. The first yacht club in the world, called the Cork Water Club, later the Royal Cork,* was established in Ireland in 1720, followed by the Lough Ree Yacht Club in 1770 (again in Ireland), and the Starcross Yacht Club in 1772 in England.

Probably the most famous of all the English yacht clubs, The Royal Yacht Squadron, was founded on 1 June 1815 at the Thatched House Tavern in St James's, London, as 'The Yacht Club' by forty-two gentlemen interested in yachting. It welcomed the Prince Regent as a member in 1817. Three

* With a clubhouse built in 1854 to the designs of Anthony Salvin, the go-to architect for the minor aristocracy.

* The 'Upper Ten Thousand' were generally taken to be those families who appeared in Edward Walford's *Country Families and Untitled Aristocracy*, first published in 1860.

The Clyde-built yacht *Thistle*, unsuccessful Scottish challenger of the seventh America's Cup in 1887. She was built for, and owned by, a syndicate of owners from the Royal Clyde Yacht Club. *Thistle* was sold to Kaiser Wilhelm II in 1891, becoming *Meteor*. *(Author's collection)*

years later, when the Regent became George IV, it was entitled the Royal Yacht Club. The club organised yacht racing as part of its annual regatta, which eventually became known as 'Cowes Week'. And in 1833 William IV renamed the club The Royal Yacht Squadron. The Squadron hosted royal visitors of many nations over the years, and maintained strong links with the British monarchy and Royal Navy. Members' yachts were given the suffix RYS to their names and permitted to fly the White Ensign of the Royal Navy.

Anybody who was, or wanted to be, anybody belonged to the RYS. Cowes Week was a key part of 'The Season' when the rich and the titled (and entitled) paraded at Goodwood, Ascot, The Derby, Henley, etc. These were the display and mating zones of the Upper Ten Thousand – the term used in the late nineteenth century to denote Britain's ruling elite – and Cowes became the social event of the season.* During the commodoreship of Edward, Prince of Wales (1882–92), Cowes week was the zenith of the social season and every August the Solent was thronged with steam yachts,

which became floating house parties for old and new money alike. There were Brasseys with *Sunbeam*, Guinnesses on *Cetonia*, Jameses with *Lancashire Witch*, Revelstokes in *Waterwitch*.

Edward himself was an annual visitor and usually stayed at Nubia House, the Isle of Wight home of Sir Godfrey Baring, scion of the banking family, member of parliament for the island, and elected to the Royal Yacht Squadron in 1892. Here, with his wife Eva Hermione, he entertained visiting royalty who enjoyed the house and its extensive grounds, tennis courts and slightly nautical air; the late evening meal was announced with the cry 'all hands fore and aft, both sides amidships, get your suppers'.[1]

The German Emperor brought his *Meteor*, the 1887 ex-America's Cup challenger *Thistle,* to Cowes in 1892. This encouraged Edward Prince of Wales to build *Britannia*, one of the most successful racing yachts of the time. Lord Crawford's* beautiful ship-rigged steam yacht *Valhalla*, built by Ramage & Ferguson at Leith, cruised far afield and was a noted visitor in Cowes Week. She was also a competitor in the 1905 Transatlantic Race for the German Emperor's Cup. RYS member Ernest Wythes paid £50,000 (around £7 million today) to build the steam yacht *St George*, especially so that he and some friends could sail around the world.

Yacht clubs sprang up all over Britain and attracted noble and wealthy

King Edward VII's yacht *Britannia*, a gaff-rigged cutter built in 1893 for him when, as Prince of Wales, he was Commodore of the Royal Yacht Squadron. Between 1892 and 1895, Wilhelm II raced *Meteor* against *Britannia* each year at Cowes Week. Being a more experienced yachtsmen and having the faster vessel, Edward won all the races comfortably.

King George V also raced in her and it was his dying wish that his beloved yacht follow him to the grave. Accordingly, she was sunk in St Catherine's deep, near the Isle of Wight, in 1936. *(Author's collection)*

* James Lindsay, 26th Earl of Crawford.

The three-masted auxiliary steam yacht *Valhalla* (1892), painted in 1901 by Antonio de Simone. She was famous for her participation in the Kaiser's Trans-Atlantic Race of 1905, when she came third. *Valhalla* had several owners, most notably Joe Laycock, a transatlantic racing yachtsman and Olympian, and Lord Crawford, who used her as a research vessel on three major voyages from 1902 to 1908. *(Author's collection)*

members and patrons. The Royal Harwich Yacht Club boasted Queen Victoria as its patron from 1847 to 1901, followed by King George V between 1911 and 1936. The Harwich Regattas had become the opening event for each season's 'Big Yacht Class' and attracted most of the famous racing yachts of the time, including *Britannia*.

Or consider the Royal Western Yacht Club. Founded as the Port of Plymouth Royal Clarence Regatta Club in 1827, it became the Royal Western in 1833. Its original aims were to hold an annual regatta, to organise an active social programme and to stimulate improvements in naval architecture through yacht racing. In its early years its principal strength was in long-distance cruising and its members' yachts, wearing the Blue Ensign* – a privilege given to them in a Warrant granted by Queen Victoria – were to be seen in many far-flung places.

* Prior to the reorganisation of the Royal Navy in 1864, the plain Blue Ensign had been the ensign of one of three squadrons of the Royal Navy, the Blue Squadron. This changed in 1864, when an Order in Council provided that the Red Ensign was to be allocated to merchantmen, the Blue Ensign to be the flag of ships in public service or were commanded by an officer in the Royal Naval Reserve, and the White Ensign was allocated to the Navy. Thus, after 1864, the plain Blue Ensign was permitted to be worn, instead of the Red Ensign, by three categories of civilian vessel. Firstly, British merchant vessels whose officers and crew included a certain number of retired Royal Navy personnel or Royal Naval Reservists, or commanded by an officer of the Royal Naval Reserve in possession of a government warrant. Secondly, Royal Research Ships by warrant, whether manned by former Royal Navy personnel or Merchant Navy personnel. And thirdly, British-registered yachts belonging to members of a defined list of yacht clubs, thirty-four in number, including eleven in the antipodes.

The Royal Corinthian Yacht Club was founded on the Thames in 1872 with the objective of encouraging amateur yacht sailing. And as a final example, the Royal Temple Yacht Club was established in 1857 by a group of yachtsmen sailing from the Temple Steps, on the River Thames in the centre of London. Club racing started on the Thames but increasing commercial traffic on the river made racing increasingly difficult. Races began to be moved further and further down the river, until eventually it was decided that a more suitable base for competitions should be found. This proved to be at Ramsgate, where a new clubhouse was opened in 1896. At the turn of the century 2,000 members dined annually at the Hotel Cecil.* The Commodore at that time was Baron Nathaniel Mayer de Rothschild, who was always accompanied by his close friend, Edward, Prince of Wales. A Royal Charter was granted in 1897 and the Admiralty Warrant to wear the Blue Ensign was given in 1898.

The growth of yacht clubs and racing brought the need for a unified code of conduct. In 1875, the Yacht Racing Association agreed a set of rules that would govern what were then called 'sailing matches' – rules that are broadly the same today.

* A grand hotel built in 1890–96 between the Thames Embankment and the Strand in London. Shell-Mex House now stands on the site.

Another painting of *Valhalla*, by Charles Dixon. It depicts the yacht at Portsmouth with HMS *Victory* in the background. *Valhalla* was reputed to be the only British steam yacht to carry a full ship rig. Designed by W C Storey, she was believed by many to have been the finest example of a steam auxiliary ever built. *(Author's collection)*

Nor was this love of yachting and sailing confined to Britain. In France, the *Société des Régates de Cannes* was founded in 1860 by Léopold Bucquet and Eugène Tripet-Skripitzine, who was French Consul in Moscow. Lord Brougham was the first honorary president. Under the persuasion of the Duc de Vallombrosa, the *Société* acquired land along the sea shore of La Croisette, Cannes, and built the *Cercle Nautique*, which was opened in 1864. Regattas were sponsored by such as the Duc de Vallombrosa, Duc de Brabant, King Léopold II of Belgium, Tsar Nicholas II of Russia and the Grand Duke of Mecklenburg-Schwerin.

In 1893, a breakaway body was formed, *Union des Yachtsmen des Cannes*, run by the Marquis de la Rochechouart. They invited Edward, Prince of Wales, to dinner at the *Cercle Nautique* when he was in Cannes. Among the guests were American financier Baron de Hirsch and the keen yachtsman Ogden Goelet, a wealthy American inheritee and member of the New York Yacht Club who for four years leased Lily Langtry's yacht *White Ladye* for socialising. He had used it to meet Edward, and also Queen Victoria when she was in Nice, and married off his daughter Mary to Henry Innes-Ker, 8th Duke of Roxburghe.

Yacht clubs sprang up in the USA, too. The most prestigious was the New York Yacht Club,* founded in 1844 and home to the prestigious America's Cup Race from 1851. It kept its caste pure by only allowing a person to be a member by invitation.

The San Francisco Yacht Club originated in 1869, the Carolina YC on Charleston Harbour in 1883 and the Annapolis Yacht Club in 1886. Soon the American littoral was crowded with yachting clubhouses and their vessels.

And in India, the Bombay Yacht Club opened its doors in 1846; it became 'Royal' in 1876 and built a seafront clubhouse five years later. Even further away, a club was established in Hong Kong in 1869 that became the Royal Hong Kong Yacht Club in 1894.

* Today it is considered one of the three most exclusive yacht clubs in the world.

An unknown (but beautiful) steam yacht moored by the pavilion of the Royal Norfolk and Suffolk Yacht Club at Lowestoft. *(Author's collection)*

The three-masted auxiliary screw steam yacht *St George* was owned by one of the youngest members of the RYS, Ernest Wythes, who commissioned it 'for something to do when he came down from Oxford'. She was built at Leith by Ramage & Ferguson to combine strength and sailing qualities for navigation in distant seas, with elegance and luxurious accommodation. Wythes and six friends sailed around the world in her between 1891 and 1892, with a crew of thirty-seven – and nine stewards! *(Author's collection)*

Running a large racing or pleasure yacht was costly. Paid crews were necessary, servants and cooks if touring; berths and moorings were expensive. Thus money, aristocracy and yachting went hand in hand. No surprise then that yacht clubs were seen as exclusive, snobbish and expensive. But an even better way to spend money and demonstrate that one had it to burn (quite literally) had begun to emerge in the 1830s – the steam yacht.

The Birth of the Steam Yacht

We might start the story of the development of the steam yacht with a man called Thomas Assheton Smith, son of a father of the same name. Born in 1775, Assheton Smith was educated at Eton, where he played cricket for the first eleven, and Christ Church, Oxford, where he joined the Bullingdon Club, and was a prominent member of the University cricket side of 1796.

He was also exceedingly wealthy, the family riches coming from their ownership of slate quarries at Dinorwig in Wales, close to their estate at Vaynol Park.* This allowed him to spend his time, typically of his class, on leisure pursuits. He was an excellent cricketer, a hard-hitting right-handed batsman and made forty-five known appearances in first-class matches up to the 1820 season, in a career limited by its spanning of the era of the Napoleonic wars. He was also a crack shot, and from 1806 to 1816 was Master of the Quorn Hunt in Leicestershire, followed by the Mastership of the Burton hounds in Lincolnshire between 1816 and 1824, before establishing his own pack at Penton, near Andover.

But Assheton Smith was also a keen yachtsman, a member of the Royal Yacht Squadron and owner of several sailing yachts especially built for him.

* At one time the estate covered a vast area of around 35,000 acres, stretching from the Lleyn Peninsula into the heart of Snowdonia. Part now belongs to the National Trust; the remainder is owned by a private company as a venue for large events.

The Royal Yacht *Royal George* at Portsmouth in a painting by John Thomas Serres. *(Author's collection)*

Smith observed that the development of the marine steam engine opened up new possibilities for leisure sailing craft, and in 1829 he engaged the Scottish engineer and shipbuilder Robert Napier to design for him what became the first of eight steam yachts he would own, the paddle steam yacht *Menai* (1830). Of 263grt, *Menai* was 120ft in length by 20ft beam, and was luxuriously fitted out internally. She was of wooden construction, built by the firm of Wood and Ritchie, Port Glasgow, with a one-cylinder beam

The small royal yacht of which Queen Victoria was very fond, HMY *Fairy*, depicted in 1865 in a painting by George Mears. *(Author's collection)*

engine, generating 110nhp, from Napier's own works at Govan. Sails were also carried.

But there was a problem. The Royal Yacht Squadron, the arbiters of sailing taste and style, banned steam vessels in 1827. A furious Assheton Smith immediately resigned his membership.

Nevertheless, Smith was very proud of his yachts, which included the renowned *Fire King* (1838), the fastest yacht of its time. Another wooden paddler, 175ft long and 525grt, she was constructed by Robert Thompson of Troon, again with a Napier power plant of two side-lever engines generating 240nhp and with sails on two masts. In 1839 Smith offered an open challenge that she could outrun any steamer afloat, for a wager of £5,000.

The RYS found it difficult to hold back the tide. More and more wealthy men found the concept of a luxurious steam pleasure vessel attractive,

Victoria and Albert I as *Osborne* with the Prince of Wales on board, going into Malta Harbour, attended by HMS *Magicienne* and HMS *Doris*, 5 June 1862, in a painting by Oswald Walters Brierly. *(Author's collection)*

HMY *Victoria and Albert III* at Portsmouth from a painting by W M Atkins. *(Author's collection)*

a vessel that could whisk them off to wherever and whenever they fancied; even Queen Victoria acquired one in 1843, the same year that the Royal Yacht Squadron gave in to royal and aristocratic pressure and started to allow the smoking monsters into membership.* When Smith died in 1858, the steam yacht was well and truly established as a rich man's toy, and a symbol of his status and wealth.

Royal Yachts

At the beginning of the nineteenth century, there were nine royal yachts. The most recent of them was *Princess Augusta*, built in 1771 at Deptford. King George III ordered new vessels to be commissioned and his son, as Regent, gained *Royal Sovereign* (1804) supported by *William and Mary III* (1807); he soon lost the latter, which was allocated to the Lord Lieutenant of Ireland in 1813. William IV had access to five large yachts together with three smaller vessels for the benefit of officers of state.

When Victoria ascended to the throne in 1837, she did not immediately make any use of the royal yachts. It was not until 1842 that she embarked on the sail-powered *Royal George* (1817) for a journey to Scotland. Owing to the weather, the ship had to be towed by two steamships, much to the queen's distaste. Moreover, when finally under way it made very slow progress and the motion made her violently seasick. The voyage took three days to cover 404 miles at an average speed of 6 knots; Victoria was not amused and let Prime Minister Robert Peel know it. On 22 September 1842, Peel wrote to his monarch that he had urged on the Admiralty the necessity of providing her with a steam vessel and that 'the Admiralty is now building a large vessel to be worked by steam power' for her use.[2] This was

* In 1843 steam yachts were permitted by the RYS; in 1844 members were allowed to own yachts with steam engines of over 100nhp; and in 1853 all restrictions were removed.

Royal George again in a contemporary etching. *(Author's collection)*

Steam yachts often had ostentatious decoration. Here is an elaborate deck fitting on the Royal Yacht *Osborne*. *(Author's collection)*

a slight exaggeration for the keel was not laid until 9 November and it was this vessel that became *Victoria and Albert I.*

Victoria's reign was the high point of the royal yacht. Three principal yachts were built during her monarchy, each named *Victoria and Albert*; in addition, there were a number of smaller vessels with clearly delineated duties.

Victoria and Albert I was a much larger ship than *Royal George* and it soon became apparent that she could not visit minor ports. Accordingly, *Fairy* was laid down in 1844 as a screw-driven iron yacht, capable of matching the larger ship's 11 knots and serving as a tender to it. She was followed by *Elfin*, a paddle-wheel steam yacht of 1848, used to ferry the queen and others from Portsmouth to the Isle of Wight or on other short journeys.

By the early 1850s, the growing size of the royal family, and Victoria's evident liking for regal cruising, led to a replacement of her maiden yacht. *Victoria and Albert II* was, anachronistically, another steam-paddle ship, laid

HMS *Fire Queen* depicted in 1851 in a painting by Philip John Ouless. Built in Liverpool in 1844 for Mackey & Co., Calcutta merchants, she was purchased by the Admiralty in 1847 and listed as a fleet tender before becoming the port admiral's yacht at Portsmouth. *(Author's collection)*

down in 1854. With two funnels and three masts, she was 100ft longer than her predecessor. The old yacht was renamed *Osborne* and continued in use as a secondary royal vessel until paid off in 1859.

Victoria liked the tender *Fairy*, thinking it 'a beautiful little steamer and charmingly arranged and filled up, with a drawing room, a nice little bedroom for us, dressing room for Albert, and several small berths for ladies and maids'.[3] But by 1863 the queen was spending considerable time at Osborne, and it was clear that a smaller craft than *V&A II*, and more comfortable than *Fairy*, was necessary to act as tender. This led to the commissioning of the paddle-wheel steamer *Alberta* at the end of the year.

In 1868 construction of the wooden steam-paddle yacht *Osborne II* commenced, a slightly smaller vessel than *V&A II* and the last of the paddle-wheel royal yachts. She was a comfortable sea boat and used extensively for cruising by the Prince and Princess of Wales, Edward and Alexandra.

All of these yachts were carried on the Navy List and the flotilla was commanded by a senior Royal Navy officer, usually a commodore or rear admiral. It was a job that required a lot of patience, tact and the ability to mix with royalty and their acolytes; royal connections helped, too.

The twin-screw schooner *Victoria and Albert III* (1899) had been launched in Victoria's lifetime but she never set foot in it. Instead, she became the yacht of choice for King Edward VII. A smaller yacht was still necessary and in 1908 *Alexandra* was commissioned, replacing *Osborne II*. George V gained both *V&A III* and *Alexandra* on his accession, together with *Alberta* and the racing yacht *Britannia*.

And, of course, the British Admiralty had its own yachts; the First Lord of the Admiralty and the Board of Admiralty had their personal vessel, *Enchantress*, and the major port admirals had theirs too, such as the two masted iron-built paddler *Fire Queen* (1844) for the CinC Portsmouth between 1873 and 1883.

Other nations followed the British lead and to a greater or lesser extent produced royal yachts (see also Chapter 9). But one country took the display of national pride as expressed through a steam yacht almost as seriously of Britain – Germany. The first German royal yacht was launched in 1878 as SMY *Hohenzollern*, built by Friedrich Krupp Germaniawerft at Kiel.

It was in this vessel that the kaiser attended a royal fleet review in his honour in 1889. It was reported: 'The Emperor of Germany, just gazetted an Admiral of the English Fleet, and the Prince of Wales, steaming down the gaily decked avenue of ironclads, and holding a reception of all the captains of the fleet on board the *Howe*, the principal flag ship.'[4] Wilhelm also held a *soiree* for commanders of all ships on board his yacht. One captain who was granted that distinction, C C Penrose-Fitzgerald of HMS *Inflexible*, later recalled that 'they had the honour of receiving a hearty shake from the unmailed fist, before it had become stained with innocent blood, and before the blasphemous hypocrite – prince of spies and father of lies – had been found out, and his villainous character exposed'.[5]

The kaiser's royal yacht SMY *Hohenzollern II* in use from 1893, seen here leaving the harbour at Venice. *(Author's collection)*

But she was an aging ship and Kaiser Wilhelm II believed he needed something more impressive to match his English relatives. So, in 1892 she was renamed *Kaiseradler* (Imperial Eagle), replaced and scrapped in 1912.

The new yacht was *Hohenzollern II*, brought into service in 1893, five years after Wilhelm II ascended to the throne. She was built by AG Vulcan Stettin and Wilhelm used her every year from 1894 for his annual cruise around Norway until 1914. Her last royal 'appointment' was in June 1914 when *Hohenzollern II* attended the Kiel regatta and was the host ship of the last state banquet, held on 25 June, to entertain officers of the British fleet whose ships had been invited to Kiel.

She was then laid up, stricken in 1920 and scrapped in 1923. A third yacht had been ordered and was launched in September 1914 but never completed.

Royal steam yachts even appeared in Africa. Sultan Bargash of Zanzibar had lost his royal yachts in a hurricane of 1872. Being a man of

A schematic of all the royal yachts of the eighty years up until the 1911 Coronation Royal Fleet Review. Drawn by G Horace Davis for the *Graphic* of 1 July 1911. *(Author's collection)*

A stern view of the Admiralty yacht *Enchantress* (1903), moored at Portsmouth. Built by Harland and Wolff, she had twin propellers, one on either side of the keel, which when cruising revolved in opposite directions. *Enchantress* was 320ft long, 40ft wide with 6,400hp. Weighing 3,470 tons, she could make 18 knots, and carried three 3pdr saluting guns. *(Author's collection)*

considerable wealth and self-importance, he decided that he should have a replacement. He had been mightily impressed by the RN frigate HMS *Glasgow* (1861) ,which had visited his island realm in 1873, and resolved that she would be the template for his new vessel.

Sir William McKinnon, founder of the British-India Steam Navigation Company, was consulted and he recommended William Denny and Bros of Dumbarton as builders. In May 1877, His Highnesses' Yacht *Glasgow* was laid down. Launched in May the following year, HHY *Glasgow* was constructed with an iron frame covered with teak planks, a keel made from rock elm, and the hull was sheathed with Muntz metal (to protect from worm) below the waterline. She had a one two-bladed lifting propellor and her single-cylinder steam engine generated 172nhp, which could drive her 736grt at 12 knots.

Internally, the yacht contained two state rooms, a dining saloon, and a bathroom and a water closet for personal use by the sultan. In all, the vessel cost £32,735 and was fitted out with seven rifled, muzzle-loading, 9pdr cannon and a nine-barrelled Gatling gun, the latter courtesy of Queen Victoria.

However, when she arrived in Zanzibar, she was laid up as the Sultan did not consider her sufficiently impressive enough to be used as a royal yacht by his exalted personage.

There she remained until 25 August 1896, when a new sultan, Khalid, ascended to the throne without first consulting the British authorities, as required by treaty. Two days later, the shortest war in history – the Anglo-Zanzibar war of 27 August 1896 – saw *Glasgow* sally out to engage a flotilla of five Royal Navy ships, headed by HMS *St George* (1892, two 9.2in and ten 6in guns). In an exchange of fire, the royal yacht was holed below the waterline and sunk, leaving only her masts protruding from the water. In 1912 she was salvaged for scrap.

So, the steam yacht was firmly established in royal circles by the mid to late nineteenth century. And where royalty led, aristocracy followed.

The Steam Yachts

There was nothing new about sailing vessels that were meant to display the owner's wealth and prestige. As far back as *c*240 BC, the Sicilian tyrant Hiero II caused a superyacht to be built, *Syracusia*. She was three times longer than a trireme and was laid out on three decks. The lowest contained cargo. On the second were thirty highly decorated cabins, with mosaics telling the story of the *Iliad*. The cooks' galley contained a seawater fresh fish tank and there were 20,000 gallons of drinking water in the bow. The top level featured a gymnasium, promenades, gardens and a shrine to Aphrodite, paved with agate and panelled with cedar, ivory and cypress. There was also a library and a bath house. But *Syracusia* proved too big for any of the dictator's harbours, so he gave it to his friend Ptolemy II of Egypt. It was a fabulous folly, which displayed Hiero II's wealth and (supposed) taste.[6]

And so did the steam yachts of the end of the nineteenth century; they were the ultimate expression of unlimited riches, swagger and status.

Perhaps because of this, they were an evanescent phenomenon, flourishing only briefly from around 1860 to the outbreak of the First World War in Britain and perhaps during 1875–1917 in the USA. They were the product of the concatenation of three events: the development of a reliable and powerful marine steam engine; the extreme concentration of wealth on a relatively small class of people owing to the industrial growth of, *inter alia*, railways, coal mining, shipping, brewing and banking; and the leisure time afforded to the rentier classes. Steam yachts became 'the most striking personal possession ever produced by man'.[7] They were a visible sign of affluence and there was scarcely an ugly ship among them.

In Britain, thirty steam yachts were registered in 1863, 140 in 1873 and 466 in 1883, but by 1913, the agricultural depression and rising costs had reduced the number to 263.[8]

Dukes were in the van, the Duke of Bedford* building the wonderful

* Herbrand Arthur Russell, 11th Duke.

Norseman at the opening of the Manchester Ship Canal. *(Author's collection)*

W H Smith's *Pandora*, from an etching in *The Illustrated London News* of 17 October 1891. *(Author's collection)*

Sapphire (his second yacht of that name) as late as 1912. The Dukes of Sutherland and Westminster were prominent, Lord Brassey (railways) was an avid owner, the Guinnesses (brewing), Inchcapes (shipping), Tredegars (coal), Singers (sewing machines) all owned multiple yachts. Samuel Radcliffe Platt, head of the engineering firm of Messrs Platt Brothers, Oldham, and quondam High Sheriff of Lancashire, owned the steam yacht *Norseman* (1890). It was the first vessel to sail along the Manchester Ship Canal, leading the opening procession in 1894. Platt died aboard her in the

Sir Thomas Lipton, grocer, America's cup challenger and yachtsman, whose *Aegusa* would be sunk by mines on 28 April 1916 while on naval service. *(Library of Congress LC-DIG-ggbain-04327)*

The Zanzibarian royal yacht, HHY *Glasgow. (Author's collection)*

Two views of the interior of the steam yacht *Niagara* (1898), owned by Howard Gould, American financier. The left-hand image shows Mrs Gould's suite, comprising a boudoir, bedroom, dressing room, and bath, in an ivory and rose design reflecting the Louis XVI period. Note the curtains at the porthole and the frieze running below the ceiling. To the right is the lower staircase on *Niagara*. *(Author's collection)*

Menai Straits in 1902, following an operation. Sir Thomas Lipton used his yachting and America's Cup challenges to promote his tea business.

William Henry Smith made his fortune as a bookseller and newsagent, expanding the family business of W H Smith. He was also first Lord of the Admiralty between 1877 and 1880, inspiring Gilbert and Sullivan's comic operetta *HMS Pinafore*. It was therefore natural that he should have a steam yacht; *Pandora* (1880) was an auxiliary steam schooner of 506 tons TM, which Smith owned until his death in 1891.

As might be expected, the fabulously wealthy European-based Rothschild banking dynasty were at the fore of steam yacht ownership. Mayer Amschel de Rothschild (born 1818), something of a playboy in the family, commissioned a truly grand house at Mentmore, largely designed by Sir Joseph Paxton of the Crystal Palace fame, and lived there from 1855. He owned SY *Garland*. His wife, Juliana, nee Cohen, had her own yacht, *Czarina*, on which she died in 1877.

Ferdinand James Anselm de Rothschild was born in Paris in 1839 but came to England to live. He built the amazing French-style country house Waddesdon Manor, designed by Gabriel-Hippolyte Destailleur, and also had the G L Watson-designed SY *Rona* (which will appear again in Chapter 6). And Lionel (born 1882) was famous for breaking the world water speed record of 28 knots in 1906 and again in the 1907 *Perla del Mediterraneo*. His motor launch *Nigella* and his obligatory steam yacht *Rhodora* were both built by Camper and Nicholson.

In France, Arthur de Rothschild (born 1851) commissioned the yacht *Eros* from Lobnitz, Coulborn and Company of Renfrew in 1875 and became a founder member of the French Yacht Club. He went on to create the Coupe de France, the country's major yacht racing prize. Arthur also provided prize money for the America's Cup. After his death, *Eros* passed to his nephew Henri.

And Edmond de Rothschild (born 1845) ordered the large (1,428grt) *Atmah* (1898, first registered at Le Havre) from the Fairfield Shipbuilding and Engineering Co. Ltd of Govan. She had twin screws, a twin-expansion engine manufactured by her builders that drove her to 16 knots, and was

The American steam yacht *Sigma* (1895), owned by the department store chain millionaires and brothers George and John Reynolds. *(Author's collection)*

289ft long. This clearly was insufficient for Edmond's needs for in 1901, *Atmah* was lengthened by Beardmore's to 314ft, increasing her tonnage to 1,573grt.

In the USA, the first steam yacht was probably the 270ft-long *North Star*, constructed for Commodore Cornelius Vanderbilt in 1853 and used by him to sail to Europe and back. William Aspinwall, president of the Pacific Mail Steamship Company, built *Firefly*, a 98ft paddler, in 1854 and the first steam-powered yachts, *Clarita* and *Bijou*, were admitted to the ultra-snooty New York Yacht Club in 1864. In the country that invented 'conspicuous

The 'game changer': the compound steam engine. These are the engines of the steam yacht *Nirvana* (1904) of 890grt and built by D and W Henderson. Two T4-cylinder engines (i.e. quadruple expansion) produced 200nhp to drive two screws. The illustration is taken from *The Engineer* of 4 March 1904. *(Author's collection)*

Cornelius Vanderbilt's paddle yacht *North Star* (1853) in an engraving from the *Illustrated London News* of 23 July 1853. Built by Jeremiah Simpson at Long Island, she was a paddle schooner. *(Author's collection)*

consumption',* the steam yacht began to replace the private rail carriage as the must have show-off item of choice. In 1870, the New York Yacht club had four steam yachts on its membership list. Twenty years later, there were seventy-one.

The technological changes that made steam yachts possible were the Scotch boiler and the compound steam engine. Scotch boilers, so called from their place of invention and manufacture, allowed a boiler to operate at a much higher pressure than before while occupying a smaller space. Compound engines were able to reuse the steam so generated, thus improving engine efficiency. From around the 1860s, they were the default options for power plants; and from the 1870s the even more powerful and efficient triple-expansion engine was usually fitted, in which a third intermediate cylinder was added to the high- and low-pressure cylinders of the compound engine.

The system works as follows; the steam is initially supplied at high pressure to the first cylinder and after moving that piston it exhausts the steam to the second cylinder. But in order to do the same amount of work to rotate the shaft the next cylinder needs to be bigger, as the pressure is lower and as force = pressure x area, then a larger cross section piston is needed at each stage. The cylinders are linked to a common crank shaft (or to multiple cranks) to turn the up and down motion to a rotary one.

Triple-expansion engines were the game changer for the steam yacht. They were probably first introduced by R Napier and Sons of Glasgow in 1874, fitting them to SS *Propontis*. But no further development occurred until Napiers installed a set of triple-expansion engines in SS *Aberdeen* in 1881 and 'the results in this instance were so satisfactory that other engines of the same type followed, and the system was soon largely adopted in the mercantile marine'.[9]

By 1885, all the Royal Navy's new ships were being fitted with 3-cylinder types and this was also the case for mercantile and steam yacht builds.

* A phrase coined by the American economist and sociologist Thorstein Veblen in 1899.

The *New York Times* commented in 1900: 'The gain in economy effected by the triple-expansion engine, worked with steam of 130 lbs to 150 lbs pressure, over the ordinary compound engine worked at 90 to 100 lbs pressure, may be taken at from 15 to 20 per cent … in consequence of the improvements effected, the consumption of coal with the most recent engines is less than one-third that required for the engines generally used before 1860.'[10]

Vibration from these compound engines could be a trouble to the owner's comfort and his accommodation had to be placed well away from the engines; this problem was not really resolved until the introduction of turbine engines into steam yachts from about 1903.

Internally, all the yachts were luxurious in the extreme, with carved wooden panelling, ornate decoration, music rooms, dining rooms, libraries; a regular home from home. The level of interior decoration and indulgence on many of the steam yachts was scarcely credible. The steam yacht *Dreamer* was constructed for the 'Copper King', Boston-based Thomas W Lawson. She had been designed by the firm of Tams, Lemoine and Crane of New York, and built at the yard of Lewis Nixon of Elizabethport, New Jersey. According to the *New York Times*, 'very few private yachts afloat or building will equal in convenience and luxury of appointment the steam yacht *Dreamer*'.[11] The *San Francisco Call* described her as 'the most luxurious yacht

The lounge/library of an unknown steam yacht, top lit and Edwardian in style. *(Author's collection)*

in the world',[12] and it detailed her beauties at length. 'The deck boudoir is finished in white, with old rose-coloured upholstery, while green is the prevailing colour in the oak rooms, the frieze panels and sofa. … Mrs. Lawson's room is finished in ivory white, the panels and bed hangings being of pink silk with linen-lace applique. The furniture in Mr Lawton's room is old mahogany, with delft blue and ecru furnishings on ecru ground.

'Blistered ash, maple, cherry and oak are used in the remaining five rooms in the family quarters … The bachelors' rooms aft are finished in mahogany, with dark blue furnishings … *Dreamer*'s electric generating plant and storage batteries are of very large capacity, so that there need be no necessity for shutting off any one set of lights or other electric[al] work, as is often the case when the decoration or search lights are in use. In the electric system are included an electric windlass, electric curling-iron heaters in all the ladies' rooms, electric cigar lighters in the bachelor quarters and smoking room, electric fans in all the main rooms and passages and in the officers' quarters.'[13]

Lawson also created a large country house and estate named 'Dreamworld'. However, his various speculations eventually caught up with him and he died virtually penniless in 1925.

Big is Beautiful

Taken as a class, the steam yachts were generally attractive ships, often with flared clipper bows, a decorated bowsprit and ornamentation at the stern; and sometimes very large. Frederick Vanderbilt's *Warrior* was a fine exemplar; 284ft long, with a beam of 32ft and a draught of 17ft, she was luxuriously furnished in an eighteenth-century French style. Her original accommodation included six guest staterooms.

Or consider William K Vanderbilt's *Valiant*, which he sailed across the Atlantic from her builder's yard on the Mersey in 1893. *The New York Times* noted that 'the *Valiant*, the largest and handsomest steam yacht in the world, anchored off Stapleton, S I, yesterday afternoon. The *Valiant* is owned by Mr W K Vanderbilt, and her owner and his secretary, W S Hoyt, made the trip across the Atlantic, and expressed themselves as well satisfied with the way the boat behaved.'[14] *Valiant* had twenty magnificent accommodation suites and a crew of sixty-two, including ten stewards and cooks.

One of the largest of the type at the time was SY *Midnight Sun* at 3,020grt. She had originally been built by Caird and Company of Greenock as an iron screw steamer for Norddeutscher Lloyd shipping company in 1874 for use as a transatlantic passenger liner and named *General Werder*. In 1886 she transferred to the Far East service and in 1893 she was sold to the Albion Shipping Company of Newcastle upon Tyne. Albion upgraded her two-cylinder engine to a three-cylinder one, refitted her as a cruising yacht and named her *Midnight Sun*, to operate on the Norwegian sightseeing routes.

In this guise it was obviously possible to charter her in part or whole, for

in November 1897 we find John Woolrych Perowne Esq* inviting Sir Arthur and Lady Arnold (politician, author and journalist) and Max Pemberton (novelist) to sail with him for Lisbon, Tangier, Gibraltar, Algiers, and the Riviera. And in December, Woolrych Perowne was joined by John Bardsley, Bishop of Carlisle, and his daughter, who boarded at Marseilles on 22 December.

Come the Boer War of 1899, *Midnight Sun* was leased by the British Red Cross to act as a hospital ship and was converted for that role by Sir William Armstrong's yard; when completed, she sailed for Southampton and then South Africa. The Princess of Wales (Princess Alexandra of Denmark) paid for the fit-out and also donated £1,000 in luxuries and comforts for the invalided soldiers. In recognition of this generosity the vessel was renamed *Princess of Wales*.

In 1901, she was returned to Albion's hands, reverted to the name *Midnight Sun* and resumed cruising the Norwegian fjords until she was scrapped in 1912.

New York-based Eugene Higgins was the enormously rich heir to a carpet-making fortune. Considered to be the handsomest and richest unmarried New Yorker, Higgins was a keen golfer, cross-country rider, fisherman, hunter, coach racer, yachtsman, fencer and amateur enthusiast in physics and mathematics. After studying fencing in France he became, in 1890, America's first fencing champion. So, of course, he had to have a steam yacht. And not just any yacht; to satisfy Higgins' need for pleasure,

G L Watson-designed *Warrior* (ex-*Wayfarer*) was built in 1904 of 1,098grt by the Ailsa Shipbuilding Company for the fabulously rich railways magnate Frederick William Vanderbilt. In 1916, she was purchased from the estate of Alfred G Vanderbilt (after he briefly owned her under the name *Wayfarer*) by the well-known yachtsman and carpet-making millionaire Alexander Smith Cochran, who reverted to the name *Warrior*. *(Author's collection)*

* Later a King's Messenger and a Gold Staff Officer at the Coronation of King George VI in 1937.

William Kissam Vanderbilt's yacht *Valiant* (1893), built by Laird Brothers in Birkenhead to a design by St Clair Byrne. She was 2,300 tons and 330ft long, and two triple-expansion steam reciprocating engines developed 4,500ihp to give the vessel a speed of 17.5 knots. *(Library of Congress LC-DIG-det-4a04779)*

G L Watson designed *Varuna* for him, named for the Hindu god associated with sky, ocean and water.

She was large and luxurious. Launched in 1896, 260ft long and of 1,573grt, *Varuna* had twin screws driven by an eight-cylinder compound engine delivering 634nhp and taking her up to around 17 knots. Built of steel throughout by A and J Inglis on the Clyde, she offered every convenience. 'It is to the size of her bridge deck that the *Varuna* owes, in greatest measure, the exceptional character of her accommodations. Her deck is 168ft in length. The dining room is about 18ft by 34ft. It is fitted up in panelled oak. The library has an area of some 187 sq ft, and a total wall length of 50ft, enough to allow of bookcases containing a plentiful supply of literature. This library is aft of a series of rooms for maids and valets and lavatories and bathrooms for guests, arranged along the casing on the starboard side, and alongside the after end of the dining room is a vestibule floored with rubber tiling. Passing abaft the engine room, you come to a drawing room 18ft square, and the fencing room, nearly as large, which is provided with cabinets, racks for foils, dumb-bells, clubs and other accessories for physical exercise. There are magnificent state rooms some in white, some in mahogany, a large bachelors' room, bathrooms, a doctor's room, and so on.'[15]

However, such splendour could not spare her from the sailor's oldest enemy. On 17 November 1909 she was wrecked off the coast of Madeira. Higgins was on board and later received an award for saving the lives of several of his guests. One crewman was lost. As for Higgins, he never married and when he died in 1948 he left the fantastic sum of $38.5 million to philanthropic academic causes.

Among other vessels, *Sapphire* was of 1,207grt and 251ft in length. *Margarita* was 1,780grt and 272ft long. For comparison, the 'L' class Royal Navy destroyers of 1913 displaced around 1,000 tons and were some 267ft from bow to stem, and the US Navy's *Cassin* class of roughly the same date were of similar displacement and about 20ft longer. The steam yachts were as big as, or bigger than, naval destroyers. A few were capable of speeds up to 20 knots. And there was a race for size, or so it seems. Newspaper reports always seemed to stress that a new yacht was 'the largest yet'.

... But So is Small

Of course, not all steam yachts were large vessels. Those whose wealth did not permit a 1,000-ton vessel made do with smaller craft. In 1913, 236 out of 272 US-registered steam yachts were less than 500 tons TM. And in Britain, 210 out of 263 were in that category.[16] Some of these lesser vessels were perhaps impractical, for in the days of coal-fired Scotch boilers, etc, most of the hull was taken up with the boiler room, engine room, coal bunkers and crew accommodation. Dixon Kemp's designs for Day Summers and Co. (see plans section) demonstrate this well; for the owner and guests, there was not a lot of privacy or space. They might be considered as 'gentleman's yachts'.

A smaller vessel, steam yacht *Xantha* (1867). Of 106grt, she was built by Palmers' Shipbuilding and Iron Co. Ltd of Jarrow for Lord Alfred Paget, Commodore of the Royal Thames Yacht Club between 1846 and 1873. Constructed in iron, she could use steam or sail power, the former coming from a two-cylinder 40hp engine. Paget already had several other yachts at Cowes. *(Author's collection)*

A good example of such a yacht is *Boadicea*. She was constructed in 1882 by John Elder and Co. at Govan as a 305grt, 170ft-long craft with a two-cylinder engine generating 90nhp and giving a claimed 14 knots from a single screw. Her first owner was one William Pearce, who gave his address as Mudhook Yacht Club. This was a small and recently founded organisation on the banks of the Clyde. Allegedly, it was formed in 1873 by six friends going off for a weekend on one of the group's steam yacht. They were having a drink before going aboard while waiting for some of the others to appear. As they were unhappy with the clubs around the Clyde area they decided to form one of their own.

Pearce did not hold the vessel for long, however, for by September 1882 *Boadicea* was registered to Mrs Catherine A Dixon of Ayr. The yacht then continued in the Dixon and Church families (1884 John Church, 1886 Annie Church-Dixon) until 1897, when *Boadicea* passed to Mrs M Morgan of London. She stayed with the Morgan family for the next thirty-nine years. In 1901, the yacht was in the hands of Lieutenant Colonel Anthony Hickman Morgan, a monocle-wearing British army surgeon who had served on *Princess of Wales* (see above) in the Boer War. He was also a member of the Royal Yacht Squadron for eighteen years, until his death in 1924. In the interim, the yacht had been taken up by the Royal Navy in 1915 as *Boadicea II*, armed with a 12pdr and a 6pdr, and used as a patrol vessel until returned to Hickman Morgan in 1919.

After his death, she was registered to Mrs Mary Morgan and remained so until purchased by the Admiralty in 1940 for use as a minesweeper (as *Seaflower*). *Boadicea* was finally broken up at Preston in 1946, a veteran at 64 years old.

Or consider the G L Watson-designed *Ituna* (1886), a small steam yacht (243 tons TM) constructed by A and J Inglis in Glasgow for one John G Mackie of Balcary House, Auchencairn, Kirkcudbrightshire. Named after the old Latin name for the Solway Firth, *Ituna* was described by *The Marine*

Smaller yachts were numerically more prevalent. The American steam yachts *Oneida* (ahead) and *Sapphire*, photographed around 1900. *Oneida* was built by Harlan and Hollingsworth at Wilmington, Delaware, for Elias Cornelius Benedict. *Sapphire* was by the Herreshoff Manufacturing Company of Bristol, Rhode Island, and was owned by Jeremiah Milbank of New York City. *(US Library of Congress LC-DIG-det-4a15645)*

The G L Watson-designed *Ituna*, depicted in US ownership in 1892. *(Robert Schemmer Maritime Library)*

Engineer as follows: 'The deckhouse is recessed 18 inches into the deck, showing less topweight than the ordinary design would have given. Forward of the engine-room have been placed the dining cabin and three state-rooms. Aft the engine room are the drawing room and three sleeping cabins, with bathroom and cloakroom. Over a dado of polished and varnished pine a richly toned cretonne design will give a comfortable and artistic finish. The dining cabin and drawing room are finished in polished hardwood. The yacht is fitted by the builders with direct acting triple-expansion compound engines of 300ihp and rigged as a pole-masted schooner.'[17]

By 1889, however, her registry was in Messina and she passed through a number of hands before being acquired by Allison Vincent Armour, playboy socialite and yachtsman, who in 1894 sailed her for Havana and the Atlantic ports of Mexico with several eminent scientists on board for a three-month study of archaeological remains. He sold her in 1901, again into American ownership.

Crewing a Steam Yacht

Crews might be kept on all year round. When the yacht was not being used by its owner, they would conduct maintenance; or the yacht might be rented out to a suitably wealthy personage and the captain and hands would operate the boat for the lessee. Occasionally they would be laid up if the yacht was not required.

The most important men in the ship's company were the captain, the chief engineer and the chief steward, the latter because he and his team (up to nine or ten strong on a large vessel) would have the most interaction with the owners and passengers when on board. This was reflected in their remuneration; the captain of the largest yachts in the first decade of the twentieth century (which might cost £55,000–55,000 to build) would be

Part of the crew of the large steam yacht *Midnight Sun*, depicted at Newcastle upon Tyne, *circa* 1908. *(Author's collection)*

paid annually around £520, the chief engineers had a weekly wage of £5, the chief steward £3-15 shillings. Captain, deck officers, first, second and third engineers and all the stewards had their food as part of remuneration. Other crew members had to purchase their own out of their wages. When wireless operator Eric Sharp joined the Duke of Bedford's brand-new *Sapphire* in 1912, he was given £3 a week, much in excess of what he had earned working on commercial passenger liners. He also had a uniform paid for by the owner, a pound of pipe tobacco and free matches with which to light it.[18] A yacht such as *Sapphire* cost around £87 (perhaps £10,600 today) a week for crew salaries alone.[19] This was quite an expense considering that the duke hardly used her; instead, she frequently carried his duchess, Mary Du Caurroy Russell, a noted ornithologist, on foreign 'twitching' expeditions.

The pre-war life of an ordinary crewman on the steam yachts could be a peripatetic one. When they sailed, journeys could be short or long or one way. And when they were taken on, crewmen were required to sign an agreement that laid out legally the terms of their engagement and the behaviours expected (see Appendix 1 for an example).

As an illustration, Arthur Shead was born at Wivenhoe in Essex in 1877 and took to a career at sea. Marriage was not allowed to get in the way of his work. He had his wedding to Gertrude on 12 May 1901 and the following day signed onto the steam yacht *Gunreda* as an able seaman for a delivery voyage to Halifax, Nova Scotia, the vessel having been purchased by a new Canadian owner.

In October that year he left *Gunreda* and returned to England, where he joined the *Marion* at Brightlingsea as boatswain and two years later signed on to *Rannoch*, again as boatswain, for the next decade. But this employment did not cover the winter months, when Shead was obliged to work on the local fishing smacks.

Rannoch was a fine yacht of 498grt built by Ramage & Ferguson in 1902 to designs by Cox and King for Thomas Valentine Smith, a director of Smith, Garrett, and Co., the Bow Brewery, the Callender and Oban Railway Company, and the Guardbridge Paper Company. He was also a famous breeder of Highland cattle. Smith died on board his yacht in August 1906, aged 81, and it passed into the hands of his nephew, Gerald Sellar. As for his vessel, she was described as 'very handsomely fitted. The dining room, drawing room, and smoking room are on the main deck, with a long shade deck above, on which are the boats, charthouse, etc, while on the lower deck fore and aft of the machinery space are a number of handsomely fitted sleeping cabins. The yacht has a steam windlass, steam steering-gear, complete electric light installation, and a system of hot-water heating throughout all the saloons and cabins ... Triple-expansion engines to give a high rate of speed will be fitted by the builders.'[20]

So luxurious was the vessel that in 1912 *Rannoch* was bought by King Victor Emmanuel III of Italy and eventually renamed *Iela*. He kept her at

The crew (with chef) of the Cox and King-designed *Venetia* (1905) wearing their 'branded' uniforms. *(Mersea Museum/ Sadie Jasper)*

Naples and it was clearly this sale that brought about the end of Shead's tenure on board.

When war came, Shead joined the hospital ship *Liberty* (see Chapter 3) at Portsmouth in 1916 and he stayed with her until December 1918, when he parted from *her* at Cowes.

Design

Early steam yachts were powered by a mixture of sail and steam and were known technically as auxiliary steam schooners. Their external design was based on that of the iron clippers that preceded them; fast sailing vessels that plied their cargo trade across oceans. As this sort of craft was replaced by commercial steamers, some of the yards that had made them turned to yachts, where the degree of craftmanship built up over the years could be put to use – it was a sophistication neither required nor affordable for quotidian merchant shipping.

Thus, early yachts looked not unlike clippers with the same sort of bows, bowsprits, decorated counters, jibs, masts and yards. With the primitive engines of the time, masters, crew and owners alike mistrusted them and preferred to have sails on hand, which were in any case useful for steadying the vessel, or when getting away from a tight mooring or reach.

As more powerful and technically more sophisticated engines, such as the three-cylinder compounds referenced above, came into use the masts and yards became largely redundant, but were retained as a preferred design feature. Then, and indeed now, few could deny that a clipper bow and bowsprit, a tasteful sheer and raking masts and funnels lend a look of refinement and elegance.

Steam yachts were essentially constructed as floating homes. They didn't need to be ultra-fast, were not required to turn on a sixpence (and thus usually possessed only a single screw); these were, of course, characteristics that ill-fitted them for naval use when the time came. They were mansions at sea with the levels of luxury and service that their wealthy owners would expect on land.

There were some important differences between US and British steam yachts. British owners tended to use their craft for extended cruises entertaining friends and family in style and often staying afloat for months. American owners, although rich, were not necessarily of the leisured class. J Pierpoint Morgan, for example, who owned a series of yachts named *Corsair*, the first acquired in 1881, was an extremely busy banker with little time to spare. He and his peers used such vessels for the weekend commute to homes on the Hudson River or Long Island Sound. Thus, their yachts sacrificed accommodation space for speed and were generally designed to be faster than their British coevals.

The yacht *Nourmahal*, meaning 'Light of the Harem' (or possibly 'Light of the Palace'), pictured in 1895. She had been built by Harlan and Hollingsworth in 1884 for William Backhouse Astor Jnr. A shade over 232ft long, she had a two-cylinder compound engine. After William's death in 1892, she passed to his son, Colonel John Jacob Astor IV. He fought in the Spanish-American War and in 1912 became the richest man to lose his life in the sinking of the *Titanic*. *(Author's collection)*

An exception to this rule was the American banker, philanthropist and close friend of King Edward VII, Anthony Joseph Drexel Jr. In 1908 he sailed his G L Watson-designed yacht *Margarita II* (1900)* from the USA to England with sixty-eight crew, a grand piano and a full-size Aeolian organ. Drexel then rented 22 Grosvenor Square in London and took a house in Cowes for the racing.

Yachts gave a measure of seclusion absent from other modes of transport. Elias Cornelius Benedict was a wealthy American banker and friend of President Grover Cleveland.† It was in the privacy of Benedict's yacht *Oneida* that Cleveland had his secret surgery to remove a cancerous growth from his jaw in 1893. In later life, Benedict became Commodore of the Seawanhaka Corinthian Yacht Club, formed in 1871.

* Watson had also designed the first *Margarita* (1896).

† The twenty-second and twenty-fourth president of the USA.

The launch of the 'cigar yacht' *Ross Winans*, as depicted in *The Illustrated London News* of 3 March 1866. *(Author's collection)*

We cannot leave the subject of design without examining one attempt to break the mould – the 'cigar yacht'.

The Winans family were railway engineers from Baltimore who had made a fortune building the Russian railways. With time and money on their hands, in the late 1850s they decided that the most advantageous shape for an ocean-going ship would be a spindle. The waves would wash easily over the decks, reducing rolling; the pointed hull would cut through the water with minimal resistance, increasing speed and improving fuel consumption. At least, that was the theory.

Between 1858 and 1864 they built three such craft, none of which worked as planned. In 1864 they came to England and had the Hepworth's shipyard on the Isle of Dogs build a fourth, the *Ross Winans*, launched in 1866. She was 256ft long, but only 16ft in diameter. A superstructure 130ft long and 10ft wide was sat on top and two nine-bladed propellers, 22ft in diameter and revolving at about 50 rpm, drove her along. *Ross Winans* was probably the first vessel to use high-pressure steam engines, forced-air ventilation, self-centring drive shafts, and derricks for lowering her boats. Additionally, she had a shifting ballast of 12 tons of lead. This was a huge pendulum that was moved by a small steam engine and allowed the ship to automatically adjust for the list created by the torque of the main engines. The family invested £60,000 in her construction.*

It was a complete failure. The vessel's deck was unusable in any weather, waves washed freely over the superstructure and the state rooms and saloon proved cramped and damp. After a few trial runs in the Solent, the Winans abandoned her and she rotted at her moorings for the next thirty years, before being sold for scrap for just £210. Not all innovation works.

... *And Designers*

In the same way as they would commission architects to build their show-off mansions of power and wealth, both new and old money used yacht designers to produce their palaces at sea. Some of these men became the

* Maybe £6 million in 2022 money.

accepted face of superyacht design. The two giants in the field were St Clare John Byrne and George L Watson.

Byrne was an early exponent of the art. Liverpool-born and the son of an Irish ship owner and a keen yachtsman, at the age of 25 he designed and built his own yacht. In 1856 he was elected a member of the Royal Mersey Yacht Club and was soon in demand by the rich and famous. Byrne designed a steam auxiliary barquentine yacht for the railway king Thomas Brassey, *Sunbeam*, launched in 1874, and three years later a yacht for Samuel Radcliffe Platt, *Norseman* (noted above). Sir Thomas George Fermor-Hesketh, 7th Baronet, was a client, as was the American newspaper mogul James Gordon Bennett and William Kissam Vanderbilt, once thought to be the richest American alive, for whom Byrne produced *Valiant* (1893), which at 2,148 tons was said at the time to be the largest yacht in the world.

When Byrne died in 1915, aged 86, not only had he set the template for steam yacht design, but he had also been naval architect to forty-one such vessels, a total that excludes his designs for boats under 100 tons.

Following in Byrne's footsteps came George Lennox Watson. Born in 1852, the son of a Glasgow doctor, Watson served his apprenticeship with the Clydeside shipbuilders and engineering firm Robert Napier and Son. Here he learned the craft he would practise for the rest of his life and in 1873, at the age of just 22, he set up a dedicated yacht design office. Watson's clients included the Vanderbilt family, the Earl of Dunraven, tea magnate Sir Thomas Lipton, the Rothschild family, politician Charles Lindsay Orr-Ewing, the fraudster James Whitaker Wright and Kaiser Wilhelm II of Germany. Watson also designed four America's Cup challengers and the largest sailing schooner of its time, *Rainbow*. His tropes were a clipper bow, two masts, a transom stern with a pronounced overhang, the symmetrical placement of deckhouses and a single funnel above the main hull.

His cousin Thomas Watson, a qualified architect, often handled the interior design work of the yachts, favouring the Scots Baronial style but also encompassing Louis XV and Arabian pastiche.

In a thirty-year career, Watson designed 432 yachts, lifeboats and other vessels, an output that averages one new build launched every three and a half weeks. He was a fanatical worker with close personal attention to detail, and it is perhaps not a surprise that he died in 1904 aged only 52. His business survived him, based in Glasgow, and a legacy company of that name is still engaged in the design, restoration and replica builds of large yachts.

Another British yacht designer who had a far-reaching impact on the yachting world was Ryde-born Dixon Kemp. Kemp was a naval architect, yachting editor of *The Field* and editor of the *Isle of Wight Observer*. His vessels included *Firecrest* (1892), which was used by French sailor and tennis champion Alain Gerbault in his 1923 solo circumnavigation of the globe, and the steam yacht *Maid of Honour* (1891) for the Earl of Cawdor.

But perhaps his most influential contribution to yachting was as the first secretary of the Yacht Racing Association in Britain in 1875, when it was formed to standardise rules and handicaps for regattas, which at the time varied from one yacht club to another. Kemp proved able to persuade these clubs that adopting common rules and standards would ultimately help the sport to grow. The organisation succeeded and in time became the Royal Yachting Association.

As an author, Kemp made a lasting impression, too. His works *Yacht Designing* (1876), *A Manual of Yacht and Boat Sailing* (1878), *Practical Boat Building and Sailing* (1881) and *Yacht Architecture* (1885) were translated into several languages and influenced generations of boat builders. Kemp died in 1899, aged 60.

In the USA, the firm of Tams, Lemoine and Crane was prominent; American-born Clinton Crane had been trained in Scotland, at the School of Naval Architecture in Glasgow. His career trajectory was unusual. Beginning as an amateur naval architect, designing for himself and his friends and relations, he established a yacht design firm that he operated for around twelve years before leaving his profession to run the family mining business full time. Crane returned to design ten years later but part time and as an amateur. From time to time, Crane and Watson co-operated on designs for US clients.

There were many others. W C Storey designed, among other vessels, *Valhalla* for Brigadier General Sir Joseph Frederick Laycock – soldier, philanderer and Olympic sailor – and *White Ladye* for Lord Ashburton. In 1880, Storey was a founder member of the Royal Portsmouth Corinthian Yacht Club. Cox and King were an innovative design company with offices and a shipyard in Wivenhoe, Essex. John Beavor-Webb was an Englishman who emigrated to the USA and designed a number of large yachts including the third *Corsair* for J P Morgan. As long as there were rich clients, there would arise men to build yachts for them!

... And a Builder

Many shipbuilders constructed steam yachts but one name will appear time and time again in this book, and will suffice to describe the many. Ramage & Ferguson was formed in May 1877 with a yard in the outer harbour area of the Water of Leith on the west side of the shore, backing onto the then relatively new Victoria Dock. Ships were launched directly into the Water of Leith, which imposed a limit on the maximum size of ship that could be built. Production moved from iron to steel in 1880 and further expansion was made in 1892.

The company was the creation of Richard Ramage, who had previously worked for the William Denny and Brothers yard at Dumbarton, on the Clyde. The 'Ferguson' is more of a mystery, clearly a sleeping partner or investor with no role in the day-to-day running of the business.

Although they turned their hand to tramp steamers and windjammers, Ramage & Ferguson soon acquired a reputation for luxury steam yachts for the rich and famous. Royalty from around the world were among their clients, including SY *Rondine* (1887) for Prince Sirignano of Naples, later renamed SY *Sultana* and then *Clementina* when chartered to King Leopold II, King of the Belgians; SY *Maha Chakri* (1892), a magnificent ship for the King of Siam, Rama V; and SY *Amélia IV* (1900) for the King of Portugal. Post-war, there was also SY *Naz Perwer* (1923), a beautiful steam yacht for Prince Youssouf Kamal of Egypt; and SS *Vyner Brooke* (1928) for the King of Sarawak.

In 1918 their yard manager, Henry Robb, left to form his own shipbuilding company, Henry Robb & Sons. With a strange circularity, when Ramage & Ferguson ran into financial difficulties in 1934, the yard was purchased by Robb, as a secondary base.

A Port and an Eccentric

Steam yachts frequented ports all over the world but were often laid up out of season, or when not in use, at a particular location. One such in Britain was Brightlingsea, at the mouth of the River Colne on England's eastern seaboard. It was historically a busy fishing port (with 100 smacks registered there in 1914); and it was famous for its oyster beds, having more advertised oyster merchants in the mid-1800s than any other place in Britain.

But it was also a busy winter laying up and repair centre for steam yachts, often at Aldous' Shipyard, and many of the yacht crewmen came from the locality.

Among those owners who patronised the harbour at one time or another were Thomas Lipton, the author Arnold Bennett, maritime and humorous writer William Wymark Jacobs, Herbert Thomas 'Bertie' Sullivan, heir to Arthur Sullivan's musical fortune and owner of the yacht *Zola*; and a famously eccentric American, McEvers Bayard Brown.

Brown was a descendant of the sixteenth mayor of New York, Nicholas Bayard. When he died in 1926, Brown was possibly the only man who ever lived on a seagoing yacht for thirty-six years, with steam up day and night, yet never sailed away.

He arrived at Brightlingsea in *Valfreya* in 1890. And never left. He kept a full crew at all times, maintained her permanently in steam and his behaviour throughout the period bordered on the insane.

To quote *Time* magazine, 'Mr Brown expended about $4,000 a month on the upkeep of the *Valfreya*. The eighteen men who comprised his crew earned their high pay and seldom stayed with him long. He possessed a large squirt gun which he delighted to fill with bilge water in the dead of night. Thus armed he stole upon sleeping members of his crew, inserted the tip of the gun in an ear, pressed the plunger. Two private secretaries left him after suffering this treatment. Mr Brown crept upon a third secretary at night, [and] clipped off his moustache without waking him.'[21]

With outsiders, his games had a cruel edge; 'Mr Brown almost daily caused his chef to heat large panfuls of gold and silver coins as hot as possible on the galley stove. The beggars of Brightlingsea, anxious to humour his whims, appeared in rowboats and caught the coins in their bare hands as Mr Brown hurled the bits of gold and silver overboard with a shovel. If the beggars attempted to use gloves, he hurled boiling water upon them instead. When the moon was full, he hurled nothing at all. Occasionally he wrapped lumps of coal in £100 notes … and heaved them at submissive heads.'[22]

Brown's behaviour never attracted the attention of the regional authorities, possibly, some alleged, because of the large donations he made to local charities. It was also stated that 'he realised that he might someday be restrained as insane and therefore kept steam up at all times, ready for instant escape'.[23] In reality it was probably to keep the electrical generators running.

As for his yacht, it had been built as *Lady Torfrida* by Fairfield Shipbuilding of Govan in 1888. Of 547grt, it had been ordered by Sir William Pearce of Cardell House, Wemyss Bay, who owned the Fairfield yard but who died before he could make use of it. Brown purchased it in 1889.

When war came, Brightlingsea became a Royal Navy base, first named HMS *Wallaroo* and then HMS *City of Perth*. The first named was an old cruiser, base ship for the boom and net craft protecting the Swin Anchorage; she was replaced by a drifter in 1916. *Valfreya* was inspected by the Admiralty but considered to be too much in need of maintenance to be worth taking up. However, they did insist that Brown and his yacht vacate their berth and she went up river for the duration.

Post-war, the vessel was drydocked, with Brown still living aboard, and then returned to her old anchorage until 1927, when her owner died. *Valfreya* was then sold to the Maharajah Jam Sahib of Nawanagar (better known as the England, Cambridge University and Sussex cricketer K S Ranjitsinhji), renamed *Star of India*, and fitted out for cruising in Eastern waters.

Two Painters

If you owned a steam yacht between (say) 1860 to 1914, you were likely to have it painted against an Italian background by someone called de Simone. Father and son, Tomasso and Antonio were Neapolitan port artists. Tomaso specialised in oils, the majority depicting warships, yachts or merchant vessels. He also created scenes of the Battles of Lissa (1867) and Alexandria (1882).

Antonio de Simone worked in watercolours, mainly gouache.* He specialised in portraits of the great society yachts of the period, capturing just about every important private yacht to visit Naples. These depictions were commissioned by the owners to show their vessels at anchor under Mount Vesuvius during their leisurely Mediterranean cruises. A smoking volcano and brilliant cerulean blue sky were features of these paintings, which also displayed a rather flat perspective.

Even today, these works can be found regularly in museums and salerooms, a frozen moment portraying a very different world, one that was soon to be changed irrevocably by American and European wars.

* A water-based paint consisting of natural pigment, water, and a binding agent (usually gum arabic or dextrin).

CHAPTER TWO

STEAM YACHTS AND THE HISPANO-AMERICAN WAR

FOR A NAVY looking at the prospect of a war that they had not anticipated or planned for, the pleasure yachts of the rich and famous represented a possible solution to a problem. And it was the US Navy that first put this thought to the test.

As the American state grew in nationhood, a proud republic free of monarchical rule, it became increasingly suspicious of the intentions of the established European nations with regard to the American continent. Particularly, American politicians worried about the empire-building activities of Britain and France. Such concerns led to the so-called Monroe Doctrine, announced in a routine annual message delivered to Congress by President James Monroe in December 1823. The announcement warned the European nations that the United States would not tolerate further colonisation or puppet monarchs in what they regarded as their 'backyard'. It was conceived to meet major concerns of that time, especially with regard to newly independent Mexico, but the Monroe Doctrine soon became a watchword of US policy in the Western Hemisphere.

Thus in 1865, when Mexico rebelled against the French-imposed regime of Emperor Maximilian, the US government invoked the Doctrine to exert diplomatic and military pressure in support of the Mexican President Benito Juárez, leading to the fall of the emperor and his execution by firing squad.

However, this policy rather ignored the fact that there was already an empire in the Americas, that of Spain. Mexico had been lost by Spain in 1821, but Cuba and Puerto Rico (both strategically important for command of the major approaches to the Gulf of Mexico) remained, as did, out into the Pacific, the Philippines and Guam.

Cuba in particular was important to Spain for the large and profitable sugar crop that it produced, income that boosted Spain's always poverty-stricken domestic budgets. But there was a strong independence movement in Cuba, struggling against Spanish oppression for nationhood and freedom; and there were frequent local revolts and insurrections.

Such an event in October 1873 led to the *Virginius* Affair, which might have resulted in war between the USA and Spain. *Virginius* was a fast American ship hired by Cuban rebels to land men and munitions in Cuba, supporting an attack on the Spanish regime there. It was captured by the Spanish, who tried the men on board (many of whom were American and British citizens) as pirates. The Spanish executed fifty-three of the crew but stopped when the British government intervened.

Strangely for a nation with two long coastlines to protect, the US government had paid little heed to its navy since the close of the internecine strife of 1861–65. Thus when, in response to the *Virginius* Affair, the navy was asked whether it could defeat any Spanish naval attack in war, Secretary of the Navy George Robeson could only reply that 'the best the navy could assemble was an assortment of rusty old hulks, most of which had not been to sea since the close of the Civil War eight years earlier'.[1] Further embarrassment came when it was realised that a Spanish ironclad, the *Arapiles,* was anchored in New York Harbour for repairs, leading to the uncomfortable realisation on the part of the US Navy that it had no ship capable of defeating such a vessel. Congress hastily issued contracts for the construction of five new ironclads and accelerated its existing repair programme for several more. In 1884, a Naval War College was established at Newport, Rhode Island, and in 1886 Congress ordered the construction of two armoured cruisers, *Texas* and *Maine.**

But Cuba continued to be an itch that America couldn't scratch. Support grew for the independence movement, fanned by the 'yellow press', especially by those papers owned by William Randolph Hearst, particularly the influential *New York Journal.* Hearst's papers sensationalised Spanish atrocities in Cuba while calling for war against Spain. And some US businessmen cast envious eyes on the riches of Cuba's sugar trade.†

* Which would not be launched, however, until 1892 and 1895 respectively.

† As they did with Hawai'i, which was annexed by the USA in June 1898.

USS *Maine* (1895), armed with four 10in guns, entering Havana harbour and passing Morro Castle on 25 January 1898. Three weeks later she would blow up there, sparking war between the USA and Spain. *(Author's collection)*

A retouched photograph of USS *Maine*, with an inset portrait of her last Commanding Officer, Captain Charles D Sigsbee USN. This was published as a memento following the ship's loss on 15 February 1898. *(US Naval History and Heritage Command NH 61674)*

By 1897, a US war plan existed that called for Cuba to be blockaded and Manila captured. With what resources was less certain. And tension continued to grow, with American public opinion swayed in support of the insurrectionists due to reports of concentration camps set up to control the populace. Then, on 15 February, the USS *Maine* blew up in Havana harbour with 261 fatalities. Underwater mining by Spanish forces was suspected and touted aggressively by newspapers.* In response, political pressure grew for war.

Recently elected President William McKinley did not want war. However, his Assistant Secretary of State for the Navy, Theodore Roosevelt,† certainly did and energetically started to prepare the USN for conflict. On 25 February 1898, he ordered ten 6in guns and twenty-two 5in to be removed from storage in Washington Navy yard and shipped to New York, where they could be used to arm civilian craft. On 9 March, the Senate passed a $50 million naval appropriations bill, approved by Congress the previous day; on the 24th, ten US Revenue Cutters (the progenitor of the US Coastguard) were turned over to the navy and fitted with additional armament. And on 4 May, Congress passed a further $63 million appropriations act, making the total the largest since the Civil War.[2]

The demand for protection of the American littoral from Spanish naval

* In fact, it is more likely that the ship's magazines had been ignited by a spontaneous fire in a coal bunker. *Maine*'s coal was bituminous, known for releasing firedamp, a mixture of gases, primarily of flammable methane which was prone to spontaneous explosions.

† Later the USA's twenty-sixth president (for two terms), and arguably one of the best.

attack in the event of war became shrill; 'chambers of commerce and boards of trade of different coast cities all lost their heads for the time being and raised a deafening clamour and brought every species of pressure to bear on the Administration ... to distribute the navy ship by ship at all points and in all kinds of ports with the idea of protecting everything, everywhere'.[3]

But the USN did not have enough small craft to blockade Cuba and provide coastal patrols. And so it turned to rich men's steam yachts.

On Patrol

Commencing in March 1898, the US Navy purchased (or had donated to it) twenty-eight steam yachts.[4] The price paid was fixed by the Navy Board. They armed them, painted them grey and put them under naval command. Some were given protective plating over the engines and boilers. On 20 April, McKinley signed a joint Congressional resolution demanding Spanish withdrawal from Cuba and authorising him to use military force to help Cuba gain independence. Spain severed diplomatic relations with the United States the following day. On the 22nd, the US Navy began a blockade of Cuba. And the steam yachts went off to war.

Six of the yachts were large vessels, over 400grt; the remainder a mixture of smaller sizes. By far the largest (and the first to be acquired) was the G L Watson-designed *Mayflower* (1896) of 1,800grt. She had been built by J and G Thompson, of Clydebank, Scotland,* as a luxurious steam yacht for millionaire Ogden Goelet, property developer and yachtsman, who died on board her in August 1897. The USN acquired her from Goelet's estate on 19 March the following year.† J P Morgan's (second) *Corsair* of 1891 became USS *Gloucester* on 23 April for a consideration of $225,000. Morgan publicly opposed the Spanish war and he loved his yacht, which was furnished to the highest standards. He vigorously protested its forced sale when the USN appropriated her.

However, William Randolph Hearst handed over his *Buccaneer* (1888) gratis, it being returned to him in September, post the war's end. He had attempted to get a commission in the USN in return, but was told that he would have to apply through the normal channels; by the time he was made an ensign, the war was over. Hearst himself hired the merchant vessel SS *Sylvia* from the Baltimore Fruit Company and fitted her out with photographic facilities, offices and a printing press; thus equipped she was steamed to the war zone around Cuba to report first hand on the conflict.

The larger yachts were fitted with two or more 6pdr guns, the smaller vessels with 3pdrs only. The latter served as despatch vessels and patrolled near to the coast, while the larger ones joined the blockade line, 'a thin grey line of warships stretching along the northern coast of Cuba from Bahia Honda to Cardenas and another off the port of Cienfuegos on the southern coast'.[5]

The US war plan was to launch an invasion of Cuba from Tampa, Florida,

* She was the largest yacht built on the Clyde to that date.

† Watson also designed a similar yacht for Ogden's brother Robert, *Nahma*; curiously, Robert too died on his yacht.

Yacht USS *Eagle*, seen in 1917. She fired the first naval shots of the Cuban war. *(US Naval History and Heritage Command NH 64949)*

covered by the US Navy. First some small-scale probing landings were tried. On 10 May, the side wheel riverboat *Gussie* was sent to Cuba to land troops and deliver aid to the rebels. The steam yacht USS *Wasp* was part of the escort for the first such land action of the war. *Wasp*, ex-*Columbia*, launched in 1893, had been acquired from Joseph Harvey Ladew Sr, one of the largest leather manufacturers in the world, on 26 March for $95,000 and fitted with four 6pdr guns. Now she fired her guns in anger protecting the land forces' retreat back to the ships, the first naval fire of the war.

The Spanish had sent out a cruiser squadron under Admiral Pascual Cervera y Topete to sail to Cuba and aid in its defence. He managed to slip the USN blockade and enter the harbour of Santiago de Cuba on 29 May, but there he was essentially bottled up and harmless unless he ventured out.

American naval forces were under the overall command of Admiral William T Sampson, with Commodore Winfield Scott Schley in charge of the 'flying squadron', conducting the close blockade of Cuba. Sailing with the commodore was the yacht USS *Eagle* (1890), once the *Almy*. She was a sluggish steamer and Schley had cause to regret that she slowed down his formation on more than one occasion. But nonetheless, on 29 June her four 6pdrs shelled the Spanish battery at Rio Honda and on 12 July she captured the Spanish merchant ship *Santo Domingo*.

Mayflower, now armed with the not insubstantial fit-out of two 5in and twelve 6pdr guns, joined Admiral Sampson's squadron at Key West, Florida, on 20 April. Two days later, the squadron sailed to blockade Havana. On passage, *Mayflower* captured the Spanish schooner *Santiago Apostol*. She also took a number of fishing boats and coastal trading vessels. Then on 11 May, she boarded a large British-flagged blockade runner, a merchant steamer also named *Mayflower*, and sent her back to America under a prize crew. On the 14th, when three Spanish warships attempted to break out of Havana

G L Watson-designed USS *Mayflower*, which later became the presidential yacht, depicted in 1898. *(US Naval History and Heritage Command NH 60646)*

harbour, they were engaged by *Mayflowe*r, driving them back to the shelter of the guns of Morro Castle.

Another successful interception of a blockade runner by an armed yacht was made by USS *Hawk*. She was once the steam yacht *Hermione* (270grt), designed by George L Watson and built by Fleming and Ferguson of Paisley in 1891 for James and Richard Allan, owners of the Allan Line steamship company. They later sold her to American chocolate king and quondam Mayor of Boston, Henry L Pierce, and in April 1898 she joined the US Navy. Her state of the art electricals and power plant could drive her at a sustained speed of 14 knots.

On her first naval deployment, in early July, now as USS *Hawk* and armed

Another view of *Mayflower*. *(US Naval History and Heritage Command NH 1037)*

with two 6pdrs, she intercepted and destroyed the British-built *Compañía Transatlántica Española* vessel, *Alfonso XII* (1888), which was attempting to beat the blockade and deliver supplies to the Imperial forces in Cuba.*

Two converted yachts that wrote themselves into history were the USS *Hist* (311grt) and *Hornet* (301grt). *Hist* had been built in 1895 as *Thespia* for the grain merchant David Dows Jnr and was acquired by the navy in April 1898, whereupon she was fitted out with a single 3pdr gun. *Hornet*, formerly *Alicia*, was built by Harlan and Hollingsworth of Wilmington, Delaware, in 1890 for Henry Morrison Flagler (a founder of Standard Oil, and a key figure in the development of the Atlantic coast of Florida). She was also taken into the USN in April and armed with three 6pdr guns.

On 30 June, both yachts were cruising off the coast of Cuba, examining the keys and inlets around the port of Manzanillo for any sign of Spanish activity. In company was USS *Wompatuck*, completed in 1896 as the iron-hulled screw tug *Atlas* for Standard Oil. She too joined the USN for the Spanish war and was armed with two 6pdr and two 3pdr weapons. The three disparate vessels would now take part in a proper naval battle.

* Twenty-one CTE ships were used by the Spanish navy during the war.

The yacht *Hermione*, which became USS *Hawk*, pictured around 1900. She remained in the navy, in various roles, until 1940. *(US Library of Congress LC-D4-22123)*

USS *Hist* under way. She was photographed on 7 June 1898, prior to her departure from the US east coast for war service off Cuba. *(US Naval History and Heritage Command NH 53539)*

Firstly, they intercepted the British-registered, Spanish-crewed schooner and blockade runner *Nickerson*, chock full of provisions for the besieged soldiers, and took her in tow. Then at 0830 they came upon the Spanish 30-ton (displacement) gunboat *Centinela* near Niguero Bay. *Wompatuck* drew too much water for her to pursue the Spaniard as she retreated into shallow water near the coast, but *Hist* and *Hornet* followed her and engaged *Centinela*. Despite gunnery support from Spanish troops on shore, *Centinela's* crew beached her.

Hornet at a quayside somewhere in the USA. *(US Naval History and Heritage Command NH 53418)*

Hist now led the three ships into Manzanillo harbour itself, where they found a number of merchant ships, four Spanish gunboats and an armed sailing vessel. Three of these vessels had been moored up as static armed pontoons. Lieutenant Lucian Young, commanding *Hist*, opened fire with his single 3pdr as soon as the range came on and *Wompactuck* and *Hornet*, second and third in line, followed his lead. They received a heavy fire in return, from both water-borne and land-based artillery, and the American weight of gunnery was weakened when after firing only seven rounds, *Wompatuck's* forward 3pdr fired sheared off the rivets at the base of the mount, forcing her to fall out of column formation to bring her other weapons to bear.

Meanwhile, *Hornet* had taken a disabling hit, which severed the main steam line, depriving her of motive power. Yachts were never designed to fight in line of battle; now the lack of any defensive armour and protection rendered her static and the escaping steam scalded three men, one of whom later died. But Lieutenant James Meredith Helm, her captain, continued to fire while the tug made efforts to fix a tow; the two ships together made a tempting target for the Spanish gunners and both came under a welter of fire.

After fifty-five minutes of action, it was time to retire. *Wompatuck* and *Hornet* crawled away from the harbour. But they were not out of danger, for

The cruiser USS *Brooklyn* (1895) mounted eight 8in and twelve 5in guns and was part of the squadron deployed to destroy the Spanish flotilla at Santiago de Cuba. *(US Library of Congress LC-B2- 4192-13A)*

Steam yacht USS *Vixen* at an unknown location. *(Library of Congress LC-D4-21079)*

J P Morgan's *Corsair* (II), his 'flagship' as commodore of the New York Yacht Club, seen here in 1892. *(US Library of Congress LC-D4-22014)*

a sloop full of Spanish soldiers approached them from their disengaged side. *Hornet*'s gunners opened fire with a 6pdr and claimed a hit and a sinking, later disproved.

All three American vessels escaped without further harm. Two pleasure craft and a tug boat had just fought a major action in a foreign harbour.

The Spanish Flotilla Comes Out

The US authorities knew that defeating the Spanish flotilla in Santiago harbour was vital to the successful conclusion of the war. As long as it stayed in port, the Spanish represented a 'fleet in being', an existential threat to US supply lines. But the Spanish governor of Cuba insisted Cervera's ships sail and attack the US ships stationed off shore. This was just what the USN wanted.

Additionally threatened by American and Cuban forces advancing overland towards Santigo, at 0940 on 3 July the Spanish squadron steamed out of the harbour to attempt to engage and escape from the waiting USN ships. Outgunned, Cervera made a desperate attempt to reach the open sea with the US forces in pursuit. Superior American naval gunnery and seamanship prevailed, and the entire Spanish force was sunk. And the steam yachts played their part.

The Spanish line was led by the armoured cruisers *Infanta Maria Teresa* (1890) and *Viscaya* (1891), both armed with two 28cm (11in) and ten 14cm (5.5in) guns; and the first American vessel to sight them emerging from harbour was the steam yacht USS *Vixen*, ex-*Josephine* (1896), once owned by financier Peter Arrell Browne Widener and now carrying four 6pdr guns, which she had used to good effect in the bombardment of Santiago harbour on 6 June. The navy had purchased her for $150,000 on 9 April.

Vixen went to full speed ahead and hard a port, which fortuitously took her away from the gunfire of her own side as the American cruiser *Brooklyn*

The armour cruiser *Viscaya*, which co-led the Spanish ships out of harbour on 3 July 1898. Note the elaborately decorated stem. *(US Naval History and Heritage Command NH 57996)*

Infanta Maria Teresa, *Viscaya*'s sortie partner. She is pictured at the opening of the Kiel Canal in 1895. *(US Naval History and Heritage Command NH 88603)*

USS *Gloucester*, previously *Corsair* (II). Her bow 6pdr gun can be clearly seen. *(US Naval History and Heritage Command NH 100294)*

Another view of *Gloucester*, forward, stern and midships guns visible. *(US Naval History and Heritage Command NH 61884)*

opened fire. Then *Viscaya* loosed a salvo toward her with her starboard bow guns, which went high.

The yacht tracked the Spanish line and when at 1105 she gained an opportunity to engage *Viscaya*, now almost battered to death by heavy shells and run aground to try to save her crew, *Vixen* opened fire. Two minutes later the Spaniard struck her flag and *Vixen*'s short artillery bombardment came to an end. *Hist* came to the rescue of 142 Spanish sailors, lifting them off their burning ship.

Another yacht was heavily involved in the battle. USS *Gloucester*, previously J P Morgan's *Corsair*, had been a luxurious vessel of 'princely comfort'.[6] But now she was armed with four 6pdr guns, four 3pdrs and two Colt machine guns, and was commanded by the quondam executive officer of the *Maine*, 48-year-old Lieutenant Commander Richard Wainwright; and he was spoiling for a fight to avenge his lost ship.

Two Spanish torpedo boats started to come out from the harbour and were spotted by USS *Indiana* (1893), which sent out a signal stating that two torpedo boats were headed seawards. Bafflingly, Wainwright chose to interpret this as being the signal for the USN gunboats (*Gloucester* was so classified by the USN) to close in.

He wheeled his ship to attack, despite her limited manoeuvrability as a result of having only a single screw – not an issue for a pleasure yacht but a limitation for a warship – and started to chase the Spaniards, who were running close to the shore in their attempt to escape. In doing so he crossed the line of *Indiana*'s field of fire, causing her to cease her bombardment and silencing for a moment her four 13in guns. It was no matter to Wainwright, however, he ploughed on, attacked the torpedo boat *Furor*, which he left disabled with a jammed rudder, caused the other Spanish torpedo boat, *Pluton*, to run herself aground under his fire, and then launched *Gloucester*'s boats to rescue forty-five of *Pluton*'s survivors. Bravely, Wainwright also sailed to the now burning hulks of the *Infanta Maria Teresa* (hit twenty-two times) and the *Almirante Quendo* and picked up more Spanish survivors.

This was not the end of the ex-steam yacht's adventures in the war. On 25 July, Wainwright took her ahead of the fleet into the defended harbour of Guanica, Puerto Rico. Single-handedly she silenced the batteries and put a landing party of her own men ashore, capturing the town and holding it until land forces could take over and fully occupy the position.

And still *Gloucester* was not finished. On 1 August, accompanied by the

USS *Frolic*, constructed by Globe Iron Works at Cleveland, Ohio. *(US Naval History and Heritage Command NH 53690)*

USS *Dorothea*, built by William Cramp & Sons in Philadelphia, and the only ship of the United States Navy to bear that name. *(US National Archives at College Park)*

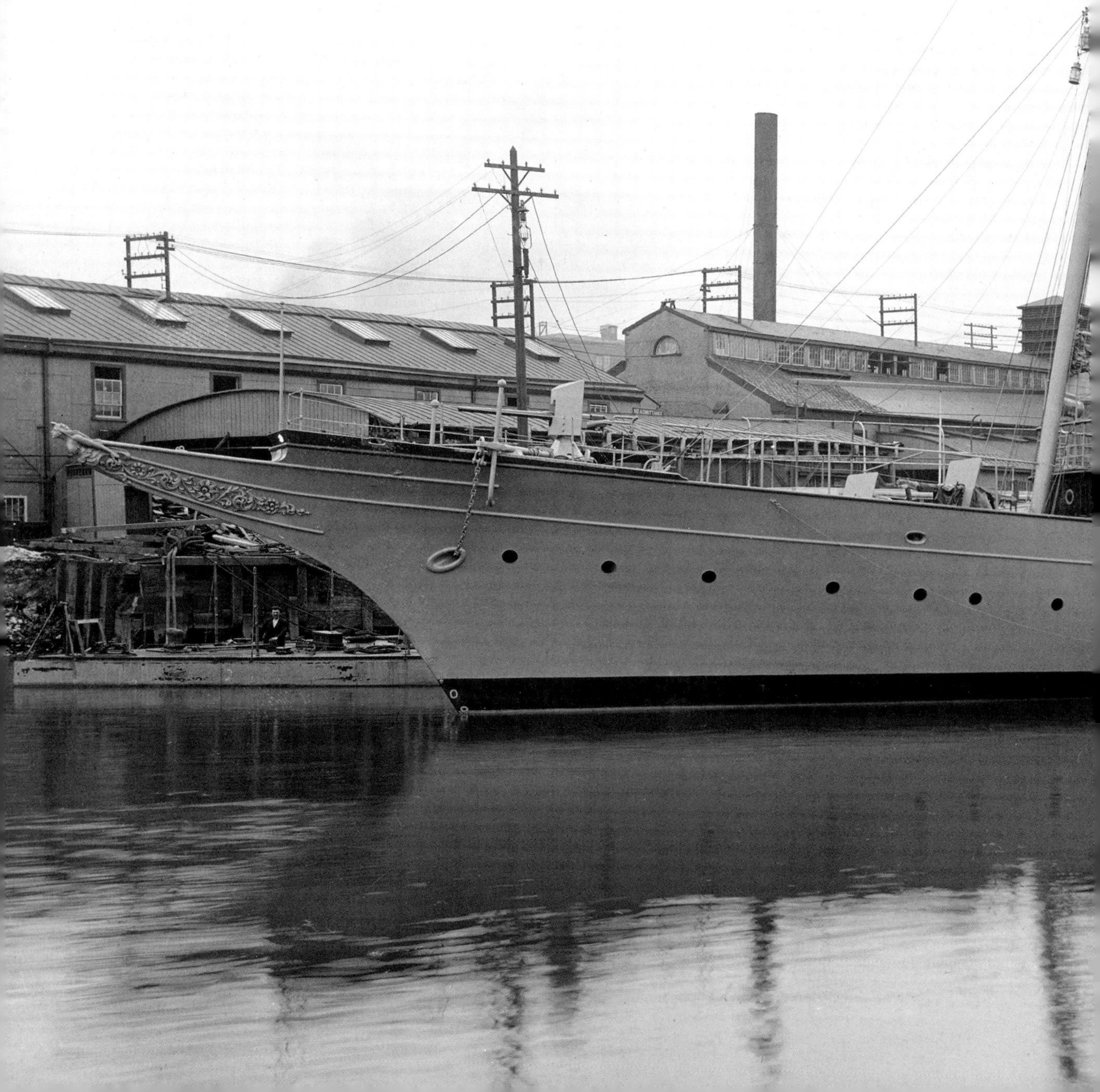

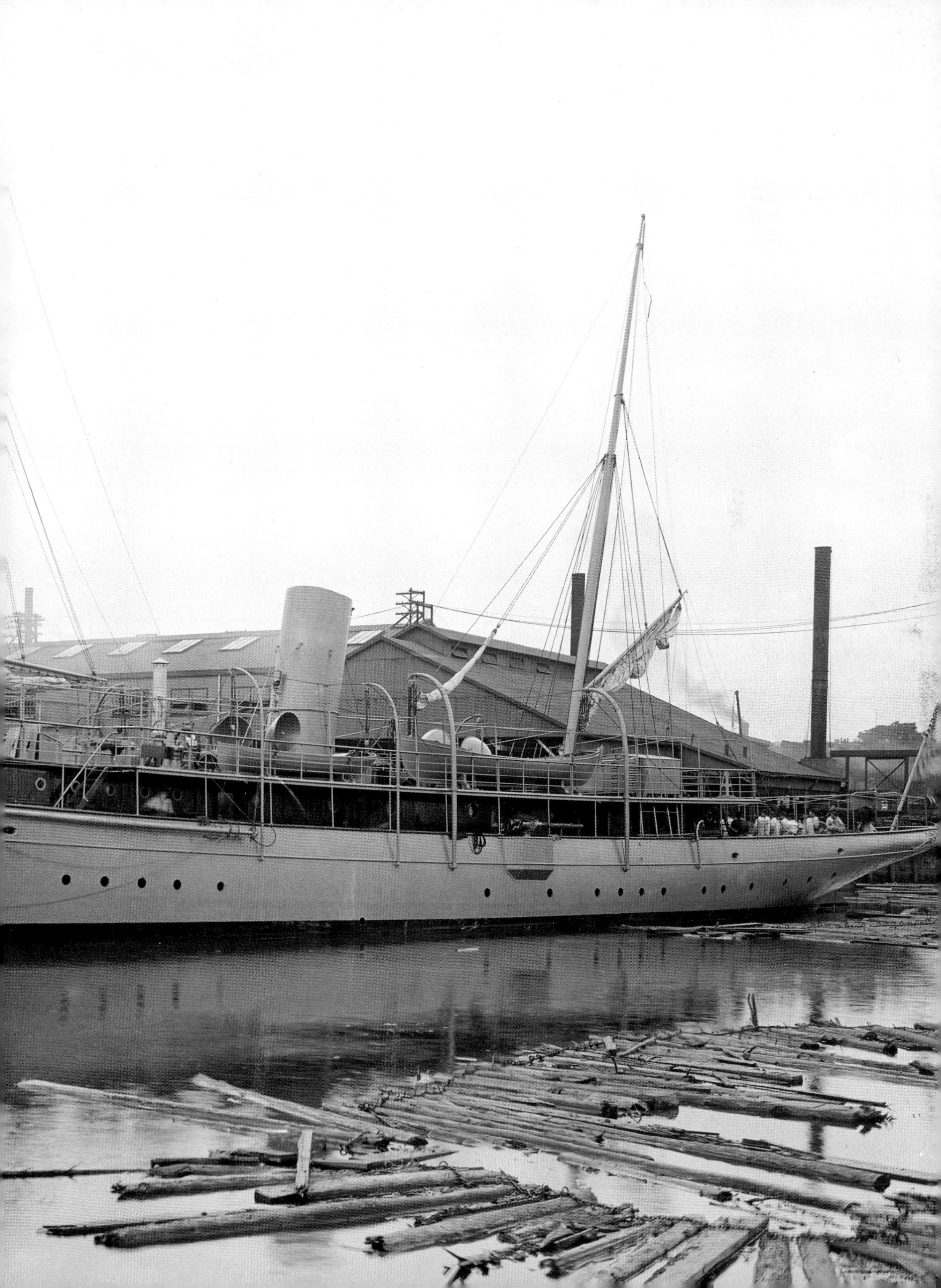

A group of petty officers of the armed yacht *Free Lance* (1895), gathered around a .65 Gatling gun, one of two that formed her main armament. From the yard of Lewis Nixon, Elizabethport, NJ, she was returned to her owner in 1899. *(US Library of Congress LC-DIG-det-4a13892)*

USS *Inca* at Boston Navy Yard, Charlestown, Massachusetts, on 9 November 1898. The larger ships in the background are USS *Vulcan* (centre) and USS *Wabash* (behind sheer legs), while a variety of rowing boats can be seen in the left foreground. *(US Naval History and Heritage Command NH 53225)*

steam yacht USS *Wasp*, Wainwright took possession of Arroyo, and hoisted the Stars and Stripes, holding the port until the arrival of the army a day later. USS *Hist* too had more work to do; she returned to Manzanillo Bay twice more during the war, on 15 July and 12 August. In the first of these engagements, ten Spanish ships were sunk and others seriously damaged. In company with *Wompatuck* and *Hornet* once more, *Hist* cut the important telegraphic cable connecting Media Luna and Quizaro Islands on 11 July and followed this up by cutting the cable between Punta Carapacho and Cayo Obispo on the 21st.

The makeshift warships had proved their worth.

They Also Served

Not all of the purchased pleasure boats had such exciting times, however. USS *Dorothea*, laid down in Philadelphia in 1897, was acquired on 21 May the following year and commissioned in June. She had been purchased for $187,000 from the estate of Philadelphia railway magnate Thomas McKean and had only been launched five months earlier. Of 433grt, she was a large vessel and able to mount four 6pdr and two 3pdr guns. But they were never fired in anger and she patrolled from Key West to Havana without incident, until returning to Hampton Roads on 28 August.

Frolic was simply overtaken by events. She had been built in 1892 for Howard Melville Hanna,* who had made a fortune in oil and shipbuilding, as the yacht *Comanche* and was commissioned by the navy on 6 July 1898. *Frolic* departed Portsmouth, New Hampshire, on 23 July 1898 with mail for ships on duty off Cuba and Puerto Rico but the war ended while she was undertaking her tasking.

Other yachts filled even more quotidian duties. USS *Yankton* (previously named *La Cleopatre, Sapphire III* and *Penelope)* was a steel-hulled schooner built in 1893 at Leith, Scotland, by Ramage & Ferguson. She was acquired by the US Navy in May 1898. Allegedly, among her previous owners was

* The younger brother of the influential power broker and senator, Mark Hanna.

Yankton was a steel-hulled schooner built in 1893 at Leith, Scotland, by Ramage & Ferguson and fitted out with a 4in and six 3pdr guns in May 1898. *(US Naval History and Heritage Command NH 67795)*

the famous actress, Sarah Bernhardt. *Yankton* spent the war serving as a gunboat, admiral's yacht and fleet tender.

Inca (1898) was a small 94grt yacht. She was equipped with an 11pdr gun and patrolled Boston Harbour, without venturing further. And USS *Aileen* (1896), of 151grt but armed solely with a 3pdr gun, was found unfit for cruising the open seas and served as a coastal defence vessel.

The short war ended on 13 August. Of the twenty-eight converted steam yachts, all survived the conflict. Four were handed over to the army and eleven were returned to their owners or sold on.

Peace and a New Empire

With the Treaty of Paris (11 April 1899), which formally ended the hostilities, the USA became an imperial power. Apart from Hawai'i, already garnered, America gained the Philippines, Puerto Rico and Guam, while Spain relinquished sovereignty over Cuba, but did not cede it. The era of the American Imperium had begun. And as Massachusetts senator Henry Cabot Lodge put it, 'the master of Manilla can make terms with every power in the East and those vast markets must be held open to the interest of our industry and our commerce, of our farmers and our working men'.[7]

The Spanish, on the other hand, called it *El Desastre*.

There was a small postscript of relevance to Britain, which had maintained a studied neutrality throughout the war. Resentful that the British government had not offered any support to its European neighbour, Spain commenced the construction of artillery emplacements that would menace the Royal Navy fleet based at Gibraltar. Acting Foreign Secretary Arthur Balfour instructed the British ambassador to Madrid, Sir Henry Drummond Wolff, to inform the Spanish that the fortification must cease immediately and that Britain would not shrink from any measures to ensure that it did. The building works stopped.

CHAPTER THREE

LET SLIP THE YACHTS OF WAR

THERE HAD BEEN an official British observer at the naval battles off Cuba; Sir Alfred Henry Fitzroy Paget.[1] He was a strange choice for a naval eyewitness, for he was a career soldier. However, he had three qualifications for the role. Firstly, he was a keen yachtsman and his father had been Commodore of the Royal Thames Yacht Club. Secondly, he was married to an American heiress, Mary 'Minnie' Stevens, daughter of the extremely wealthy Massachusetts hotel proprietors Paran Stevens and Marietta Reed Stevens. Minnie was a noted society hostess, well-known for her jewels and expensive costumes, and Paget was thus welcome in the highest Stateside circles. And thirdly he was there at the time. He would have been able to provide some first-hand feedback to the authorities in Britain of the utility of the armed yachts.

The Auxiliary Patrol

Britain's nineteenth-century navy had largely been configured on the principle that France would be the foe. The major naval bases were Portsmouth and Plymouth, looking towards the adversary across the English Channel. There was little in the way of defence facing Germany across the North Sea.

Furthermore, Britain's naval strategy had been to follow the Nelsonian doctrine of 'close blockade'. The fleet would be deployed close up to the enemy's ports, preventing exit of its ships, or forcing it to seek battle, and stopping the inflow of war materials. Close blockade had some advantages, the best perhaps being that it was legal under the dictates of the Hague Convention.

But the *matériel* changes such as the torpedo, mine, submarine and small, fast torpedo boats, undermined this strategy completely. They redefined the rules. Admiral Sir John 'Jacky' Fisher, First Sea Lord from 1904 to 1910, was one officer who recognised this and with it the realisation that close blockade would be impossible in modern conditions. Fisher was one of the few Royal Navy leaders who saw clearly that the advent of new technologies had revolutionised naval warfare.

More than anyone, Fisher understood that the coming of the torpedo-armed submarine, and the availability of mines, meant that the narrow waters of the North Sea and English Channel became a high-risk environment for large and expensive capital ships. Rather than chance battleships in such a situation it was better, he argued, to police those waters through 'flotilla defence', using large numbers of torpedo boats (surface vessels carrying on-deck torpedoes), submarines and torpedo boat destroyers (more usually abbreviated to 'destroyers') to render the waters uninhabitable for enemy battleships or potential invasion fleets.

It was also clear to Fisher, and increasingly to Britain as a whole, that Germany was the more likely adversary and the North Sea would be the battleground. By 1912, this change of thinking had led to the acceptance that distant, not close, blockade was the solution, bottling up the North Sea.

So distant blockade became the *de facto* strategy, driven by fear of the submarine and mine menace in the closed waters of the North Sea. But this required a large number of small vessels to police the east coast waters, and they did not exist.

In recognition of this, in 1911 the Admiralty formed the RNR(T), the Trawler Reserve, and approval was given to recruit 1,278 ratings to man 142 trawlers. Over the course of the coming war this would grow to more than 3,000 fishing vessels on (primarily) anti-submarine or minesweeping duties.

On the outbreak of war, defence of the east coast of Britain was vested in the Admiral of Patrols, who commanded destroyer flotillas, designed to act as a mobile force that could be deployed anywhere along the littoral. By December, there were also twenty-seven patrol areas, each under a senior naval officer, often a 'dug out' (a retired senior officer recalled to duty) with a shore base and again under the overall supervision of the Admiral of Patrols.* There were also eleven patrol areas in the Mediterranean, variously under British, French or Italian (after 1915) control. A random assortment of vessels was entered into the organisation; trawlers, drifters, tugs and motor launches. And to this mix, no doubt with the US Navy's experience somewhere in mind, the Admiralty added hired or purchased steam pleasure yachts, initially as command vessels. These civilian craft were known collectively as the 'Auxiliary Patrol'.

From 1914, hunting patrols, based on the Admiralty patrol areas, sought the foe. They generally comprised an armed yacht, furnished with wireless, four more or less armed trawlers or drifters and possibly a motor boat or two. Such patrols continued throughout the war. Admiral Reginald Bacon, commanding the Dover Patrol between 1915 and 1917, thought that 'the yachts attached to the drifters and trawlers did good work. For the drifters they acted as wireless stations and as links of communication, and did much the same services for the trawlers before these vessels were fitted with wireless. Of course, for defensive purposes they were useless, but at the same time their size in some manner gave a feeling of support to the smaller boats. Psychology in war is not to be ignored.'[2]

* The post of Admiral of Patrols was originally created in May 1912 to protect the coasts from invasion or raid. It was abolished in 1915 and the patrol destroyers and the auxiliary vessels then came under the direct control of the admiral commanding the local district.

Even in 1917 there were 150 such Auxiliary Patrol groups, often made up of one yacht and up to six armed trawlers. The latter were often equipped for minesweeping as well and generally had 6pdr or 12pdr guns. One or more of the trawlers were also fitted with radio and named as second and third leader. Armed yachts were also formed into specialist yacht squadrons, where their speed, superior to a trawler, might be more useful in fixing an enemy. Just as in the USA sixteen years earlier, the rich men's playthings were going to war.

Steam Yachts Join the Navy

War was rather inconsiderately declared in the middle of Cowes week. James Butler, 3rd Marquess of Ormonde, Commodore of the Royal Yacht Squadron (and also Vice Admiral of Leinster) and his wife had been in residence at 'Solent Lodge' since 11 July. Among his guests was the Primate of Ireland. Edward Guinness, Viscount Iveagh, with Viscountess Adelaide arrived at their house 'Thornhill' a little later. His 204-ton schooner *Cetonia* appeared regularly at Cowes. Evelyn Seymour, 17th Duke of Somerset, and his duchess were in residence at 'Hardwicke' for the month of August. And Admiral Sir Francis Bridgeman, a former First Sea Lord (1911–12), member of the RYS and a regular competitor in his younger days, was at 'Cliff Side' with Lady Bridgeman.[3] All of society was gathered on the Isle of Wight, many arriving directly from the racing week at Glorious Goodwood, when Kaiser Wilhelm interrupted the proceedings.

Immediately, yachts were volunteered for naval service by their owners or requisitioned from them by the Admiralty. In both cases, promises were made to return the vessel in a decent state, and in the latter case a lawful transfer of ownership or hire was arranged. According to First Lord of the Admiralty Winston Churchill, the 'intention of the Admiralty is to obtain the vessels which they require on conditions as little onerous to the owners as possible'.[4] Financial compensation was certainly made but the process failed to satisfy everyone. The 11th Duke of Bedford, Herbrand Russell, writing from Woburn Abbey on 16 January 1915, complained bitterly to Churchill that he had been informed that his yacht *Sapphire* was about to be requisitioned for service. 'I am further informed,' he expostulated, 'if I like to voluntarily to make a magnanimous offer of my yacht, I shall not only avoid requisition and escape a heavy pecuniary penalty but receive a handsome *douceur* in cash … I do not know how the Admiralty are justified in promising pecuniary rewards and other advantages to owners who voluntarily offer their yacht and in threatening pecuniary penalties to those who prefer the less obtrusive method of legal transfer.'[5] Churchill told him that he had misunderstood the process.

At first yachts were offered up free of charge, with the Admiralty paying all equipment and running costs. If at the end of three months the yacht was still required for naval service, she was hired by the Admiralty at a fee of £1 per ton per month.

Boats were donated or taken from members of all the major yacht clubs. The Royal Yacht Squadron, for example, provided no fewer than thirty-eight vessels. Of these, four were sunk by mines, one was lost in a collision, one was wrecked while chasing a submarine in heavy weather and all the others survived the war. Four other yachts served as hospital ships and the club's headquarters, Cowes Castle, was opened up for the care of convalescent naval officers.

The yachts taken up by the Royal Navy were of many and varied types. The steam yacht *Molly* was built in 1897 by Camper and Nicholson as a gentleman's yacht. Built of pitch pine on an oak hull with teak topsides on oak, her boiler and engine room occupied most of the midships area. *Molly* was requisitioned by the Admiralty in 1914 and renamed *Undine*. She was unarmed and used for harbour-guard duties, patrols and general 'maid of all work' inshore duties in the Solent because, as a coal-fired steamer with limited endurance, she could not travel far from base.

By contrast, the 437grt Clyde-built *Tighnamara*, launched in 1890 by Fleming and Ferguson's yard, was a 165ft-long, twin-masted schooner with a single amidships funnel. Commissioned by Alexander Allen, joint owner of the Allen Lines steamship company, most of her fittings were solid brass and even her toilets were highly decorated with blue flowers and curling blue foliage running riot around the china washbasins. Passing through a succession of owners, her name was *Verona* when she was taken up by the Admiralty in November 1914. Fitted with radio and armed with two 6pdr guns and depth charges, she was set to work on anti-submarine patrol in the Moray Firth.

The wealthy Paisley-based cotton thread manufacturer George Coats (later George, Baron Glentanar) volunteered his steel screw steamer schooner *Minona*. Of 199grt, she was a G L Watson-designed, Ramage & Ferguson-built, vessel originally launched in 1906 for one Robert Stewart of Glasgow and acquired by Coats in 1909.

Hecate (1903), 434grt, was built for Andrew Coates by D W Henderson of Glasgow. She entered the Royal Navy in October 1914 and served until March 1919. *Hecate* was armed with a 12pdr and a 6pdr and later served in the Second World War as *Aarla*. *(Author's collection)*

The Admiralty took up *Minona* on 7 October 1914, fitted her with two 6pdrs and deployed her around the coast of Britain on patrol duty; she survived the war (and the next one) and her later owners included Elizabeth Taylor and Richard Burton.

Hecate was built in 1903 by D and W Henderson and Co. for Andrew Coats. Coats was another member of the wealthy Paisley thread-making family, in his case with a personal penchant for polar exploration. Of 424grt, she was taken up by the navy in October 1914 and fitted with a 12pdr and a 6pdr weapon. She too survived to fight in the next global conflict.

The yacht *Monsoon* (1897) offered a Coats connection, too. Her owner was Thomas Julius Hirst, of German parentage and education, who was a director of J and P Coats and of Messrs Jonas Brook and Brothers, sewing cotton manufacturers of Huddersfield. She was also a G L Watson vessel, built by the Ailsa Shipbuilding Company of Troon. She was taken up in May 1915 and fitted with two 12pdr guns.

Zaza was the twin-masted, 423grt, personal yacht of William Beardmore* of Tullicheun Castle, sole proprietor of the William Beardmore shipyard at Govan since 1886. She was unsurprisingly built by his yard and launched in 1905 with a single-screw engine of Beardmore's own manufacture. William Beardmore had sponsored Ernest Shackleton's 1907 Antarctic expedition, and Shackleton named the Beardmore Glacier after him. He was also a member of the Royal Yacht Squadron.

* Sir William from 1914 and Lord Invernairn from 1927.

William Beardmore's *Zaza*, painted by Antonio de Simone and wearing the flag of the Royal London Yacht Club. *(© National Maritime Museum PY8806)*

North Star II, taken up in November 1915 and armed with two 3in guns. *(Author's collection)*

In September 1914, *Zaza* was requisitioned as a patrol vessel, fitted with a 12pdr and two 6pdr guns, and continued in that role throughout the war, being returned to her owner in March 1919. She had a brief moment of fame during the first raid by the German navy on Great Yarmouth on 2 November 1914, which was watched by a naval reservist from his hotel window. The yacht was trying to dispose of a mine by gunfire when suddenly the old gunboat *Halcyon* and a destroyer were observed to take off seawards and then quickly return seeking shelter in the harbour from a hail of gunfire that pursued them, and more that was directed at the town. The destroyer zigzagged laying smoke and both survived while the town was hit and seventeen civilians killed. *Zaza* was seen to have carried on her mine disposal work while hell broke out around her.[6] She would be purchased by the Admiralty for service again in 1939.

In 1893, Francis Denzil Edward Baring, 5th Baron Ashburton, commissioned W C Storey to design, and Naval Construction and Armaments Ltd (later Vickers) to build, the large steam yacht *Venetia*,* 819grt. She was named after his first-born child, the Hon Venetia Marjorie Mabel (born 1890).† A renowned yachtsman, Ashburton sold her five years later, when she became *Sybarite* and then *Cherokee* before General Cornelius Vanderbilt purchased her in 1902 and renamed her *North Star II*. Vanderbilt was an experienced sailor and during his ownership she served as the flagship for the New York Yacht Club and cruised extensively abroad.

When war came, *North Star II* was lying at Cowes. Sources differ as to her role in the conflict. Dittmar and Colledge have her fitted with two 3in guns and taken up in October 1915. Other sources suggest that she was turned over to the navy in 1914 and converted to a hospital ship, for which her size would fit her. Possibly she fulfilled both roles. Whatever her part, she was dropped from the Lloyd's registry in 1920.

Owned by Royal Yacht Squadron member Herbert A Foster, managing

* *Venetia* seems to have been a popular name for a steam yacht and there are a confusingly large number of vessels so named in the period.

† Later, Maid of Honour to Queen Mary.

The armed yacht *Portia* (1906) painted by W L Wylie. This watercolour shows *Portia* as an armed patrol vessel leaving Portsmouth Harbour, with a three-stacker 'L' class destroyer on the same course between her and Camper and Nicholson's yard at Gosport on the left. HMS *Victory* is in stern view on the right at her usual mooring off the Clarence Victualling Yard. *Portia*, built by Cammell Laird at Birkenhead, was hired into Admiralty service on 8 October 1914 and equipped with a 12pdr and a 6pdr gun. She was renamed *Portia II* in December 1915 and was returned to her pre-war owner on 1 April 1919. (© *National Maritime Museum* NMM PAF1139)

director of the engineering firm John Foster and Son, *Portia* was a 433grt steam yacht built in 1906 to the designs of St Clare John Byrne. She joined the navy in October 1914, had her name changed to *Portia II*, and was armed with one 12pdr and one 6pdr. She served until April 1919 and was based around the Orkney Islands.

And *Vanduara*, an all-steel screw schooner, was another from naval architect George L Watson, built by D and W Henderson in Glasgow in 1886. Originally owned by Stewart Clark of Dundas Castle, South Queensferry, for nearly twenty years, she was 170ft long with a 24ft beam. She was sold to J Mann-Thomson in 1905 and he loaned her to the Admiralty in September 1914 for wartime duties as a submarine depot ship. But *Vanduara* proved unsuited to the task and in February 1915 she was returned to her owner.

Initially, it was not uncommon for the owners of the yachts to serve on them, or even command them, once they had joined the navy; such men would be commissioned into the RNVR. *Aries*, 201grt, was the yacht of the vice commodore of the Royal Yacht Squadron, George Godolphin Osborne, 10th Duke of Leeds, who pre-war held the honorary rank of captain in the RNVR. She was one of the first yachts to be taken into service and the duke, although aged 53 at the time, served in her in the North Sea.

Maid of Honour (1907, 419grt) by Ailsa of Troon for wealthy stockbroker William King Millar. In April 1915 she was taken up as a patrol vessel from her then owner, Marion G Thornton of Cavendish House, Ryde, Isle of Wight, fitted with two 12pdrs and used as a patrol vessel. *(Author's collection)*

And the 5th Duke of Sutherland, George Sutherland-Leveson-Gower, commanded his 688-ton yacht *Catania* (1895) in the yacht patrol around Cromarty until he was sent to serve with the British Military Mission to the Belgian Army in 1915. However, on his return he resumed command of his vessel, this time in the Mediterranean.

But the employment of yacht owners in such roles fell into disuse owing, according to Edward Keble-Chatterton, to 'one or two incidents that occurred which made this undesirable'.[7]

James Cleland Burns, 3rd Lord Inverclyde, put his vessel forwards, the 1,042grt *Beryl*, built in 1893. She was taken up in January 1915, armed with one 3pdr and one 12pdr and used by the Director of Naval Intelligence until October 1915. Subsequently she served at Queenstown, Portsmouth, Kirkwall and Dundee and survived the war.

John Graham Hope Horsley de la Poer Beresford, 5th Baron Decies, international polo player, yachtsman and RYS member, had the large *Atalanta*, a 1,303grt steam yacht built in 1903, requisitioned in June 1915.* She was fitted with two 3in guns and for the remainder of the year served as an examination, rescue and patrol vessel based at Milford Haven, before transfer to the Mediterranean as an anti-submarine unit.

At the other end of the size scale, the 126grt *Rhiannon* was a ketch owned by Lord Howard de Walden. *Rhiannon* had been the private steam yacht of Thomas Evelyn Scott-Ellis, 8th Baron Howard de Walden, 4th Baron Seaford, landowner, writer, patron of the arts and a participant in the power boat races at the 1908 Olympics. After succeeding to his family titles in 1899, Howard de Walden received his inherited estates when he came of age in 1901. These included a large part of Marylebone, London, and earned him the title of 'Britain's wealthiest bachelor'. And the equally small *Cecilia*, the property of Sir Charles Wyndham Murray, Gentleman Usher of the

* It is not clear that the yacht was actually owned by Decies, although it was registered to him at the Royal Yacht Squadron. *Atalanta* had been first owned by the American engineer and steam pioneer A L Barber as *Lorena*, then was purchased in 1907 by another American, the railway magnate George Jay Gould. It was to Gould that the Admiralty returned the vessel in 1919. Lord Decies was married to Gould's daughter Helen, so that is the probable route by which the vessel came into his care.

Scarlet Rod of the Order of the Bath and a former MP, was used under her owner's command as a transport for taking parties of convalescing soldiers for joy rides out from Netley Hospital, Southampton.

The Admiralty's stock of patrol vessels was sometimes added to from abroad. For example, the famous French yachtswomen and racer Madame Virginie Hériot sent her 1903, G L Watson-designed, *El Salvator* (ex-*Katoomba*)* of 646grt to Britain, both to serve in the naval war but also to avoid capture by the occupying German forces.† In naval service, she became just *Salvator* and was fitted with two 12pdr guns.

An armed yacht of exotic provenance was *Safa-El-Bahr* ('Joy of the Sea' in Arabic), a single-screw, 14-knot, 487grt twin-mast steamer built in 1894 by A and J Inglis of Glasgow to the designs of their managing director, Dr John Inglis. The client was His Highness The Khedive of Egypt, Abbas II, who registered her at Alexandria.

Safa-El-Bahr was constructed of Siemens steel with teak bulwarks, railings and deck fittings, and the Khedive's room was panelled in English oak, while his bathroom was marble with silver fittings. His Highness was so pleased with his new toy that Inglis was made a Commander of the Imperial Order of the Osmanie.

In 1900 she passed into the ownership of Argentinian-born, American Civil War veteran Colonel Francis L Leland and was then acquired two years later by Charles M Schwab, steel magnate and president of the Bethlehem Steel Corporation. In 1915, she was hired by the Royal Navy, armed with two 3in guns and commissioned into service on 23 August.

And so it went on; by the end of the war, a total of 159 yachts had been enrolled by the Admiralty.

Steam Yachts as Hospital Ships

Britain operated many hospital ships during the war. Steam yachts played a part here, too. *Liberty* had been built by Ramage & Ferguson at Leith to the designs of George L Watson in 1908. She had been commissioned by Joseph Pulitzer, the American politician and publisher, after he had suffered loss of sight and developed an acute sensitivity to noise, and was one of the largest private yachts of her time at 1,607grt. She was especially fitted with ramps and soundproofing and was nicknamed 'The Tower of Silence'. Sailing in her, Pulitzer was able to travel the globe in a cocoon of calm, served by a forty-five-man crew, and a twelve-man staff of personal assistants to read aloud, play music, or provide conversation. This, one assumes made her ideal as a hospital ship.

Pulitzer died on board at Charleston, South Carolina, on 29 October 1911 and *Liberty* had only just been purchased by Lord Tredegar, Courtenay Charles Evans Morgan, when war broke out. Tredegar loaned her to the Admiralty and accompanied her to war as her commander; he also paid for her fit-out for medical purposes.

Unusually, originally she was a Royal Navy hospital ship. Most hospital

* In which she had spent her honeymoon, post marriage to Viscount François Marie Haincque de Saint Senoch.

† Her original owner had been Kenneth Clark of Paisley.

Liberty off Brownsea Island, Poole. *(Author's collection)*

ships were controlled by the army under the Red Ensign with a mercantile marine crew and army personnel (Royal Army Medical Corps and Queen Alexandra's Royal Army Nursing Corps) as medical staff. But when she first came into service the idea was that she could care for sailors in remote anchorages.

Another hospital vessel was the yacht owned by the future Liberal politician Henry Graham White, who contributed *Paulina*, 264grt, with his brother Arnold in command. Both these vessels were used to bring wounded men to Dover from Calais or Boulogne; to indicate their humanitarian purpose they were painted, as were all hospital ships, white with yellow funnels, a stripe of green round the sides and with a row of green lights. (*Liberty*, as a Royal Navy hospital ship, wore a red stripe and red lights.)

The St Clare John Byrne-designed steam auxiliary barquentine yacht *Sunbeam* was constructed for Thomas Brassey of railways fame. She was 532 tons, 159ft in length, built by Bowdler and Chaffer's in Seacombe, on the Wirral, and launched in 1874. *Sunbeam* became one of the most famous

Liberty, built for Joseph Pulitzer to the designs of G L Watson, and here seen as a hospital ship. *(Nottage Maritime Institute)*

Another picture of *Liberty* as a hospital ship. *(Nottage Maritime Institute)*

private yachts of the late Victorian era. Brassey took her on a world cruise with his wife Anna and their children, after which Anna wrote a book describing their travels that became a bestseller, reprinted many times and translated into many languages. When war came, Brassey himself sailed *Sunbeam* to Mudros Bay in 1915 to act as a hospital ship during the Gallipoli campaign.

Albion was launched in 1904 by Swan Hunter at their Tyneside Neptune yard. Fitted with three screws driven by three 300nhp Parsons turbines, she was designed by Sir William Henry White* for Sir George Newnes MP, a wealthy publisher and keen yachtsman. Of 1,116grt, she was taken up by the navy as a hospital ship in September 1914 but converted to an armed patrol vessel five months later. And *Queen Alexandra* was a small steam yacht of 267grt, built in 1902. She served as a hospital ship from March 1915 until the end of the war.

Sheelah, constructed in 1902 for William A Donaldson of Glasgow by John Brown and Co. Ltd at Clydebank, was a fine yacht of 466grt. In 1913, she had been purchased by Admiral David Beatty through the funds of his millionaire heiress wife, Ethel. When war came, the Beattys loaned her as a hospital ship, pennant number YA11, and Ethel paid for the conversion. In November 1914, *Sheelah* was honoured by a royal visit; 'Princess Christian†

* Director of Naval Construction at the Admiralty from 1885 until 1902.

† Queen Victoria's fifth child, Princess Helena of Britain and Princess Christian of Schleswig-Holstein.

Thomas and Annie Brassey's yacht *Sunbeam* (1874). She served as a hospital ship from 1915 but proved of limited utility and was handed over to the Indian government. The image below shows *Sunbeam* in Sydney Harbour, Australia, pre-war. *(Author's collection)*

David and Ethel Beatty's yacht *Sheelah*, converted to a hospital ship. *(Author's collection)*

last week paid a visit to the Queen Mary and Princess Christian Hospital at South Queensbury on the Firth of Forth where there are at present a number of sick cases from the Fleet in the wards,* and afterwards visited Lady Beatty, wife of Rear Admiral Sir David Beatty, on board the steam yacht *Sheelah* which is now equipped as a hospital ship.'[8] She was not returned to the admiral until 1923.

However, the use to which the Beattys' yacht was put seems to have been less than meets the eye. The Labour party MP for Blackburn and prominent anti-war socialist, Philip Snowden, attempted to capitalise on this when in August 1918, in the House of Commons, he asked the Secretary to the Admiralty 'if a yacht owned by the wife of a British admiral has been lying in Bo'ness Docks for the past two years; if this yacht was taken over by the Government early in the War for the purposes of a hospital ship; if practically no work of this character has been done; if the Government are paying the full cost of maintenance; if the captain and crew are standing by the vessel; and whether, in view of the importance of utilising every available ton of shipping, this vessel can be put to a useful purpose?'

The reply from Dr Thomas Macnamara, Parliamentary Secretary to the Admiralty, deflected the question with a reply that praised the generosity of the donors; 'The vessel in question is a yacht which has been used in emergency as a hospital ship, and will, if occasion arises, be used again. The Admiralty is at no expense in connection with the vessel which was offered free of cost, fully manned and equipped as a hospital ship in 1914, and so accepted. I am sure Lady Beatty would not desire me to say this, but

* There were actually 200 in-patients at the time of the visit.

Surf, pictured in peacetime. *(Author's collection)*

in view of the form of the question, I take occasion to say that we owe the gracious act of placing this vessel at our disposal to the kindly generosity of the wife of the Commander-in-Chief, Grand Fleet.' It was also explained that *Sheelah* 'does not accommodate many, but it has been used on different occasions, and will be used again. We are very much obliged to Lady Beatty.'[9]

American yachts became hospital ships too once the USA entered the war. *Surf* was built in 1898 by Ramage & Ferguson for one E D Lambert of Berkshire. He sold her to an American shoe manufacturer, who in turn passed her on to John Alton Harriss, a New York businessman and former physician. Harriss offered her to the USN as a hospital ship but only if he could serve on board as the chief medical officer. He also covered all the costs for painting her in Red Cross livery, her maintenance and the salaries of the doctors and nurses assigned to her. As converted, she could accommodate twenty-five patients.

Not on Admiralty Service

These vessels and owners, and all the others, answered their country's call. Even Royalty and the First Lord of the Admiralty gave up their yachts, although in these instances, the vessels did not serve in the war. The royal yachts *Victoria and Albert* (1899, the third of that name) and *Alexandra* (1907)* were laid up at Portsmouth in 1914 and the Admiralty yacht *Enchantress* (1903) was laid up at Sheerness.

Some experienced sailors wanted to lend assistance but found their way blocked. George S Bryan was a master mariner who had 'given up a very good position' by sailing from New York having been advised by the British consulate that he 'should receive a temporary commission in the RNR'.[10] He applied to the yacht patrol in February 1915, only to be told to try again in six weeks' time. By 26 April he was moved to write to Winston Churchill

* Some sources claim she was used as a hospital ship but this is probably a confusion with the yacht *Queen Alexandra*, referenced above.

Irish-born but American naturalised, renowned tenor John McCormack is photographed here singing on board *Surf*, with owner Dr Harriss sitting with folded arms by the piano. *(US Library of Congress LC-DIG-ggbain-27505)*

himself to seek a role in the war. Telling Churchill that 'he was not an American in any way but I am related to Mr William J Bryan, Secretary of State for the USA',[11] he asked to be given a reason why the navy didn't want him. Clearly at this point in the war, supply exceeded demand.

Others thought themselves deserving of greater recognition. Lord Dunraven, Windham Wyndham-Quin, 4th Earl of Dunraven and Mount-Earl, had been the owner and co-owner of the 1893 and 1895 America's Cup yachts *Valkyrie II* and *Valkyrie III*. He was a keen yachtsman and held an 'extra master's certificate' from the Board of Trade together with a commission as a lieutenant in the RNR.

The Admiralty had taken up his 108grt yacht *Scadaun* in 1914, fitted it with a 6pdr gun and paid him for its use. He had also equipped the 351grt yacht *Grianaig* as a hospital ship (Transport Hospital Carrier no 2806) at his own expense and paid for the crew and an on-board surgeon. Additionally, Dunraven had provided another smaller yacht, *Greta*, which he fitted out as a hospital vessel and intended to command himself. In early 1915 he wrote to Churchill suggesting that this generosity might be rewarded with an increase in naval rank. On 13 April Naval Secretary Captain Charles Martin de Bartolomé, poo-pooed the notion. 'His yacht is not on Admiralty service,' he wrote to the First Lord 'and I think it would be wrong and somewhat out of place to make him a commander RNR for such a small vessel.' In a separate note he added that 'if you so make him a temporary commander you will be in for a good deal of trouble – he really appears to have not a vestige of a claim'.[12] Dunraven remained, at least in his own mind, unrecognised. But he continued to skipper *Grianaig* at the age of 73 in her duties as a hospital ship at Dover.

Fitting Out

Once an owner had agreed to lend his yacht for the duration of the war, his vessel was taken to a naval dockyard – usually Portsmouth or Devonport – to be fitted out for war service. Names were sometimes changed and the prefix HMY – His Majesty's Yacht – applied.

Steam yachts had been designed for comfort, luxury and sometimes speed – but certainly not for war. Substantial modification was required to fit them for war service. Furniture and decorations were removed, and the

Surf converted and liveried as a hospital ship. *(US National Archives at College Park 45511205)*

mahogany, teak and oak panels were taken down and replaced by mountings for small arms. The hulls received coats of grey paint, while storm shutters replaced plate glass in the portholes and viewing panels. Crews were required to improvise sleeping berths. Yachts with sails had their masts shortened or removed and canvas-screened platforms or crow's nests erected. Galleys were enlarged to fulfil a different sort of catering requirement to their intended purpose. The bows, quarterdecks, and fantails now mounted guns, depth charge racks, and other equipment of war that required the strengthening of bulkheads and decks, the fitting of additional supports and the firm screwing down of the gun mountings.

But their basic deficiencies remained. They had no armour, were not necessarily constructed for constant use and heavy seaways, and were often less manoeuvrable than their likely adversaries. 'Many of the steam yachts were only single screwed,' wrote Edward Keble Chatterton, who himself served in the Auxiliary Patrol, 'extremely unhandy ... and anything but ideal for anti-submarine work.'[13] And an anonymous contributor to *Yachting Monthly* magazine noted that 'as a patrol flagship or an executive headquarters, the modern steam yacht is certainly well adapted but one must recognise the type's commercial inadaptability when in competition with, say, steam trawlers or drifters'. The same writer went on to note that 'steam yachts ... are the most costly of craft and, apart from their engines and boilers, contain little that is usable for rough work. They are incapable of sustained speed in heavy weather and I should put 10 knots as their working average speed.'[14]

Manning the Yachts

In many cases, the original peacetime crew was 'volunteered' with the yacht. Where men stayed on, they were required to sign a T-124Y form. This protected their 'terms and conditions' of remuneration etc, but made them subject to naval discipline and orders, specifically stating 'any offence committed by any such person shall be tried and punished as the like offence might be tried and punished if committed by any person in or belonging to His Majesty's Navy, and borne on the books of any of His Majesty's ships in commission'. Generally, they became members of the MMR – Mercantile Marine Reserve. As their civilian pay was likely to be better than the rates for a regular RN sailor, this was a considerable benefit although, as will be seen in Chapter 11, it had disadvantages when the war was over.

There was a general shortage of engineers; six or so seamen ratings, usually RN, were put aboard to man the guns and often one or more RNVR radio operator, too. Any remaining needs were met from the RNR, MMR or ex-fishermen. SY *Lorna* provides a good example; half her crew was comprised of the original peacetime members, the rest were RNR or RNVR and two pensioners.[15]

As for the officers, 'generally speaking, the captain was a retired naval officer, sometimes a mercantile officer: the navigating officer and watch keep-

The wonderfully elegant royal yacht *Alexandra* (1907) seen at Malta. A triple-screw schooner of 1,728grt, built and partially designed by A J Inglis of Glasgow, she could achieve a speed of 18.8 knots. Laid up for the war, she was sold in 1925 to become the Norwegian cruise ship *Prince Olaf. (Author's collection)*

ers being selected from … the Royal Naval Reserve'.[16] They were drawn from the RNR, RNVR and to a surprising extent from reactivated Royal Navy retirees. Of the latter, one example that can stand for many was Charles James 'Billy' Barlow, a much-loved admiral who retired from the navy in 1911. But he volunteered to return, first ranked as commander RNR then as an acting captain, and in November 1914 the 66-year-old Barlow took command of the large steam yacht *Valiant* (1893, 1,855grt), originally built for W K Vanderbilt and previously noted herein, which now mounted four 12pdr guns. With her he patrolled in the North Sea until a mishap narrated in Chapter 5.

On 20 February 1915, Barlow was appointed to command Auxiliary Patrol Area XVII, based at Larne. Here he oversaw the net-laying drifters, which were in the process of creating an anti-submarine barrier that extended from the Mull of Kintyre to Rathlin Island, where a rectangular area 30 miles long and 12 miles wide was completely closed to navigation by the laying of nets from 23 February. A small passage 3 miles wide was left between Rathlin and the coast of mainland Ireland through which all traffic, neutral and Allied, had to pass, and then only between the hours of sunrise and sunset, and where it could be stopped and searched as necessary.

Additionally, Barlow 'was given a flying squadron of six large armed yachts, *Valiant*, *Jeanette*, *Marynthea*, *Medusa*, *Narcissus* and *Sapphire*'.[17] In all, it was a significant command for a man of his age and that is perhaps why he was replaced in the post two months later. Instead, he became the Admiralty representative for the supply of ammunition in Manchester and Leeds. His spirit was willing but the body was possibly not.

Arming the Yachts

In general, the yachts carried either 3pdr, 6pdr or 12pdr guns (or a mixture of the types); later in the war, machine guns and depth charges may also have been aboard.

The 12pdr had started life in 1904 as an anti-torpedo boat weapon on pre-dreadnought battleships. Of 3in/40 calibre (the Mark 1 was 3in/50), it fired a 12.5lb shell with a 3lb charge to a range of around 8,500–9,000yds. It became the standard armament for pre-war destroyers and as they were retired there were so many on hand that, from April 1912, as existing ones wore out no more were ordered. However, the wartime demand to arm auxiliary craft, including fishing vessels, was such that from May 1915 large quantities were once more requested of manufacturers and guns were taken from larger ships to be used in their smaller brethren.

The 6pdr gun most likely to be found was the Hotchkiss-made version, its use in the RN dating from 1890. It was widely fitted to destroyers and other small craft. Of 2.24in/40 calibre, it fired a shell of 6lb. In the latter part of the war, some were installed on high-angle mountings for use against Zeppelins and Gotha bombers. There was also a Nordenfelt version of 42.3 calibre.

The 3pdr (1.85in/40 calibre) was a product both of the Nordenfelt and Hotchkiss companies, first ordered for the Royal Navy in 1885. With a calibre of 1.85in/50, it delivered a 3lb 3oz shell over a range of 7,500–8,900yds. They were often used as saluting guns and when war came the battleships surrendered their 3pdrs for mounting in trawlers and drifters, particularly minesweepers, where they were used to sink swept mines. With a high muzzle velocity, they were considered a better anti-aircraft gun than the Hotchkiss 6pdr and began to appear in high-angle mountings from 1915.

None of these weapons were of the latest type but at least they were available. Initially 3pdrs and 6pdrs predominated; later 12pdrs began to be installed. It is estimated that sixty-nine of the latter were fitted to the yachts by the end of the war, usually just one, sometimes two and, in two cases, four (the yachts, *Valiant* and *Valhalla*). A total of seventy-three 6pdrs were fitted mainly in twos; and twenty-four 3pdrs were deployed.[18]

But as gun platforms, yachts were generally deficient; 'if they fired their guns, the decks became damaged and windows [were] smashed by the concussion'.[19] Nor were the hulls ever designed to withstand the stresses imposed by a gun firing; warping or damage was an ever-present risk.

Perhaps the last word on the suitability of steam yachts for war should be given to an American reservist officer, Ensign Joseph Hubbard USNRF; he thought that they were 'manned in a large measure by relatively inexperienced reserve officers, and themselves being by construction entirely unfitted for the service'.[20]

CHAPTER FOUR

STEAM YACHTS ON PATROL

YACHTS WERE PRIMARILY USED AS PATROL VESSELS. This could mean stopping cargo ships to check for contraband (goods intended for the enemy), investigating suspicious sightings, searching for floating mines, and looking for, and attempting to sink, U-boats. Because the Admiralty had not taken the threat posed by the submarine entirely seriously, neither had it aggressively pursued means of countering it. An *ad hoc* anti-submarine committee had been formed by the navy in 1910 under the presidency of Rear Admiral Cecil Burney, and reported its views at least fifty-five times to the Admiralty Board. But it went through five presidents in four years and, although some future needs were identified, a number of blind alleys were explored comprehensively. As Admiral Percy Scott commented, 'with regard to attacking submarines, as the Admiralty before the war regarded them as little more than toys, it was only natural that no progress had been made in the direction of taking measures for destroying them'.[1] Scott himself recommended putting rams on trawlers and destroyers, a measure harking back to the Greek wars in the Mediterranean of some 500 years BCE.

There was practically no such thing as a depth charge at the beginning of the war. Scott advocated 'a bomb which could be thrown down onto a submarine if she was on or near the surface'[2] from the deck of a ship. And indeed, one was developed, the lance bomb. This was a hand-thrown weapon comprising a 7lb charge of Amatol attached to a wooden handle some 4½ft long. It was a contact weapon, designed to explode when it hit a hard surface, such as a U-boat's hull, and was to be swung around the head of a strong seaman and then hurled at the enemy; an effective range of 75ft was claimed. The device was introduced in April 1915 and supplied to trawlers and other small craft. Lance bombs were not withdrawn from use until early 1917; in that time 20,000 units had been produced but no U-boat had ever been sunk by the method.

It was not until January 1916 that the first really effective depth charge, the Type D, became available. These were barrel-like casings containing a high explosive, TNT or Amatol. There were initially two sizes, Type D, with a 300lb charge for fast ships, and Type D-star with a 120lb charge for those ships too slow to clear the danger area of the more powerful charge. A hydrostatic pistol set to a pre-selected depth detonated the charge and they were supplied with two depth settings of 40 or 80ft. But they were in limited supply and most auxiliary vessels so equipped made do with only two until 1917.

Yachts Against the U-boats

Lord Dunraven's yacht *Scadaun*, the subject of his correspondence with Churchill, was taken into naval service on 7 October and despatched to Queenstown (now Cobh) on the south-west Irish coast. Armed with a single 6pdr gun, she was sent out in the wake of the sinking of the *Lusitania* by *U-20* on 7 May 1915 to search for survivors. Although *Scadaun* stayed out for forty-eight hours, she found only one empty life raft and some bodies.

Her commander, New Zealander Lieutenant Commander Wybrants Olphert RNR, had a chance to avenge the loss the following month when, on 21 June, *Scaduan* encountered a submarine off Fastnet and fired on her before she dived. Arriving over the spot where the U-boat disappeared, Olphert discovered a large quantity of oil on the surface, part of a cigar and bubbles among the oil. But after a search for several hours proved unsuccessful, he saw no more and departed, claiming a sinking. The Admiralty ruled that the attack had been successful and Olphert was Mentioned in Despatches and awarded the DSC. But in fact, post-war records showed that no U-boat had been lost on that day.*

His medal was part of a larger award to twenty-four captains from the Auxiliary Patrol recognising that 'the Lords Commissioners of the Admiralty have received with much satisfaction from the officers in charge of the Auxiliary Patrol areas at home and abroad in reports on the services performed by the officers and men serving under their orders during the period 1st January, 1915, to 31st January, 1916. These reports show that the officers and men serving in Armed Yachts, Trawlers and Drifters of the Auxiliary Patrol during the period in question have carried out their duties under extremely arduous and hazardous conditions of weather and exposure to enemy attack and mines with marked zeal, gallantry and success.'[3] It was a public affirmation of the service that the yachts were providing. Olphert was later awarded the Distinguished Service Order (DSO), and in 1919 a bar to his DSO.

The steam yacht *James Fletcher* was designed by R A Richardson of Liverpool and built by Messrs G. Philip and Son Ltd of Dartmouth at a cost of £12,900. She had been ordered by the Lancashire Sea Fisheries Committee, based at Fleetwood, and served them for nearly thirty years, interrupted only by the war. Taken up by the navy in September 1914, she was fitted with two 6pdr and one 3pdr guns and sent to patrol off the Kent coast.

Her captain was a retired naval officer, 38-year-old Commander Evelyn Leonard Beridge Boothby, who had been placed on the Retired List at his

* In 1917 the decoy ship *Q-15*, commanded by Olphert, was sunk and he was taken prisoner.

own request on 31 May 1912. Early in January 1916, *James Fletcher* was on a night patrol off the south Goodwin Sands when she came upon a U-boat travelling towards the west on the surface and at speed. In the dark, the submarine was only spotted at the last moment, 10yds off the starboard bow, the crew's voices audible before the enemy could be seen.

Deliberately or otherwise, Boothby contrived to ram the U-boat, striking it twice and dragging along the hull for a few seconds. The second strike was so hard that it virtually stopped the yacht's progress. Boothby and his crew were convinced that they had sunk the predator and claimed that it must be so for all the U-boat's hatches were open when they hit.

The Admiralty agreed and awarded prize money of £1,000; and Commander Boothby received the DSO for the action, in the same group as Olphert. But modern scholarship can find no U-boat sunk at that time.

It was not the yacht's last encounter with an enemy submarine, for in August 1918 *James Fletcher* and the drifter *J Burn* launched a depth charge attack against *UB-103* near the Dover Barrage. *UB-103* was commanded by the German submarine ace *Kapitänleutnant* Paul Hundius, who boasted seventy kills to his name and was the holder of the *Pour le Mérite*. The U-boat escaped but was sunk off the coast of Flanders on 14 September; she had been discovered by the British airship SSZ-1, which signalled the position of the U-boat to the drifter *Young Crow*. The submarine was already in trouble as she had lost oil, possibly through hitting a mine, but dived anyway. The crew of the *Young Crow* dropped depth charges where they had seen the U-boat submerge, resulting in two explosions and a third, large, explosion half an hour later. Hundius and all his men died.

As for Boothby, he had been relieved of his command on 8 March 1916 and undertook an appointment in the Yacht Patrol Office until the end of 1916. As an acting captain, Boothby was then appointed in command of the second-class protected cruiser *Hermione*, which spent the war at Portsmouth as a depot ship for motor launches.

One armed yacht played a part in protecting a damaged capital ship from U-boats. On 1 June 1916, the *Queen Elizabeth*-class battleship HMS *Warspite* (1913) was limping back to Rosyth, damaged in the Battle of Jutland the night before and being steered from the engine room. She had no escort and at 0935 was attacked by *U-51*, which fired two torpedoes, only one of which left the tubes and, in any case, missed. *Warspite* radioed for escort to come to meet her around forty-five minutes later. At 1142, just as the escorts began to arrive, the battleship was again being tracked, this time by *U-63*. But before the submarine could get a firing solution, *Warspite* fired on her, forcing a steep dive in which the U-boat hit the bottom and bounced up, becoming visible to the newly arrived torpedo boats and patrol yachts of the escort. They chased her off and attacked with depth charges but *U-63* escaped at around a depth of 100ft.

HMY *Mingary II* was one of the patrol vessels involved. She was a G L Watson-designed, Ailsa Shipbuilding-built, yacht of 1899, the second of

Watson's creations for diamond magnate Charles Durnell Rudd of Shielbridge, near Ardnamurchan, the business partner of Cecil Rhodes, and named after the thirteenth-century castle in the village of Kilchoan, the most westerly point of the British mainland. Of 591grt and over 179ft long, *Mingary II* was taken up by the Admiralty in January 1915, fitted with two 6pdr guns and sent to patrol the northern North Sea, where she helped save a battleship.

A month earlier, in the same area, the yachts *Semiramis* and *Portia* had succeeded in chasing off the German Schütte-Lanz airship *L-11*, which was trying to attack Rosyth.

Narcissus was an 816-ton steam yacht, built in 1905 and owned by Alfred Edward Miller Mundy, Squire of Shipley and Mapperley in Derbyshire and owner of Shipley Hall.* His family fortune came from coal; in 1899, Shipley's pits were excavating 420,000 tons of coal per annum and 2,000 miners were employed. Mundy played no part in the running of the family business, leaving that to his agent, but he took a keen interest in horticulture, sport, especially cricket (he built his own cricket ground), and yachting; inevitably, he was a member of the Royal Yacht Squadron.

Narcissus was taken into service in January 1915, had her name changed to *Narcissus II*, was armed with two 12pdrs and became part of the Auxiliary Patrol based on Gibraltar. Here she had several 'near-miss' encounters with U-boats.

On 25 August 1916, for example, the yacht spotted an enemy submarine at 1505, heard gunfire, and opened fire herself at extreme range. The U-boat submerged successfully but left behind a French steamer, the Sunderland-built SS *Socoa*, 2,772grt, damaged and sinking. *Narcissus II* searched for the escapee fruitlessly.

U-boats were also sighted and chased on 24 April and 19 May 1917, in the latter case when *Narcissus II* went to the aid of the Ellerman Lines SS *Mardinian*, 3,222grt, after hearing gunfire. The attacker had been *U-34*. No warning had been given but all the crew were saved before the merchantman sank.

* Built in 1700 and famous for its beautiful gardens under Miller Mundy's ownership, the house was demolished in 1943 and the grounds turned into a country park in the 1960s.

Alfred Mundy's yacht *Narcissus*, later *Narcissus II* in naval service, which caused *UB-49* to seek shelter in Cadiz in 1917. *(Author's collection)*

However, her closest encounter was on 7 September that year. Under the command of Captain John Philip Rolleston RNR* and steering east at about 10 knots, a submarine was seen about a mile ahead crossing the streak of light thrown by the lately risen moon. Her conning tower and a small portion of the hull were clearly visible and she appeared to be in diving trim and heading slowly south-east.

Rolleston sounded 'action stations' and rang for full speed. At 2343 and a range of 800yds he opened fire with common shell from the bow gun and claimed a hit at the base of the conning tower. There was only time to fire twice (the second fell short) as the submarine submerged swiftly, but Captain Rolleston held his course and speed until a little past the spot where she disappeared, which was still obvious owing to the disturbance of the water. Here he dropped a type D depth charge, which failed to explode.

Nonetheless, *Narcissus II* had caused considerable damage. Her prey was *UB-49*, which was forced to make for neutral Cadiz and was interned there. *Kapitänleutnant* Hans von Mellenthin and his crew gave their parole but then broke it, taking his boat back to sea to the fury of the Spaniards. A claim by Rolleston for prize money was supported by the Senior Naval Officer at Gibraltar but disallowed by the Admiralty.

Nor was this the end of the yacht's work in 1917. On 15 September she again heard heavy gunfire and, on going to investigate, found a sinking steamer with a U-boat on the surface. The enemy submerged before *Narcissus II* could get in range but she was able to rescue the victim's crew, who had taken to their boats.

The following year, on 29 April 1918, she was escorting a convoy from Genoa when it was attacked by a submarine. *Narcissus II* responded with depth charges, without effect. Then finally, on 23 September 1918, she was escorting a convoy from Gibraltar to Genoa when she again attacked a U-boat after it had sunk a steamer, but with the same negative result.

Narcissus II continued to serve until February 1919, when she was returned to Miller Mundy. But the presumably grateful owner did not enjoy her for long, dying on 15 April 1920, aged 70.

More Near Misses

Built in 1902 and of 526grt, *Rosabelle* was the third yacht of that name to be owned by Irish-born stockbroker and Quaker Theodore Pim. She was a very luxurious boat, even down to an allegedly gold-plated bath! Pim, whose family had made money in trade and broking in Dublin, was a well-known yachtsman, Commodore of the Royal Thames Yacht Club for eighteen years from 1905 (and where there is still a racing trophy named for him) and a member of the Royal Yacht Squadron. *Rosabelle* wintered at Wivenhoe on the River Colne, from whence her crew was largely drawn. She was taken up by the yacht patrol in February 1915 and, as was usual, many of her peacetime crew stayed with her.

Her first wartime commander was 47-year-old Ernest G H Brady RNR,

* Rolleston was a retired (March 1914) naval officer whose last appointment had been in charge of the naval establishment at Sydney, Australia, from 1908 until 1912.

who took *Rosabelle* over at Brightlingsea. Brady had retired from the mercantile marine in 1908 to work for the Weston-Super-Mare Pier Company but retained his RNR rank of lieutenant. When hostilities commenced he reported for duty and seven months later *Rosabelle* became his responsibility. Her peacetime captain, Mr Wenlock, was there to greet him, as were her two mates, and they stayed with the vessel under Brady's command. She was configured for war duty at Marrin's Yard on the Isle of Wight and the navy fitted her with three 6pdr Hotchkiss guns, later changed to two high-angle 6pdrs and a 3in.

Rosabelle's service life began in Falmouth and ended in the Orkney Islands; in both locations, she came close to sinking a U-boat. In March 1915, shortly after leaving Portsmouth, she spotted a U-boat and tried to ram it but a rapid crash dive took the submarine out of harm's way.

Then on 10 April 1916, the crew observed a merchant ship to starboard that suddenly exploded before them, torpedoed by a U-boat; *Rosabelle* steamed at top speed towards the scene and rescued two of the crew before making for Penzance to put them ashore.

The beginning of 1917 saw the yacht based at Kirkwall, one of six assigned for duty there. In January, while on patrol from Kirkwall, she observed an enemy submarine and opened fire with her aft gun, but the U-boat submerged, unharmed.

Next, in May *Rosabelle* sighted a U-boat that was attacking two steamers with its gun. She opened fire with her 3in but again the U-boat crash-dived. This time, however, the enemy was reluctant to leave its prey, and *Rosabelle* sighted the periscope, at which she directed a hail of 3in and 6pdr gunfire from fore and aft. But the futility of trying to attack a submarine under the water, without detection systems, was proved when the U-boat pressed home its assault and sank both the intended victims with torpedoes; they sank only 500yds distant from the yacht. She dropped the two depth charges she carried without effect.

Theodore Pim's yacht *Rosabelle*, seen in civilian days flying the White ensign, to which, as a member of the RYS, she was entitled. *(Nottage Maritime Institute)*

The crew of *Rosabelle* during the war. *(Nottage Maritime Institute)*

Finally, on 24 July 1917, *Rosabelle* saw yet another U-boat on the surface, this time off Stromness. Again, it submerged before she could reach it. Hydrophones were still in their infancy and finding a submerged submarine was difficult for all navies at the time. As for Brady, he was reassigned and promoted to captain in recognition of his service. He had been 'an excellent officer, thoroughly zealous and entirely trustworthy'[4] during his time in command.

Pim regained his yacht in March 1919 and enjoyed her for another ten years until his death. But *Rosabelle* went on to fight in the next war, too; she was purchased by the Admiralty in 1939 and used as an armed boarding vessel in the Mediterranean. *Rosabelle* was sunk by a U-boat off Gibraltar on 11 December 1941. A luxury cruiser, a doughty warrior and in the end a victim of the underwater weapon she tried so hard to sink herself.

The 1,421-ton yacht *Sapphire*, owned by the Duke of Bedford, had featured in the Duke's correspondence with Churchill (noted in Chapter 3). Built by John Brown and Co., she was described at the time as 'of the conventional type, though both the bow and counter appear to have somewhat less over-hang than is to be seen in many modern yachts by the same designer [i.e. Watson]. Of course, the clipper bow is generally fitted to yachts as a matter of looks, as a curved stem is undoubtedly more graceful than a straight one. It has, however, other advantages; for instance, more room can be obtained on deck for a given water-line length, while in the event of a collision less serious results are likely to occur to the rammed boat. Besides this, a clipper bow provides a beautiful flare to the forward sections, thus making a better and drier sea boat; generally speaking, in fact, it may be said that a yacht is probably a better sea boat than a commercial type of ship of the same size.'[5]

Taken up by the navy in January 1915, she had her name changed to *Sapphire II*, and was armed with one 4in and one 12pdr.

She served until February 1919, first of all in the Irish Sea as a patrol and escort ship before performing the same role when based on Gibraltar. By 1916, *Sapphire II* was escorting convoys between Gibraltar and Malta. While on this duty she made three unsuccessful attacks on U-boats.

In July 1917, she sighted a U-boat but it dived before she could strike. The next time was in January 1918 when a steamer in the convoy she was escorting was torpedoed. *Sapphire II* attacked the U-boat with depth charges but without effect. Finally, in May 1918 while escorting a convoy from Genoa to Gibraltar, the wake of a submarine was spotted but before any action could be taken two steamers were torpedoed and sunk.

Sapphire II drove in to attack with depth bombs but in doing so collided with another escort, badly damaging it and leaving her own forepeak full of water. Despite this, she was able to pick up the survivors, sink the crippled escort with gunfire, and make Toulon under her own steam.

One luxury yacht had the doubtful pleasure of a surface engagement with a U-boat. This was, of course, something her designers had never contemplated, and a hit on any yacht's thin planking would invariably be fatal.

Venetia was owned by the redoubtable Harold William Swithinbank. He trained as a veterinarian but also had a largely military career, beginning as a lieutenant in the 11th Hussars, then as a captain in the Middlesex Yeomanry (Cavalry section). By the end of his long life, Swithinbank had been awarded the distinctions of FRS, FRSE, FRGS, FSA, DL and held the positions of Governor of the Royal Agricultural Society and Vice President of the Royal Veterinary College. A keen yachtsman, Swithinbank was also a

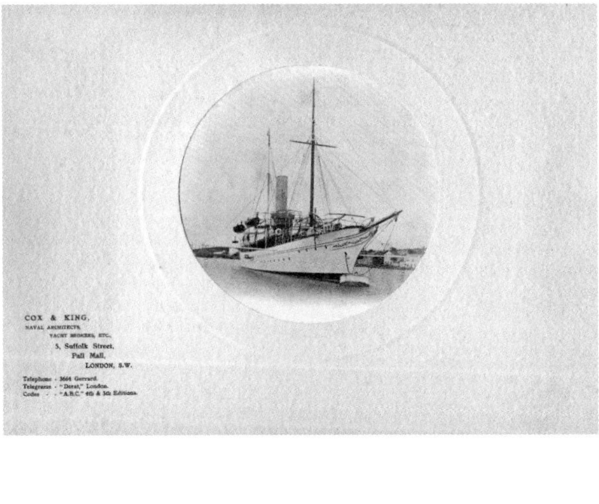

Venetia as the front page of a Cox and King's catalogue in pre-war times. *(Author's collection)*

HMY *Venetia* in wartime. Her forward gun mounting can just be made out. *(Nottage Maritime Institute)*

member of the Royal Naval Volunteer Reserve and during the war, despite being 56 years old at its onset, he served in the rank of commander on the battleship HMS *Orion*.

His yacht had been built in 1905 by Ramage & Ferguson with a single screw driven by a triple-expansion engine, originally for F W Sykes of Lyndley in Yorkshire, whose fortune came from the manufacture of card clothing. She was of 577grt, 189ft long, and joined the navy in August 1914. Armed with a 6pdr and two 1pdr guns, *Venetia* served firstly around the Orkneys and then from Falmouth.

In September 1917 and now named *Venetia II*, she was picking up

Venetia in dazzle camouflage sometime in 1917 or 1918. *(Nottage Maritime Institute)*

survivors from a torpedoed steamer when a submarine surfaced. She opened fire with all guns, but the submarine stood and fought on the surface. Most shots from either vessel fell short and after thirty minutes the U-boat decided that discretion was the better part of valour and disappeared under the waves. *Venetia II* depth charged the area, again without result.

As for Swithinbank, he suffered from acute sciatica, being found unfit for sea service on three occasions until, in January 1916, he was reported as 'unfit for further active service'. Even then, he requested that he be 'allowed to retain his commission without pay in the hope of being fit for some duty'.[6] It was not to be and he was demobilised.

Success at Last

Other luxury yachts had success where *Rosabelle*, *Sapphire* and *Venetia* had failed.

In 1916 the yacht *Diane* became the first yacht to play a part in the sinking of a U-boat. *Diane* was a 194grt steam yacht built in 1902 and taken into the navy in September 1914. Her owner was 51-year-old Captain Cecil William Paulet Slade, a wealthy stockbroker and grandson of Sir John Slade, 1st Baronet, who had fought under Wellington in the Peninsular War. Cecil Slade had served with the British South African Police in Mashonaland and became a captain in the 3rd Battalion of the Wiltshire Regiment in 1890.

On 24 April 1916, *Diane* was employed in the Dover Patrol guarding the 11th Division of drifters in the area of the Dunkirk Roads. An anti-submarine net and mine barrier had been laid there about 10 miles off the coast and the drifters were involved in maintaining it.

At about noon, the drifter *Arndilly Castle* reported that a submarine had fouled her first two nets, dragging them across the tide about 400yds. Division senior officer Lieutenant D Watson RNR, in the drifter *Chrysanthemum*, hastened to her assistance and found the nets still being towed by the entangled U-boat slowly across the water in a south-easterly direction. His only effective armament in this situation was a lance bomb and two were thrown where Watson thought the submarine might be; neither exploded.

At this point Watson signalled to *Diane* to come to his support. She threw two more two lance bombs and then First Mate Dunstan rolled a depth charge off the aft position. This detonated under *Diane's* stern and shattered it. But it also mortally wounded the U-boat. 'A heavy explosion took place, followed by a large eruption of air bubbles and oil. The air bubbles became much reduced later, but oil continued to come to the surface; and when *Diane* returned through this position at 1725, she passed through pools of oil.'[7] They had sunk *UB-13*. All seventeen of the U-boat's crew were killed.

In June 1917, *Diane* again made the news when a drifter shot down a German seaplane and the yacht subsequently rescued and took the two pilots prisoner; *Diane* attempted to tow the seaplane to harbour but it broke up and had to be cast adrift. The yacht continued to serve at Dover until she was handed back to Slade on 23 November 1917.

As for her owner, he served on the Headquarters Staff (Musketry) at Aldershot between 1915 and 1919, was appointed a Fellow of both the Royal Geographical Society and the Zoological Society and died having never married, aged 79.

Lorna *Sinks a U-boat*

Lorna was a 427grt yacht built by Scott of Greenock in 1904 with twin triple-expansion engines. Originally, she was ordered by Wyndham Francis Cook, son of the 1st Viscount of Monserrate, who had made his money in textiles and in the late nineteenth century was one of Britain's three richest men. But Cook died in 1905 and she was purchased instead by shipbuilder John Burns, the first Baron Inverclyde, who named her *Beryl* (seemingly his second yacht bearing that name). Inverclyde sold her to Samuel Morley, 1st Baron Hollenden, a former Governor of the Bank of England (1903–05), in 1911 and he renamed the yacht *Lorna*.

She was requisitioned by the Royal Navy at the outbreak of war and armed with two 6pdr guns and, eventually, depth charges. *Lorna* served in the Stornoway area in the first years of the conflict but moved to Portland in 1916 and it was here she rescued Leading Mechanic Bill Argent and his pilot when their Wright Seaplane came down in the water. *Lorna* towed it to safety at Poole.

She spectacularly gained her claim to fame in 1918. On the evening of 26 May, *Lorna* was under the command of Lieutenant Charles Loftus Tottenham RNVR and employed escorting a convoy at the eastern end of Lyme Bay. Tottenham was by now an experienced armed yacht command-

The U-boat killer *Lorna* seen in 1911. She was completed in October 1904 at Scott's Shipbuilding and Engineering Company, Greenock on the River Clyde, and was originally named *Beryl*. *(Mersea Museum/John Leather Collection)*

er, having served since 1914 on *Wintonia*, *Amethyst III* and from October 1917, *Lorna*. At 2050, Tottenham picked up a signal from SS *Julian*, screaming that she had been torpedoed 2 miles off Portland Bill and asking for help. Tottenham rang for full speed and rushed off to render assistance, but was forestalled by a follow-up message that stated the torpedo had misfired and *Julian* was proceeding to port.

Tottenham spent the next hour alerting various cargo vessels he encountered as to the possible danger of a U-boat until at 2155 he sighted a periscope steering west, 150ft off his port bow. Immediately he ordered a course to ram and as *Lorna* passed over the spot where he had seen the periscope the whole ship jarred as if she had hit some underwater obstruction. Presuming this to be the U-boat, he dropped a D-type depth charge, set at 50ft and then a second a short distance further on.

Circling the disturbed water in the dark, he observed four objects that he assumed to be wreckage. As *Lorna* approached these resolved themselves to be four men in the water shouting '*kamerad*'. And in the middle of them was a disturbance in the water caused by the rush of escaping air from the damaged submarine.

The time in the war when humanity might have stayed a captain's hand and rescued the survivors was well past. The real and perceived atrocities of the U-boats had long hardened British sailors' hearts. Tottenham drove into the area and dropped another depth charge and a can buoy. The charge killed three of the survivors, two of whom were blown completely out of the water. They picked up the remaining man, Wilhelm Wendland, but he died from internal injuries. *Lorna*, a rich man's plaything, a toy for the leisured classes, had proved just as deadly as a purpose-built warship. And *UB-74* had been destroyed with her thirty-four crewmen all dead.

Lieutenant Tottenham was awarded the DSO for the action, for 'Honours for Services in Action with Enemy Submarines'.[8] And the crew received

Another view of *Lorna*, showing off her graceful lines. *(Author's collection)*

£1,000 prize money from the Admiralty, notified on 21 December 1920.[9] But by then it was too late for Charles Tottenham. He died of the Spanish influenza on 27 November 1918 at the age of 35, still in command of *Lorna*, and was buried in Brompton Cemetery.

The yacht was returned to her owner in February 1919 and sold to Walter Preston, Conservative member of parliament for Mile End, Chairman of Platt Brothers and an innovative engineer. She would serve again in the next war, between 1939 and 1943.

Makeshift Convoy Escorts

As has been recounted above, yachts found themselves acting as convoy escorts, a role in which they were every bit at risk as their merchant charges, given the nature of their construction. Convoy was introduced in 1917, in May generally and in March–April on the Scandinavian route.* It was recognised that yachts were not the ideal vessel. But it was a problem to find enough close escorts.

* Convoy had been operated on the cross-Channel coal run to France since 6 February 1917.

A newspaper illustration depicting two steam yachts escorting a convoy of three merchant ships. *(Author's collection)*

Commander in Chief Coast of Scotland Admiral Sir Cecil Burney wrote to the Admiralty on 22 February 1918 that he had to designate the yacht *Shemara* as convoy leader 'as no more suitable vessel was available for the purpose'. He added that 'it is important that the vessels allocated permanently for the duty should be ready at the earliest possible date; at present only two Armed Boarding Streamers are available'.[10] *Shemara* was clearly of limited use in the role; she was launched as *Victoria*, 477grt, built by Ramage & Ferguson in 1899 and was at one time owned by the government of New South Wales. Now the property of Earl Fitzwilliam, she was taken into service in September 1914 and armed with a 12pdr and a 6pdr gun. With his seat at Wentworth Woodhouse, 'Billy' Fitzwilliam, William Charles de Meuron Wentworth-Fitzwilliam, 7th Earl Fitzwilliam, had inherited his family's extensive coalfield holdings, employing more than 2,000 colliers at their peak, along with industrial interests in glass, pottery, tar, chemicals and cars.

Or consider convoy OZ 14, of twenty-eight vessels, from Methil to Scandinavia, which departed on 4 March 1918. Once again there was an issue with providing close escorts and the convoy leader was the yacht *Zoraide*, ex-*Sylvabelle*, armed with a 12pdr gun and a 6pdr anti-air weapon.

It proved a trying job. SS *Mortlake* stopped with steering problems and a trawler had to be detached to watch over her. Then the vessels *Cito* and *Fidda* were unable to maintain the speed of the convoy – a common problem for the escort commanders – and another trawler had to be dropped astern to guard them. But the unique feature of this convoy was that it was escorted part way from Methil by two seaplanes, a first for the Scandinavian route. Yachts, seaplanes and convoys working together – unthought of before the start of the war.

... *And Other Uses*

Yachts found many usages apart from that of patrol and escort vessels. Some became depot ships, providing accommodation and maintenance facilities for smaller vessels. One example was the old yacht HMS *Resource II* (1865). She was hired as a depot ship for the newly commissioned Elco-built motor launches at Portsmouth in October 1915. Originally the 'Fast Paddle Despatch' steam paddler HMS *Helicon*, she was renamed HMS *Enchantress* when used as the Admiralty yacht. Sold off in 1905 to the Royal Motor Yacht Club (RMYC), she became their floating clubhouse until the navy hired her back. Such luxury as she offered the motor launch crews did not last long, for she burnt out six weeks later.

The steam yacht *Catania*, noted in Chapter 3, a steel screw steamer owned by 28-year-old George Sutherland-Leveson-Gower, 5th Duke of Sutherland and a leading light in the Royal Yacht Squadron, had been patrolling in the Cromarty area. But in mid-1916 she was despatched to Taranto to be a depot ship for the motor launches sent to work the

The G L Watson-designed, D and W Henderson-built *Catania*, used as a depot ship for motor launches at the Otranto barrier. *(Author's collection)*

Vanduara (1886) served as a depot ship for submarines. She is seen here in a painting by Antonio de Simone off Naples in 1906 flying the Royal Victoria Yacht Club flag. *(Author's collection)*

Otranto barrier, a sixty-mile-long barrage between Brindisi in Italy south-east to Corfu off the Albanian coast. *Catania*, armed with two 12pdr guns, reached Taranto at the end of July and remained there for the rest of the war.

And *Vanduara* (1886, 376grt) was an all-steel screw schooner, designed by G L Watson and built by D and W Henderson at Glasgow. She was owned by Stewart Clark of Dundas Castle, South Queensferry (whose fortune came from the Clark Brothers thread empire he founded), until 1905 when she was sold to a J. Mann-Thomson. From September 1914 she served as a depot ship to the 9th Submarine Flotilla at the Clyde until she was returned to her owner in early 1915.

The 9th SF was also supported by the yacht *Mairi* (1911, just 59grt) armed with a single 3pdr and apparently acting as a depot ship between September 1914 and July 1915, when she was redeployed as a tug. She was not a steam yacht but a steel motor vessel schooner built by Ritchie, Graham and Milne of Glasgow for the Marquis of Graham.

Another yacht deployed as a tug was the small (44grt) but beautiful *Mauna Loa*. Built in 1907 by J Armour and Sons of Fleetwood and with steam engines by another local company, James Robertson and Sons, she had been commissioned by Henry Calvert, who had made a fortune in textiles. Her name was after the Hawaiian volcano that erupted in the year of her launch. The designer was Armour employee William Stoba, a perfectionist who finished the yacht to a very high standard. Overall 92ft long, *Mauna Loa* had pitch pine on oak planking with a teak superstructure. The interior with ten berths was fitted out in Honduras mahogany and her hull was lined with copper.

Her captain was one Robert Rawlinson, who was still in charge when in November 1917 she was taken up by the Royal Navy at a lease of £2 7s 0d a day; Rawlinson stayed with his vessel by dint of joining the RNVR as a temporary sub lieutenant. The navy listed her as a 'harbour and inland service tug' and she was used for towing barges in the River Mersey, with occasional forays into the Irish Sea as a minesweeper. By the war's end, painted grey and with a broken mast, *Mauna Loa* was in a sad state when returned to Calvert, but he had her restored and returned to his cruising.

Yachts played other vital support roles. The strangely named *NYKR* was a G L Watson-designed steel screw steam yacht built by John Reid's Jordanvale Yard in 1893. She had been commissioned by London-based barrister Maurice Bernard Byles, son of Sir John Barnard Byles, with Byles senior a British legal expert, judge and author of books on law and the economy. Of only 30grt and 59ft long, by the outbreak of war *NYKR* was owned by a Major Adam Boyd of Douglas Street in Glasgow, who seems to have been the proprietor of a bleaching and finishing works. She was taken up in 1916 and was used, in common with a number of steel drifters, as a hydrophone tender, supporting those ships equipped with sound-detecting equipment for tracking submarines.

Later, Byles also owned *Saevuna* (1901), again designed by Watson, built by Scott and Co. of Greenock. She was a small (62grt) single-screw vessel with a two-cylinder engine that could take her to around 9 knots. *Saevuna* was converted to a tug in 1916 and became part of the Ministry of Munitions.

Then there was *Don Frederic* (1884, 37grt), used as a fleet messenger having been gifted to the Admiralty by her owner, and *Mustard* (1887, 112grt), which was put to use at the end of the war as a torpedo range support vessel at Weymouth.

Seven yachts operated as Armed Boarding Vessels, stopping cargo ships at sea to check their manifests for contraband and, if necessary, putting a prize crew aboard to sail the potential offender to a port of inspection. Four smaller (less than 100grt) yachts were used as examination vessels, performing similar tasks closer to shore.

The luxurious finish of some vessels rendered them attractive to high command. The steam yacht *Triad* was built by the Caledon Shipbuilding and Engineering Company of Dundee and launched in 1910. She was a twin-screw, twin triple-expansion engine vessel of 1,212grt, capable of 16 knots and commissioned by George Alfred Shenley of Warsash House (near Southampton), a keen yachtsman and Royal Yacht Squadron member.

Triad was fitted with every modern luxury; sleeping berths were under the dining room and lighted and ventilated by large skylights, on the shade

HMY *Triad*, seen when serving as the yacht of the Senior Naval Officer, Persian Gulf. Note the 12pdr gun mounted right in the bows. *(© Imperial War Museum Q 75499)*

deck there was an apartment set aside for governesses and children, and a saloon was made up in the poop for the use of the ladies' maids.

Electric fans were provided in all the enclosed rooms, the drawing room had a parquetry floor, and black and white rubber 'silent' tiles lined the corridors. The walls of the lavatories were covered in tiles of 'a Dutch design' and 'the vessel is equipped with a large drying room and laundry with all the latest machines for washing, electrically driven'.[11]

Technically, she had unusual vertical bows, 'an indicator on the steam windlass showing what length of cable had been run out' and 'a patent electrical arrangement connected to the captain's bridge whereby this officer can tell at a glance whether one or both sets of engines are running ahead or astern and he can also observe the number of revolutions'.[12]

Such luxury did not serve Shenley for long, for by 1911 *Triad* was being refitted at Dundee and in 1912 was sold to one A Grech in Constantinople, where she was often used by the Turkish navy.

In 1915, the Admiralty purchased her for £40,000, fitted her with two 12pdrs, and she served as the naval commander in chief's flagship and headquarters vessel in two eastern war theatres. Firstly, as the yacht of Vice Admiral John de Robeck in the Gallipoli Campaign, where she also formed part of the Seventh Squadron blockading Smyrna during the Allied troop landings of April 1915; and then as the yacht of the Senior Naval Officer, Persian Gulf.

Sagitta (1908) was a 744grt yacht built by Camper and Nicholson at Gosport that had been ordered by Paul Louis Marie Archambault Boson de Talleyrand-Périgord, 6th Duke of Talleyrand and Duke de Valençay. She was

A contemporary half block model of the steam yacht *Ivy* (1895). *(© National Maritime Museum F7723)*

requisitioned by the Admiralty in December 1914, fitted with two 12pdrs and a 6pdr AA, and spent the first part of the war as a patrol yacht (with occasional minesweeping) in the North Sea, off the East Anglian coast. But in March 1917, after a refit at White Brothers' Yard, Southampton, she was despatched to the White Sea to become the headquarters ship for Commander (later acting Captain) Henry Albert le Fowne Hurt, a retired officer (he had left the navy in 1911) recalled for the war and SNO in charge of a group of minesweepers. *Sagitta* had been built for pleasure cruises in the warm waters of the Mediterranean; the freezing wastes of north-west Russia must have come as a shock to her and her crew. Certainly, one able seaman recorded that, 'I am sure not one of *Sagitta's* crew would ever forget the voyage from Aberdeen to Kola Inlet. We were ill-equipped to face the dreadful weather – no protective clothing in those days. I had a pair of seaboots, a Balaclava helmet and a second-hand raincoat that I bought in Aberdeen for ten shillings.'[13] They stuck it out until 30 November when *Sagitta* was ordered home.

Then there was SY *Ivy*. She was built in 1895 by Earle's Shipbuilding and Co. of Hull (more usually associated with ships for the Wilson Line) as an 870grt steam yacht for the Niger Coast Protectorate Government. *Ivy* was 220ft long, 34ft in the beam and came complete with small QF guns for policing duties. Her top speed was 13.5 knots.

Apart from ferrying important colonial officials in luxury, *Ivy* was responsible for patrolling the Niger delta. In 1900 the Protectorate was joined to the Lower Niger, to become the Protectorate of Southern Nigeria, which was later renamed Nigeria in 1914.

With war declared, by the end of August *Ivy* was painted grey, fitted with wireless and armed with a 12pdr and two 6pdrs. So equipped, she became part of the riverine force (the cruiser *Cumberland*, gunboat *Dwarf*, a steam lifeboat, some lighters and a few launches) that assisted General Charles

Dobell's Cameroon Expeditionary Force in the capture of German Cameroon, where fighting did not end until March 1916.

Next *Ivy* was sent in December 1916 to join the murderous Mesopotamian campaign, with British and Indian troops still reeling from the fall of Kut earlier in the year. She left Lagos for Simonstown and then Basrah and in March 1917 commissioned there as a headquarters ship. Her operations included visits to Dar-es-Salaam and Zanzibar but by August neither yacht nor crew seemed to be in good condition. On 28 August the Director of the Inland Water Transport (RE) section at Basrah reported that there had been a mutiny on board, and that *Ivy* was 'practically unseaworthy' and he intended to send her to Bombay for repairs.[14] Despite her obvious degeneration, she was eventually returned to Nigeria and served in her old capacity until 1923.

Warrior was requisitioned in 1917 and served as Admiral Sir William Lowther Grant's (CinC North American and West Indies Station) flagship from 16 February 1918. On 28 March she arrived in Washington DC from Halifax and remained there until the very end of the year.[15] Here HMY *Warrior*, her crew and Admiral Grant all took part in a Memorial Day (then called Decoration Day) ceremony honouring those who died at sea during the First World War, including the victims of the *Lusitania*. She had been built for Frederick Vanderbilt in 1914 by Ailsa at Troon and was later owned by carpet millionaire Alexander Smith Cochran. *Warrior* left seven of her crew on American soil when she departed at the end of the war, buried at Arlington cemetery, as victims of the so-called 'Spanish' Influenza.

Surf, a 496grt yacht built by in 1902 by Hawthorn and Co. to designs by Cox and King, became the post-Armistice flagship of the Dover Patrol, providing a luxurious berth for Admiral Sir Roger Keyes or his deputy Rear Admiral Cyril Dampier. She had previously served at Dover as the depot ship of the rear admiral in charge of controlled minefields.

The Spy Yachts

Often steam yachts passed through many hands in their career, gaining and losing new names as they went. Few however, ended up working for spies.

Sir John Denison-Pender was chairman and managing director of the Eastern Telegraph Company (which became Cable and Wireless). He was also very keen on steam yachts called *Maretanza*, of which he had five in total. The fifth became *Zarefah*, which we will meet later, while the fourth, built in 1904, was a 206grt vessel from the yard of Bow, McLachlan and Company of Paisley. She had a single screw, could manage 12 knots, and was 119ft long.

Denison-Pender kept her for only a year and in 1905 she was renamed *Hildegarde* and sold to Albert Holden Illingworth, later 1st Baron Illingworth. He was British businessman from Bradford, partner in the family firm of Daniel Illingworth and Sons, spinners, and subsequently Postmaster General during the war and MP for Heywood and Radcliffe.

By 1911 *Hildegarde* was registered to the egregious future MP, Noel Pemberton Billing. Billing had purchased a steam yacht, *Violet*, for £50 and sailed to the Isle of Wight with the intent of selling it. As there was only him and his wife to crew it, they somehow ended up in Le Havre! Finally reaching Cowes, Billing sold the yacht for £275. The broker dealing with the trade was so impressed that he set Billing up in a joint venture business as a yacht dealer in Southampton, and *Hildegarde* came into his hands for sale.* Finally, in 1913 she was purchased by the Egyptian government for use as a survey vessel.

War came, and in January 1917, *Hildegarde* was hired by the Admiralty as patrol yacht for the Eastern Mediterranean Special Intelligence Bureau's espionage activities off Syria and Palestine – and became a spy ship.

The battle for the Ottoman Middle East had taken a poor turn with the failure to seize Gaza, and on 27 June 1917 General Edmund Allenby, large and irascible, known as 'The Bull', took command of the Egyptian Expeditionary Force. His mission, as given to him directly by Prime Minister Lloyd George, was to take 'Jerusalem by Christmas'.

Aaron Aaronsohn was a famous botanist who had received wide acclaim for discovering a weather-resistant form of primitive wheat. With the support from an American-Jewish organisation and the US Department of Agriculture, Aaronsohn established an experimental agricultural station at Atlit, a small coastal village next to the Carmel Mountains, in what was then Turkish Palestine, and where he conducted research on dry farming.

But Aaronsohn was also a Zionist patriot who believed that the Jewish cause would be favoured if the British and their Allies won the war in the east. To this end he established an espionage group, pro-British in nature, named NILI.† From February to September 1917, *Hidegarde*, now renamed HMY *Managem*, and armed with a single 12pdr, called regularly at Atlit and collected intelligence as to Turkish positions and strengths in the Beersheba and the Negev desert, in preparation for a British attack inland. Details on

* In 1916 Billing founded the scurrilous weekly journal *The Imperialist* (later rebranded as *Vigilante*), which in January 1918 asserted the canard that 47,000 highly placed Britons were in a German intelligence service book, naming them as perverts of one sort or another, which prevented them from fully supporting the war effort through fear of blackmail.

†An acronym of the Hebrew phrase from Samuel 1 15:29 'Netzah Yisrael Lo Yeshaker', which translates as 'the Eternal One of Israel will not lie'.

weather patterns, Turkish fortifications and troop movements, railways, desert routes, and water-source locations were all passed to *Managem* for intelligence use.

In October 1917, the British army, combined with Australian cavalry, surprised the Turks with a raid on Beersheba, and opened the way into Central Palestine. Jerusalem surrendered in December. *Managem* and the NILI spy network had undoubtedly assisted in the victory.

But the yacht's work was not yet done. Allenby was forced to wait to pursue his attack and it was not until September 1918 that he began a drive along the coast. Haifa was taken, then Damascus, Tyre, Sidon, and, on 8 October, Beirut. The first vessel to nose into her dangerously mined and obstructed harbour was a Royal Navy motor launch, *ML-240*. And the second was *Managem*.

Then there was *Sayonara*, a yacht that had already passed through a large number and variety of owners. She was launched in 1880 as a 455grt steam yacht from the yard of Robert Steele and Co. of Greenock, who also built her two-cylinder, 110nhp engine. Her first owner, who named her *Catarina*, was James Houldsworth of Coltness, Lanarkshire, who kept her at Cowes. In 1886, she passed into the ownership of the Duke of Sutherland, as *Sans Peur*, and then rapidly through eight owners until in 1907 she was Spanish owned, by Ramon de la Sota of Bilbao, and renamed *Goizeko-Izarra*, Basque for 'Morning Star'. In 1911, Anthony Drexel acquired her and then came the war.

Now she entered on a new and different life – that of a spy ship. Captain Reginald 'Blinker' Hall was Director of Naval Intelligence at the Admiralty. Together with the Head of the Special Branch, Basil Thomson, he chartered *Sayonara* from Drexel, recruited a fifty-man crew who were trained to pose as Americans, with as captain a RNR officer, Lieutenant F M Simon, who was versed in American behaviour from many years of Cunard Line service, and sent her to the west coast of Ireland. Ostensibly she was the pleasure yacht of another fake American, Major Wilfred Howell, who had in fact been educated in the USA, and who pretended to be 'Colonel McBride' of Los Angeles, a German sympathiser.

Their objective was to investigate rumours of German U-boat pods off the Irish littoral (mythical, as it transpired) and gather intelligence on the activities of Irish revolutionaries.

They played the part so well that the yacht and its crew were placed under arrest by Captain Charles Le Mesurier of the cruiser HMS *Cornwallis*. When Hall ordered its release, an enraged Marquis of Sligo, George Ulick Browne, left Ireland for London and the Admiralty to protest the release in person and threaten to take the matter to the House of Lords. Hall had to let him in on the secret, sworn to secrecy.

In June 1915, the Admiralty requisitioned *Sayonara* as a patrol yacht and her spying days were done. Fitted with two 3in guns, she took to more quotidian tasks.

Hall repeated the trick with the 316grt yacht *Vergemere*, this time off the coast of Spain. Designed by A Cary Smith, *Vergemere*, was built by Harlan and Hollingsworth in Wilmington, Delaware, for Albert Carlton Bostwick, son of one of the founders of Standard Oil, and himself a member of the New York Yacht Club, the American Yacht Club, and former Commodore of the Larchmont Yacht Club.

The yacht came into Hall's hands in June 1915 and he selected an eccentric Irish baronet and keen sportsman, Sir Hercules Langrishe, to play the part of owner. A keen yachtsman, a RNVR commander and a member of the Royal Yacht Squadron, Langrishe cruised from port to port throwing lavish champagne parties for local dignitaries and collecting information on German activity in neutral Spain as he went. This charade lasted until the end of the year, when the yacht disappears from the Admiralty record.

Yachts Around the World

The armed yachts served all over the world. Taking the Admiralty 'pink lists' for 30 June 1917 as a snapshot, HMY *Eileen* and *Warrior* were on the North American and West Indies station. *North Star* and *Drama* were on the East Indies and Egypt station and a yacht squadron comprising *Atalanta, Iolanda, Jeanette II, Marynthea, Narcissus II, Sapphire II* and *Valiant II*, was based at Gibraltar.

These stories and deployments represent just a small sample of the actions involving armed yachts during the war. Built for peace, they acquitted themselves well in war, as did their crews, when the country's need was greatest.

CHAPTER FIVE

YACHTS AND MEN

Henry Thomas Gartside Tipping. *(Author's collection)*

AS IMPORTANT as the yachts themselves were the gentleman volunteers who manned or commanded them. Henry Thomas Gartside-Tipping could be taken as the exemplar of their sangfroid and *noblesse oblige*.

Gartside-Tipping was born on 11 June 1848 in Dublin. He was the son of Gartside Gartside-Tipping, whose family had made a mercantile fortune in Manchester. Henry joined the navy at *Britannia* in 1860 and by 1870 had been advanced to lieutenant after a tour in the Royal Yacht *Victoria and Albert*, but he proved sickly. In 1871 this was declared to be heart disease, serious enough to keep him from 'manual labour',[1] and by 1884 he had been placed on the retired list with the rank of lieutenant commander, owing to non-service. In 1890, Gartside-Tipping married Mary Jane Pilkington, a 'lady of considerable musical talent',[2] who came from a wealthy Southport family. Her stepfather, a surgeon, was *inter alia* a Liberal MP, mayor of Southport and High Sheriff of Lancashire. That same year Gartside-Tipping senior died and left Henry a valuable inheritance and property in Bolton, Lancashire, as well as County Fermanagh in Ireland and on the Isle of Wight. The newly-weds set up home in the latter location, living at Quarr Wood in Binstead. Henry became well known as a yachtsman, a passion he passed on to his eldest daughter Phyllis.

Apart from yachting, Gartside-Tipping was a stalwart of the Lifeboat Service. He held the post of Inspector of Lifeboats (Irish District) between 1879 and 1892 and was awarded the Royal National Lifeboat Institution Medal in May 1892, the citation for which read 'in high appreciation of his zealous and efficient services … in acknowledgement of the risk of life he frequently incurred in the Lifeboat Service'. He was also the inventor of 'Tipping Plates', named after him, which enabled a heavy lifeboat to be transported on her carriage over deep and soft sand.

When war broke out, Gartside-Tipping was already 66 years old but with 'undemonstrative patriotism'[3] he immediately volunteered for duty and badgered the Admiralty until he was given command of the armed yacht *Aries*, previously owned by the Duke of Leeds, of 201grt and now armed with two 3pdrs.

In January 1915, Gartside-Tipping was made officer in charge of Auxiliary Patrol Area XIX on the West Coast of Ireland, a command he exercised from another armed yacht, *Sanda* of 300grt, built in 1906 as the

St Serf for the linoleum king Sir Michael Nairn of Rankeilour and now armed with two 6pdr guns.

He was superseded in this command in May 1915 and transferred with his vessel to the Dover Patrol. When King George V inspected the Patrol on 23 September that year, he was presented to the king as 'the oldest officer officially engaged in the British Navy'.[4] *

The following day, Admiral Reginald Bacon (commanding the Dover Patrol) took his monitors and escort craft out to bombard the coast around Zeebrugge and Ostend, in response to a request from the army to create a diversion while they carried out an offensive on the Western Front (which became the Battle of Loos). *Sanda* was among the craft so employed and was screening the monitors engaged in bombarding shore positions when German artillery batteries at Blankenberge responded and found in *Sanda* an excellent target. An 8in shell struck the yacht below the deckhouse and she was sunk with thirteen officers and men out of twenty-six lost; all her executive officers, including Gartside-Tipping, were killed. Among these were two reservist officers from Sunderland, socially very distant from Gartside-Tipping but sharing his volunteer spirit. They were Sub Lieutenant David Brown RNR, 24 years old of Eldon Street, who held a master's certificate, and Sub Lieutenant Norman Middleton RNR of Cleveland Road, aged 22, who held a first mate's ticket and had gone to sea at 15. Both had attended St Gabriel's Sunday School at Bishopwearmouth.[5] And numbered with the dead ratings was a 15-year-old lad, Signal Boy Clement Kendrick RNR.

Admiral Bacon later wrote of Henry Gartside Tipping that 'this gallant officer returned to the navy on the outbreak of war at an age when most men are beyond active service …, and undertook the duties of captain of a yacht in the Dover Command in spite of the arduous work and exposure which the performance of his duties entailed'.[6]

This was not the end of the family's loss to the war. Mary Gartside-Tipping 'had worked for nearly a year at the Munition Workers' Canteen, Woolwich, and last January joined the Women's Emergency Corps for service in the war zone in France, where she was shot by a soldier whose mind was disordered. The French military authorities have done everything possible to express their sympathy,' reported the *Suffolk Gazette*, 'the Croix de Guerre, which had been withheld from women since last November, was conferred at once; and a full military funeral accorded.'[7]

The concept of gentlemanly sacrifice is writ large in both Gartside-Tipping deaths. They could have chosen to sit the war out in retirement and no one would have blamed them. But they knew that was not the 'code'. And they died.

A Family of Service

Another family who knew where their duty lay were the Pagets.

Lady Alexander Paget (née the Hon Hester Stapleton-Cotton) was the

* This is a disputable claim. William Balfour Forbes (born 1845), for example, was commissioned with the rank of commander at age 70 and given command of a dummy battleship off Mudros and then a group of some thirty armed drifters at Ramsgate.

relict of Lord Alexander Victor Paget, son of Henry Paget, 2nd Marquess of Anglesey, who had died in 1896 leaving his 191grt yacht *The Evening Star* to his widow. At the outbreak of war, Lord Alexander's cousin, the white-bearded, monocle-wearing, 62-year-old Admiral Alfred Wyndham Paget,* who had retired from the navy in 1911 after three years as Senior Officer Coast of Ireland Command, volunteered the yacht – and himself to command it – for naval service.

The brother of the Cambridge member of parliament Almeric Hugh Paget, 1st and only Baron Queenborough, the admiral had last served afloat in 1906 but this did not stop him answering his country's call. The Admiralty accepted both the yacht (renamed *Evening Star*) and the admiral, giving him the rank of commander in the RNR on 18 September 1914,[8] and sent them to the Humber to serve on anti-submarine duties in the swept coastal 'War Channel'.

Paget chronicled his adventures in letters to his wife Alpina Viti MacGregor, known as Viti, who was serving in France as a volunteer nurse in the Hospital Anglais, at Nevers. They had married in Newfoundland, where the bride's father was governor, when she was 21 and Paget thirty-three years her senior.

It would appear that the yacht did not handle the conditions of the North Sea well, with it being recorded: 'Steamed well, but under heavy seas sweeping along deck seas poured down [into the cabins].'[9] And after two days on patrol Paget was moved to report: 'I don't think I can possibly stay out more than three days as navigating is anxious to work in the offing, honeycombed with shallows and all shore lights put out.' Four days later, he added 'she is a devil to steer and going into the long lock [at Immingham] crowded with destroyers with a swishing tide race outside is a hard trial'.[11]

Of course, what he really wanted was to bag a U-boat. 'I am longing to spot a German submarine. Still there is always something exciting … I feel that I am just doing something for the country.'[12] Quite how his two ancient 6pdr guns would have fared against a U-boat's deck gun and torpedoes is open to question. But the effrontery of the Germans amused him. 'German U-boats have recently surfaced alongside trawlers to ask for fish,' he noted.[13] But he was fairly happy with his lot. 'I would love a faster and bigger yacht but I love all my officers,' he told his wife.[14]

A victory over a U-boat was not to be, but it was in *Evening* Star that Paget was able to help another admiral, and a distressed one at that. The steam yacht *Valiant* (1893) was the property of Lord Pirrie, a leading British shipbuilder and businessman. He was chairman of Harland and Wolff, shipbuilders, between 1895 and 1924 and also served as Lord Mayor of Belfast from 1896 to 1898. *Valiant* had originally been built by Laird Shipyards in Birkenhead in 1893 for the railroad magnate William K Vanderbilt. She was one of the largest and most luxurious steam yachts in the world at the time, with a tonnage of 1,855grt tons and a service speed of 17.3 knots.

* Younger brother to Sir Alfred Henry Fitzroy Paget, noted in Chapter 3. Their father, Lord Alfred Paget, was an inveterate yachtsman and Commodore of the Royal Thames Yacht Club, 1846–73, and Vice-Commodore, 1845–46 and 1874–88. He owned several yachts, one of which, *Violet* (built by Ramage & Ferguson in 1886) was equipped as a trawler yacht, with powerful trawling gear, suitable for fishing on the North Sea banks. He enjoyed trawl fishing, sending the choice fish to the Royal Family and the bulk of the catch to London hospitals. Lord Alfred died on board her in 1888.

G L Watson-designed *Eileen* (1910), originally *Doris*, owned by Solomon Barnato Joel, was a twin-engined, twin-screw, 274nhp yacht built by John Brown and Co. at Clydebank. A lovely looking vessel, she was converted to a passenger ferry in the 1930s. *(Author's collection)*

Taken up at the beginning of the war and fitted with four 12pdr guns, she was under the command of 'Billy' Barlow, a retired officer met in Chapter 3. On 20 December 1914, *Valiant* was mined off Filey. Leaking badly, she was taken in tow by *Evening Star*, firstly back to the Humber, then to Cowes for repair; 'but the moment I sight a submarine' the doughty Paget informed Barlow, 'I shall let you go and chase the enemy.'[15]

Alfred Paget's wish for a bigger vessel came true the following April, when he took command of the Immingham-based yacht *Eileen* (1910), 910grt, armed with two 12pdr guns and originally built in Glasgow for Solomon Barnato Joel, a South African-based millionaire financier. The yacht was firstly named *Doris* after his daughter and when requisitioned became *Eileen* after another of his children.

Between April 1916 and February 1917, Paget served as Senior Officer of the Auxiliary Patrol in area XVII (North Coast of Ireland) but was then forced to retire for a second time owing to ill health, quite probably brought on by the stress and strains of his role. The Admiralty acknowledged the contribution he had made with the award of a DSO after his retirement 'in recognition of [his] services in the prosecution of the war'.[16]

Admiral Paget did not recover and died on 17 June 1918; his 33-year-old wife followed him to the grave three months later; worn out by her nursing duties, she died of pneumonia.

Admiral Sir John Jellicoe, CinC Grand Fleet and later First Sea Lord, certainly appreciated the efforts of the old admiral and his ilk, writing: 'Sir Alfred, in common with many other officers who took up this work, was over 60 but age did not discourage these gallant seamen from facing the hardship and discomfort of service in the North Sea.'[17]

The Paget family service did not end here. Brother Almeric, who had made a fortune in coal and iron in the USA and Nova Scotia, was a highly successful yachtsman* who had taken the first prize in the open handicap race from Cannes to Monte Carlo in 1902, and won the Tsar's prize at Cowes Week in 1909. He now served his country by founding the Almeric Paget Massage Corps (renamed the Almeric Paget Military Massage Corps in December 1916, and the Military Massage Service in 1919) for the treatment of wounded soldiers. Initially fifty masseuses and masseurs were recruited, rising to over 100. The corps established clinics in every hospital in the United Kingdom, with central direction from Paget's London townhouse at 39 Berkeley Square.

The Wreck of the **Mekong**

Another yacht based at Immingham was *Mekong*, which was acting as a sort of flagship for the random collection of small Auxiliary Patrol boats that worked from the port. She had a colourful history. Built as the *Maund* in 1906 by Ramage & Ferguson of Leith, she was 199ft long and of around 900grt, with two boilers and a single screw. Her initial owner was Adam Mortimer Singer, son of the founder of the Singer Sewing Machine empire and a British citizen since 1900. For her first voyage, Singer sailed her to Stockholm, where King Oscar II paid a visit to the vessel.

She then passed through several hands before becoming the property of Ferdinand d'Orléans, Duc de Montpensier, younger brother of the Orléanist claimant to the throne of France.

In April 1915 the Admiralty found her docked at Southampton and promptly requisitioned her under wartime emergency powers. She was commissioned into the Royal Navy as HM Yacht *Mekong*, fitted with two 3in guns and put under the command of another 'dug out' (as reactivated retired officers were unflatteringly called), retired Admiral Frank Finnis, with a crew of forty-nine.

Finnis, who had left the navy in February 1909, returned to the sea as a captain RNR in April 1915 and became *Mekong*'s first (and only) naval commander at the age of 64. Now based on the Humber, armed and with a relatively powerful wireless as befitted her command position, she and her consorts maintained a patrol of the Yorkshire coast between the Humber and Berwick, looking for U-boats.

But it was not submarines, or even German surface vessels that brought about her tragedy. The weather was sometimes a much worse foe. On 9 March, Finnis had sailed to his patrol area. The weather was poor but by the 11th it had deteriorated significantly with a fierce north-easterly gale driving heavy rain before it.

Just after midnight a particularly big sea struck the vessel and water entered via the ventilators, filling the cabins below. Finnis decided to make for shelter between Flamborough Head and Filey Brigg but at 0430 *Mekong* ran onto rocks with rough seas now breaking over her. Cliffs could be seen about 150yds away and signals were made by Very light and gunfire. At 0520

* And Rear Commodore of the Royal Thames Yacht Club, 1905–10.

a boat was lowered with five men in it, but it was immediately swept from sight, although the men did struggle to the shore.

There now followed three of those sporadic acts of bravery that seem, in retrospect, to deserve more attention than they attracted at the time. Thirty-one-year-old William Chaplow, a fireman MMR from Southampton, attempted to swim ashore with a line but was instead washed against the rocks and drowned. Undeterred, Able Seaman Roger Piper MMR, 21 years old, attempted the same thing and suffered the same fate. Finally, an engine room man, Ernest Thorn, succeeded in getting ashore and raising the alarm, an act of courage that was rendered nugatory by the arrival of the Filey Rocket Brigade, a coastguard rescue unit. As the waves continued to drive the boat ashore at a spot known as the Chimney Hole, they managed to get a line out to the stricken boat and set up a breeches buoy to haul the crew up to safety onto the shore. Even now, disaster was lurking and Able Seaman John Davies MMR fell from the line to his death. Because of his age, Finnis was spared the traditional requirement that the captain is the last man to abandon his ship, his first lieutenant taking that role.

The subsequent court of enquiry decided that no one was at fault, a verdict with which the Admiralty disagreed. They thought that faulty navigation by Lieutenant George Parker RNR was to blame and that 'the mistake indicated ignorance rather than negligence'.[18] Parker's commission was cancelled and he was discharged from the navy. Regarding Fireman Chaplow, Finnis wrote to his wife of just eight months, Gertrude, 'his gallant efforts to get onshore to render us assistance will never be forgotten, and you may rest assured that his death was as noble as if he had been killed in action'.[19]

As for Frank Finnis, he was appointed Senior Naval Officer, Buncara, a minor naval base at the extreme north of Ireland, a post he held from June 1916 to May 1917, whereupon he once more retired from naval service. Finnis died on 17 November 1918, aged 67, another who had selflessly given his all.

Three Yachts, No U-boat

As has been seen, yacht commands were often given to dug out officers who had accepted a lower rank in order to get into the war. None came stranger than Admiral John Locke Marx. He had joined the navy in 1866 and was eventually promoted rear admiral in 1906, after a career spent afloat, mainly in independent commands. He retired in 1909 and was subsequently promoted to vice and then full admiral (in 1913) on the retired list.

At the start of the year, he attempted to re-join the navy but was rejected. Refusing to take such a refusal, he camped out on the steps of Whitehall in protest, occasioning an article and poem in his favour in the magazine *Punch*. Eventually his services were accepted and he was gazetted as a captain RNR, aged 62. His first command was a trawler, *Stephen Furness*, but in November 1914 he transferred to the armed yacht *Agatha* (1905), of

353grt and built by Day Summers of Southampton for Sir Walter Greene, brewer* and Conservative politician. When launched she had the rare distinction of electric lighting on board. Greene offered her to the Admiralty in September 1914, whereupon she was fitted with two 6pdr guns, and Marx and his new command were deployed as part of the Cromarty-based vessels of the Auxiliary Patrol.

Marx was less than enamoured of his new vessel, for she had, among many other defects, a problem with both the furnace and the boiler. Moreover, there was no first lieutenant – so Marx advertised for one (specifying that the post would be unpaid) in the personal columns of *The Times*!

Nonetheless, Marx was game for the fight: 'They gave me this yacht as a submarine chaser. I've made her ship shape. There is a useful gun on the fo'c'sle and two depth charges aft … but if they don't work, I've still got a shot in my locker. The old way – ram the submarine. Run her down, sir!'[20]

But the engine was an issue. When a fisherman reported a submarine sighting, they sailed out to find it and promptly broke down. Moreover, the six trawlers that comprised the patrol group Marx led were reluctant to bow to pukka naval ways. One day there was a mini mutiny when they refused to go out and the men concerned eventually walked off their boat, not having signed the articles of service (form T-124), and were never seen again.

On leave, Marx bumped into Captain Cecil Lambert, Fourth Sea Lord, and asked him for a faster vessel. He was vaguely promised *Atalanta* but in fact the Admiralty told him that 'we have an even better yacht for you than *Atalanta* – a Russian vessel called the *Iolanda*'.[21]

Designed by Cox and King and Leith-built by Ramage & Ferguson in 1908, *Iolanda* (1,647grt) had thus far had an interesting career. Owned by Elizabeth Terestchenko, in 1912, the yacht was described by the *New York Times* as 'the second largest steam yacht in the world, once the property of Commodore Morton F Plant† but now owned by Mme Elizabeth Terestchenko of St. Petersburg and Kieff [*sic*], Russia'.[22] She had sailed to

* He was a scion of the Greene King brewing dynasty.

† Plant was an American financier, railway and steamship magnate. He was a member of the Atlantic Yacht Club, Corinthian Yacht Club, the New York Yacht Club, and the Larchmont Yacht Club, the latter of which he was commodore.

The Cox and King-designed *Iolanda*, seen pre-war, 1,647grt and 310ft long with twin engines and screws, capable of 18 knots. *(Author's collection)*

New York for repairs before heading for Cannes (where Elizabeth had a home, the Villa Mariposa).

When war came, *Iolanda* had been interned in Trondheim. But her skipper, Captain Bertun, secretly chartered the yacht to the British Admiralty in 1915, and then escaped from Trondheim on the excuse of needing dry dock repairs in Bergen. In fact, he sailed the vessel to Southampton, where she was commissioned on 21 May and fitted with two 3in guns. Marx was appointed on 24 June 1915 and joined the Auxiliary Patrol at Milford Haven.

In November, *Iolanda* was ordered to Gibraltar and ran into a heavy gale; in his diary for 12 November, Marx recorded 'the ship rolling heavily, the men seasick and unable to keep steady, taking in much water … a large quantity of water got into stokehold and engine room'. A day later he noted 'we have to keep our nose to a mountainous sea. The ship had more than 150 tons of water in the stokehole … steam pinnace washed into the sick house and badly damaged.'[23] They were lucky to survive. But in Gib, Marx fell foul of the authorities for his independent and less than deferential manner and was sent back to Britain. Here he was given command of another large yacht, HMY *Beryl*, (1,042grt) built in 1893 as *Princess Alice* and once owned by Lord Inverclyde. When he left her in August 1916, Marx took command of a Q-ship, having commanded three armed yachts but sunk no U-boats (or even encountered one).

So far in this chapter we have examined officers who had some naval training, or had previously achieved high naval rank. But many of the yachts were manned and officered by laymen.

The Blues

The yacht *Zarefah* was taken up by the navy in August 1914 and employed minesweeping off the Belgium coast by the December. Her crew at this

Zarefah, which at the beginning of the war was crewed exclusively by Cambridge graduates. *(Mersea Museum/ Andrew Brown)*

time comprised mainly Cambridge rowing men, including several Blues, while her skipper was Lieutenant Commander W H Stuart Garnett RNR, himself a Wrangler,* the founder of the Sea Scout movement and a keen amateur yachtsman. Stuart Garnett was 'an enthusiastic Alpine climber, and an ardent yachtsman, with a practical knowledge of seamanship and of the navigation of the Channel and North Sea, such as is possessed of few amateurs'.[24] He was the ultimate 'gifted amateur'. When war broke out, he had 'obtained from Mr Steane Price the loan of his yacht *Zarefah*, which he manned, both as to officers and men, mainly with Cambridge graduates and undergraduates'.[25]

In summer 1915, Stuart Garnett left the navy and joined the Royal Flying Corps, home to would-be heroes since the start of the war. He was killed in a flying accident on 21 September 1916, aged just 34.

Norman Carlyle Craig KC, member of parliament for the Isle of Thanet, was another outstanding university man who joined up at the beginning of the conflict as a sub lieutenant RNR. Forty-six years old in 1914, he had been a classical scholar at Peterhouse, Cambridge, was called to the Bar in 1892, appointed King's Counsel in 1909 and elected a Unionist MP in 1910.

Craig had the peculiar distinction of having been presumed dead in 1912 when he cancelled a planned voyage on the *Titanic* so close to her departure time that he was thought to be on board when she sank.

When war came, he joined the yacht *Lorna* and then in April 1915 was transferred to the staff of Rear Admiral Reginald Tupper at Stornoway; next he was appointed to the yacht *Iolaire* in the same role. However, his health seemed suspect and sick leave for six weeks followed. It was then proposed to cancel his commission, presumably for reasons of health, and he was officially thanked for his service. But the cancellation was rescinded and he continued to serve, now as a lieutenant commander RNVR, in a variety of shore-based roles. He was demobilised on 2 January 1919 but died ten months later, after failing to recover from a medical procedure.

The Amateurs

Francis Fitzpatrick Tower was a gentleman of leisure and keen yachtsman. Born in Florence, Italy, in June 1859, he had attended Wellington College and Trinity, Cambridge. At the outbreak of war, he lived in London at the highly desirable address of 66 Princes Gate and also possessed property on the Isle of Wight. His family had owned Weald Hall in Essex and various country estates having made money, as far as can be ascertained, in the law.

He had purchased at least one yacht, *Gossamer*, a 3-ton gaff sloop designed by A E Payne and built in 1892 by Camper and Nicholson at their Gosport yard. Tower sold it in 1896 and doubtless bought another. In 1884, Tower had married Laura, the daughter of Sir Thomas Butler, 10th Baronet Cloughgrenan (and would in 1915 marry off his daughter Isolde to Fitzwalter George Probyn Butler, 17/27th Baron Dunboyne).

* He appeared as eighth Wrangler in 1902 and in the first class of the Mechanical Sciences Tripos in 1903. A Wrangler is a student who gains first-class honours in the final year of the University's degree in mathematics.

Fifty-five years old at the start of the war, Tower immediately volunteered for service in the RNVR and after training at *Vivid* was given command firstly of the armed yacht *Oriana* (1896, 122grt), which proved too slow for the purpose, and then *Ceto*. She was a 140grt steam-powered vessel, owned by Lord Iveagh, Edward Cecil Guinness, and lent to the war effort by him in 1914, whereupon she was fitted with one 6pdr high angle and one 3pdr. Iveagh had kept her at the Isle of Wight, although she does not appear in the Royal Yacht Squadron listings for the time.

Ceto and Tower became part of the Dover Patrol, specifically the Downs Boarding Flotilla. With some of the original crew and a smattering of fishermen, *Ceto* was used to stop and search merchantmen and escort particularly valuable cargoes, such as oilers, through the Dover Strait. They were often out at sea for ten days at a time, especially after the first of the Downs net barriers were laid, when she acted as guard ship for a period.

The yacht was not in very good condition, with a patch on her boiler that constantly gave problems, and on one occasion she lost a propeller while coaling and had to go out on patrol with only one screw. Frustrated at the bureaucracy involved in obtaining a new one through official channels, Tower telegraphed the supplier direct for one and paid for it from his own pocket. On another occasion *Ceto*'s steering gear broke down as she was entering Ramsgate harbour. It was a bit hairy and Tower noted 'thank one's stars grief didn't result'.[26]

Tower enjoyed his time in command. He regarded it as an 'adventure'. On 28 December 1914, SS *Montrose* (famous for being the ship on which Dr Crippen and his inamorata were captured in 1910), loaded up with concrete for blocking one of Dover Harbour's entrances as protection against attack, broke adrift and drove right through Dover harbour from the western entrance to the eastern entrance without touching anything. It was blowing a gale that night and *Ceto* was ordered out to try to rescue the two men on board. Tower described it: 'as we opened out the South Foreland poor *Ceto* took it on board heavily and though we cruised about for hours, we did little good. [*Montrose*] drove ashore on the Goodwins, the crew being taken off by a tug.'[27]

One of the duties that Tower enjoyed most was when the first net defences were placed in position at the north end of the Downs and ships had to be taken through the gateway. The Admiralty had instructed on 5 March 1915 that 'compulsory pilotage will come into effect at 0600 March 10'.[28] However, there was a marked shortage of pilots and so Tower was ordered to do it himself. 'My method was to steam up alongside the waiting ship, hail her and ask her if she wanted to be taken through,' he wrote, 'and then steam ahead with "follow me" in international code flying at the masthead.'[29]

Once he was ordered to take an arrested trawler into harbour for inspection. The trawler was anchored near to *Ceto* and her anchor dragged, fouling *Ceto*'s cable, which made the ships fast to one and other and 'driving about Deal in the dark'.[30] Eventually the trawler winched the tangled mess on board and they were able to clear the chain.

Tower's adventure came to an end when the Admiralty instructed that all captains of such vessels should have a Board of Trade certificate. Tower did not possess one, and stood down from command in April 1915.

It had been fun and he had enjoyed it. 'What a pleasant and interesting time it all was and a good old ship,' he commented.[31]

It wasn't the end of his naval service, however. He went on to serve as assistant to the Senior Naval Officer (SNO) Auxiliary Patrol Area XIV, was Mentioned in Despatches by that officer 'for excellent work and untiring energy and devotion to duty' in May 1917,[32] having been advanced in rank to commander the month before, served in the Q-ship *Lisette*,* and became the assistant to the SNO at Kingstown, Ireland. For these 'valuable services as assistant to the Senior Naval Officer, Kingstown' Tower was awarded the OBE after the war.[33]

Charles Edward Evans was a successful businessman who owned the coal export and pit prop import firm of Evans and Reid (Coal) Limited of Cardiff. His father had been a master mariner and Charles had been born at sea, 100 miles south of Lima on the full-rigger *Rhea Sylvia* of which his father was master. Evans was also the owner of a splendid sixteenth-century manor house in Nailsea, Somerset. This was Nailsea Court, which he had restored over a seven-year period commencing in 1906 and working with the renowned Tudor specialist Arthur James Stratton. Additionally, Evans was a founder member of the Penarth Boating and Yachting Club and owned or leased the American-built steam yacht *Idaho* (1910, 43grt), which had at one time graced the New York Yacht Club.

Fifty-six years old when war broke out, Evans immediately volunteered both himself and the yacht to the Admiralty. Their Lordships rejected the yacht as being too small but accepted him, giving Evans the rank of (unpaid) sub lieutenant in the RNR and appointing him to the steam yacht *Hersilia* (1895), based at Aultbea on the shore of Loch Ewe, in north-western Scotland.

Here the yacht and its twenty-six crewmen patrolled with their two 6pdr guns at the ready, undertaking a variety of jobs including mine sweeping, examination vessel, escort, and U-boat hunting, largely in the Minch, a strait in north-west Scotland separating the north-west Highlands and the northern Inner Hebrides from Lewis and Harris in the Outer Hebrides.

Hersilia was a 'comfortable boat although rather wanting on the ventilation side and rather ancient'. Evans thought that she, painted slate grey like her yacht sisters, resembled 'pretty women in badly fitting widow's weeds'.[34]

The yacht was frequently pressed into service to dispose of floating mines. On 29 December 1914, they were tasked with finding one, discovered the offending object, and at 1430 fired seven 6pdr rounds into it to no effect, until one Able Seaman Kirwan hit it with a rifle shot. 'The smoke and water shot up to a great height and after some seconds a ring of

* She was not a steam-powered vessel but a 116grt top sail schooner, built in Cowes in 1873 for Francis Robertson Reid (d. 1899), who once ran the Stonelaw Colliery (in Rutherglen, Scotland) and was a colonel in the 5th volunteer battalion of the Glasgow Highlanders. The navy took her in June 1916 and converted her to a decoy ship with three concealed 6pdrs.

Steam yachts were rarely used as minesweepers but if they located one would often try to destroy it. Here *The Illustrated War News* of 19 January 1916 imagines such a scene. *(Author's collection)*

projectiles fell all around, evidently a top dressing of the charge.'[35] Some of the fragments fell on the church at nearby Canna Island. Four days later, Evans took some men in a gig to sink a mine found wedged against some rocks. They fired at it with rifles from 200yds, then 100 and then 60, all to no avail, which left them rather chastened. Two weeks later, the yacht *Vanessa* found the mine riddled with bullets and waterlogged, which made Evans feel a little better.

The charms of north-west Scotland palled on Evans and in February 1915 he wrote to the Admiralty once more asking them to take *Idaho* with him to command it. On 30 March he was ordered south and in April, Their Lordships asked if *Idaho* was still available. He sailed her to Milford Haven, where the little yacht became headquarters ship for the port SNO. He was provided with naval signal flags but no ensign, and so Evans acquired one for eighteen pence. Neither had they weapons, apart from a few revolvers, and so Evans purchased an elephant gun, which he demonstrated could make a dent in steel plating.

Here Evans served out the war. He was appointed a lieutenant commander RNVR (honorary – he was still to be unpaid) at the end of March 1916[36] and was demobilised on 2 June 1919. Their Lordships returned his yacht with an expression of their pleasure 'for placing the yacht at their disposal and to thank him for services undertaken by him in the RNR and RNVR'.[37]

The route to armed yacht command was sometimes surprising. One of the more interesting commanders was Limerick-born Edward Conor Marshall O'Brien. He was a boat builder and naval architect whose designs included *Saoirse* (in which he would single-handedly circumnavigate the globe between 1923 and 1925). A committed Irish republican, another of his boats, *Kelpie*, was used for gun running in 1914. On 26 July, 600 rifles were brought by *Kelpie*, and another 900 guns plus 25,000 rounds of ammunition by the yacht *Asgard* (owned and skippered by Erskine Childers of *Riddle of the Sands* fame), to Howth harbour for the use of the Irish Volunteers (of which O'Brien was a member).

When war came, amazingly, Conor O'Brien eventually joined the RNVR. It was not necessarily a happy time for either him or the service. As a sub lieutenant in April 1916, his service record indicates that his conduct was reported twice – but for what we will never know for a large ink blot obscures the missing words.[38] In September he was on the books of the depot ship *Hermione* for a course of instruction on the American-built motor launches (MLs) coming into service, after which he took command of *ML-425* in November, *ML-102* in December and then *ML-551* before eventually becoming captain of the armed yacht *Sayonara* (see Chapter 4) in March 1917. A month later he passed his seamanship and navigation exams and was advanced to lieutenant. *Sayanora* remained under O'Brien's

Norman C O'Neill's *Adventuress*, which spent most of the war in the Coast of Ireland Command at Queenstown. Her forwards 12pdr is clearly visible. She served in the Second World War as *Anglia*. *(© National Maritime Museum GO5437)*

Stephanotis (1903, 120grt), also owned by Norman O'Neill, was originally built for Chatham brewer Charles Arkoll by Hawthorns and Company of Leith. Arkoll was a keen yachtsman and Commodore of the New Thames Yacht Club at Medway. She was named for the Madagascar jasmine, *stephanotis floribunda. (Author's collection)*

command until she paid off in October 1918 and O'Brien remained in the navy until March the following year.

Adventuress (1913, 342grt) had been built by Hepple and Co. in South Shields as a single-screw steel yacht capable of 12 knots and commissioned by one A M Tree of New York. By 1914 she was owned by Norman Clark O'Neill and registered at Southampton, from whence she joined the navy in November 1914. *Adventuress* is the only one of the yachts taken up by the Admiralty to be designated as a minesweeper, according to Dittmar and Colledge, although yachts did occasionally turn their hand to sweeping. She was armed with two 12pdrs and survived to fight again in the Second World War as *Anglia*.

O'Neill owned several yachts, including *Noti* at Southampton and *Stephanotis* (of which he was the third owner). He had inherited a fortune based upon the O'Neill family's sugar interests and the Clark cotton thread business. He seemed to have lived mainly for boats (he held a master's certificate) and motoring and enjoyed the life of a gentleman of leisure in London.

But when war came, 30-year-old O'Neill responded to the clarion call. On 3 August 1915, he was granted a temporary commission in the Royal Naval Volunteer Reserve as a lieutenant and included in the Navy List as Transport Officer Second Grade, having held a sub lieutenant's position since December 1914. By 29 July 1915, O'Neill was assigned to the yacht *Vanessa* and on shore to assist Captain Arthur Reginald Raby (a dug out officer commanding Auxiliary Patrol Area XXII, Eastern Irish Sea and west of the Mersey, based at Holyhead) and from 25 September 1917 to 25 February 1918 he was at Dunkirk as a 3rd Grade Transport Officer,[39] an exposed post for Dunkirk was shelled and bombed frequently at this time. Idle rich he may have been, but like many of his kind he knew where his duty lay.

At the other end of the social scale to Tower or O'Neill was Harry Chadwick-Smith. He was typical of the young men who joined the RNVR and were specifically trained to be signalmen or radio telephonists. Many of the men serving in such a role in the auxiliary forces were RNVR and of tender years.

Born in 1899, the son of a mill worker, in the Lancashire town of Leigh, famous for its spinning of cotton and silk, he was educated at Leigh Grammar School (on a scholarship). When war broke out, he wasn't old enough for military service but in April 1917, Chadwick-Smith cycled to nearby Warrington to enlist in the RNVR.

He and many others were sent to the Crystal Palace for basic training and then after six weeks he was ordered to Signal School, which he passed out of in January 1918, and went to Chatham barracks for drafting. From here Chadwick-Smith was ordered to Granton, Auxiliary Patrol Area VII, to serve on an armed trawler as a signalman.

After further service on a Q-ship, he swapped jobs with a friend and found himself in the yacht *Zoraide*, where he became second signalman.

Zoraide was the property of Kenneth Mackenzie Clark,* whose great-great-grandfather had invented the cotton spool, and whose business, the Clark Thread Company of Paisley, had grown into a substantial enterprise, one that allowed the founder's great-great-grandson to live a life of luxury.

She had been built in 1894 of 532grt and a year later the marine artist Antonio de Simone painted her in the Bay of Naples. But in September 1914 she was hired by the Admiralty, fitted with a 12pdr and a 6pdr AA gun and sent off on patrol. Now she was one of six yachts based at Granton, under the ultimate command of another dug out officer, retired Admiral James Startin, now a commodore RNR.

Chadwick-Smith was moving in famous company, for the commander of *Zoraide* was the famous yacht racing skipper Archibald Hogarth, who had sailed Sir Thomas Lipton's *Shamrock* in the America's Cup of 1899 without, however, securing the trophy. The son of a Scottish fisherman, 54-year-old Hogarth was a yachting legend, now detailed to patrol the edge of the minefields around the Scottish east coast, looking for drifting mines, German or British.

It was Chadwick-Smith who took in the signal announcing the Armistice. *Zoraide* was on patrol off May Island, in the outer Firth of Forth. At first light Signalman Chadwick-Smith RNVR observed the mechanical semaphore arms on the island in action, trying to contact his ship, and a flag flying. To his surprise, as he took in the signal from the semaphore machine, he realised that it read 'Armistice to be signed at eleven o'clock this morning'. His mind whirled; 'would miracles never cease? It was astounding news. It was unbelievable,' he thought.[40]

He rushed to give the glad news to his captain, Archibald Hogarth, who

* His son was the art historian Kenneth Clark of the television programme *Civilisation* fame. Along with the yacht, in 1904 he purchased Sudbourne Hall in Suffolk for the pheasant shooting.

he found in his pyjamas sitting on the edge of his bunk. On being given the message, Hogarth simply said 'good', and dismissed him. But the news spread like wildfire among the crew and, perhaps unsurprisingly, they felt that they could now return to base and enjoy the festivities that were bound to be resultant on such a declaration. But when they reached Granton, Commodore Startin was furious at such dereliction of duty and sent them out again to complete their mission. 'So back we went,' Chadwick-Smith remembered, 'feeling very sorry for ourselves knowing that we should miss all the fun and jollification of Armistice Day ashore.'[41]

But recompense came some weeks later. Shortly after midnight on 21 November, the 'C'-class cruiser HMS *Cardiff*, wearing the flag of Rear Admiral Edwyn Alexander-Sinclair, commanding the 6th Light Cruiser Squadron, stole quietly out of the Forth of Forth to meet the German battle fleet and lead it to a pre-arranged rendezvous with Admiral David Beatty, CinC Grand Fleet and his ships, code-named 'Operation ZZ'. Later that morning, *Cardiff* met and led the German High Seas Fleet – fourteen capital ships, seven light cruisers and forty-nine destroyers – towards the coast of Scotland. They were greeted by the entire Grand Fleet, some 192 ships in total, which formed into two flanking lines of escort. Led by HMS *Cardiff* and her admiral, the Germans sailed to internment and a formal ceremony of submission at Rosyth. There Beatty signalled 'the German flag will be hauled down at sunset today and will not be hoisted again without permission'.

Zoraide was there to see the spectacle. 'It was a marvellous sight,' thought Chadwick-Smith, 'but in some ways a sorry spectacle, for these great ships looked dirty, uncared for, salt encrusted ... ships that had never dared venture to sea.'[42]

And there was another yacht witnessing the event, too. Admiral Beatty's *Sheelah*, despite being a hospital ship, had been hurriedly summoned with Ethel Beatty on board in order that she could observe her husband's triumph. She was unwittingly the cause of some light relief in an otherwise sombre ceremony when the hastily prepared *Sheelah* passed close to the German battlecruiser SMS *Seydlitz* and received 'a derisive demonstration from the crew'.[43]

CHAPTER SIX

ROYAL NAVY YACHT LOSSES

GIVEN THEIR DESIGN and intended role when built, it is small surprise that the armed yachts were easily sunk if mined, torpedoed or hit by bad weather.

Mines were invariably fatal to the armed yachts. On 6 July 1915, the *Portsmouth Evening News* reported a Lloyd's message: 'The Norwegian steamer *Peik*, from Cherbourg for Warkworth, in ballast, when abreast of the Sunk Light Vessel, at 1000, was torpedoed, and the vessel foundered in five minutes. The crew left in one of the boats, and were afterwards picked up and landed at Harwich.'

Two weeks later the armed patrol yacht *Rhiannon*, in peacetime owned by Lord Howard de Walden and now based at Harwich, was sent to patrol in the Thames Estuary in company with the trawler *Strathspey*.

Taken up by the navy in 1914, *Rhiannon* was fitted with two 3pdr guns and became part of the Harwich Auxiliary Patrol. On 20 July 1915, she was sailing towards the wreck of the *Peik* when at 1040 there was a large explosion under her bows. She had hit a mine. The forepart was blown away but the aft section floated for some time before sinking.

The area had been swept for mines after the loss of the Norwegian and the Admiralty became concerned that *Peik* might have been a German decoy that was now releasing mines on a time delay. Equally, her insurers, Bowring's Insurance Agency and Lloyd's of London, seemed to think that she may have been deliberately scuttled.[1] What is certain was that five of *Rhiannon*'s crew died, including her captain, Lieutenant Commander George William Wellburn RNR. Forty-seven-year-old master mariner Wellburn had joined the RNR in March 1898 and retired in 1912, but he volunteered for active duty straightway war was declared and had been appointed to *Rhiannon* in the December.

Another yacht was lost to a mine three months later. The Duke of Leeds' *Aries*, 197ft long and of 268 tons, was attached to the Dover Patrol. On 31 October, she received reports of the sinking of the Norwegian SS *Eidiva* and later the British SS *Forward*, 2 miles south-east of the South Foreland, probably to mines. *Aries'* captain, Lieutenant Commander Harry R D Calder RNR, a merchant mariner from Leith, proceeded to the area and

Aries, sunk on All Saints' Eve, 1915, pictured here in happier times. *(Author's collection)*

was able to pick up several survivors from the British ship, transferring them to trawlers; one of these vessels reported that she had seen a mine floating nearby, off Leathercoats. Calder decided that he would investigate and mark or destroy the hazard. He posted extra lookouts and sailed towards the potential minefield. It proved to be a rash decision. At 1100 there was a large explosion under the yacht that broke her back and she sank quickly. Mine clearance was not necessarily a patrol yacht's task; Calder's decision, possibly influenced by the fact that as a master mariner he would have hated to see good cargo ships sunk, killed twenty-two of *Aries'* crew and forfeited his own life, too. Thirteen of the dead were MMR, mainly members of the original crew. One who wasn't was 46-year-old Francis Bacon, a professional county cricketer who played seventy-five matches for Hampshire as an all-rounder.

The court of enquiry indicated that Calder had made a misjudgement in entering the mined area.[2] It turned out that the field had been laid by *UC-6*; three ships in one day was not a bad haul for her commander.

Or take the example of *Aegusa*. HMY *Aegusa* was originally built by Scotts of Greenock in 1896 for Ignazio Florio who, at the age of 22, had inherited one of the greatest fortunes in Italy. She was a screw schooner powered by a steam engine of 2,500ihp, which gave her a top speed of 15.5 knots. In 1898, Florio sold her to Sir Thomas Lipton, 'The King's Grocer' and famous yachtsman, who had made it his ambition to win the America's Cup. He didn't achieve his heart's desire but his well-publicised efforts to win the trophy, which earned him a specially designed cup for 'the best of all losers', made his tea famous in the United States. He renamed her *Erin* and used her as a tender to his various racing yachts called *Shamrock*,* and for personal pleasure; 'Sir Thomas Lipton largely entertained on board the *Erin* during the America Cup trials and races.'[3]

* There were five in total.

Thomas Lipton (fifth from left, second row from front) and nurses on their way to Serbia on board Lipton's steam yacht *Erin*, as depicted in *The Times History of the War*. *(Author's collection)*

When war was declared he volunteered her to ferry medical staff to France and then in 1915 to Serbia. In the latter case, Lipton himself sailed the vessel, carrying Red Cross stores, doctors, and nurses, and then toured Serbian hospitals bringing cheer and supplies to the patients.

On 3 July 1915, *Erin* was commissioned under her original name as HMY *Aegusa* and placed under the command of a retired vice admiral, now enrolled in the RNR as a captain, 63-year-old Thomas Philip Walker. On 27 April 1916, while closing in on the sloop HMS *Nasturtium*, which appeared to be in distress, she struck a mine in a field laid off Grand Harbour, Malta, by *U-73*, although at the time it was believed she had been torpedoed. Six crew lost their lives, all of them MMR and probably members of Lipton's original crew, five of them firemen. Mine explosions against yachts were invariably fatal for engine room crew. *Nasturtium* sank in the early morning the next day, mined in the same field, which had also accounted for the pre-dreadnought battleship *Russell*.

Walker survived the sinking and went on to take command of the armed yacht *Marynthea*, also at Gibraltar, the following month. His dedicated service was remembered by Sir John Jellicoe in his post-war writings, when he noted that: 'Admiral T P Walker, DSO, had his yacht sunk under him.'[4]

As for Lipton, despite his wealth and generosity (and his friendship with King Edward VII), his low-born Scottish provenance did not make him a natural member of the British upper class and the ultra-exclusive Royal Yacht Squadron only admitted him shortly before his death in 1931.

The loss of the *Aegusa* also occasioned a question in the House of Commons nearly two years later, when in January 1918, Sir Bertram Falle, MP for Portsmouth, rose to ask a question on behalf of one of his constituents. 'Is he aware,' Falle began 'that James Horner, of 48 Meyrick Road, Portsmouth, signed on as AB [able seaman] in one of His Majesty's yachts in July 1915, and was with the yacht when she was sunk* … and that he had shortly before handed to his officer the sum of £28† which sum was lost with the ship, the fact of which is acknowledged in writing by the

* Falle actually gave the wrong day in April for the sinking, but only one armed yacht was lost in April of any year, and that was *Aegusa*.

† Just under the average annual wage for an agricultural worker at the time.

officer, and that the Admiralty, Foreign Office, and Treasury decline to assist Mr. Horner or to repay the money; that Mr Horner is now 68 years of age; and if he will have the matter inquired into and compensation paid to Mr Horner?'

The reply would have done justice to Charles Dickens' Circumlocution Office. 'My hon and gallant Friend brought this case to my notice in October last, and I informed him, after inquiry, that as the money lost was in the form of Treasury notes the question of allowing compensation for the loss should be addressed to the Postmaster-General, whose Department deals with compensation in such cases. The matter is now under the consideration of the Postmaster-General, to whom evidence in support of the loss is being furnished by the Admiralty from the reports of the officers under whom Mr Horner served.'[5]

Commander Samuel Robson Crabtree RN was captain of Lord Rosebery's yacht *Zaida*. Before the war, *Zaida* had boasted wooden fittings of teak, wall-to-wall carpeting, and a triple-expansion engine by J S White of Cowes. Now she was a warship under 50-year-old Robson, who had retired from the Royal Navy on '14 March 1911 with a step up in rank'[6] but re-joined on 21 August 1914. He was sent to Peterhead for 'special service', which probably meant Q-ships, was commended by Their Lordships on 10 May 1915 for 'chasing a submarine',[7] and appointed to *Zaida* on 1 June 1916.

Special service work obviously suited Crabtree, for *Zaida* was attached to the Intelligence Department at Alexandria, where at the end of May 1916, he was given orders to destroy Turkish petrol stocks at Iskenderun in the Gulf of Alexandretta.

What happened next is something of a mystery. *Zaida* failed to return, and the Turks reported her as sunk with her surviving crew members prisoners of war, including Commander Crabtree. It was presumed that *Zaida* had been sunk by a submarine, and this is how her loss was recorded, but later it was concluded that she had hit a mine at 0845 on 17 August, causing her to break up and sink within minutes, with only her masts showing above the water. These the Turks cut off, so they did not give away the location of the minefield.

Crabtree was Mentioned in Despatches on 14 July 1916 'for Services in the Auxiliary Patrol';[8] but by then he was already an internee of the Turks. The Turks treated their prisoners notoriously badly; Crabtree died in captivity on 30 September 1916 and was followed on 15, 17 and 25 November by three other survivors of the mining held as POWs. Altogether thirteen crew were killed in the incident, including Lieutenant Edwin Griffiths RNR, the former master of *Zaida* in peacetime, who died in the mine explosion.

One who survived was an artillery officer, Lieutenant Charles Leonard Woolley RFA. Woolley appears to have been in charge of a group of spy ships operating in the area. He ran agents on the Syrian coast from a motley collection of small ships, ranging from *Zaida* to a lateen-rigged Turkish schooner; in order to pass unnoticed in those waters the crews were dressed up as pirates. This would suit a former Q-ship man such as Crabtree, too. Woolley seems to have been ordered to take leave and so had taken passage in *Zaida* as some form of recreation from his day job. He spent the rest of the war as a POW.

HMY *Verona* (1890) had originally been built by Fleming and Ferguson of Paisley for wealthy Australian brewer John 'Jack' Robert Wood as a wedding present for his Shakespearian actress bride, Elizabeth Jennings (aka Essie Jenyns), and subsequently went through multiple ownerships. Of 331grt and capable of 14 knots, she was taken up by the navy in late 1914. Fitted with guns at her counter and bow, which she never fired in anger, she was later modified to take a single depth charge.

On 24 February 1917 *Verona* was returning from a night patrol, between Lossiemouth and Helmsdale, to Tarbet Ness. At 0817 there was a tremendous explosion abreast the funnel that broke her back and she sank stern first, the bows standing proud of the water for some time before slipping beneath the waves.

The Admiralty was initially concerned that she had hit a drifting mine from a defensive British field but it was later determined that it was a German weapon, laid by *UC-33*.

All twenty-tree of her crew died, including her captain, Commander Charles Peter Wilson RNR. His wife erected a tablet to his memory in their local Teesdale place of worship, The Church of the Barn, in the tiny hamlet of Laithkirk. A marble scroll-like plaque on a surround reads: 'In proud and tender memory of Charles P Wilson, Commander RD RNR lost with the destruction of HMS *Verona* Feb 24th 1917. Aged 48 years. This tablet is erected by his wife. Nought but well and fair and what may comfort in a death so noble.'

The last yacht to be mined during the war was *Zarefah*. She had given stalwart service since 1914. On 8 May 1917, *Zarefah* was employed as part of the Kirkwall local defence force and was now commanded by Lieutenant Alfred Stephen Gilbert RNR.

At 1900, off Mull Head in Deer Sound (Orkney), she reported spotting a floating mine. Gilbert took his vessel close to the object and fired on the mine with a rifle, which exploded it. In doing so, lookout focus was lost and suddenly another mine was seen under the bows. There was no time to avoid it; a massive explosion devastated the 129ft yacht and she sank within minutes. Sixteen men of a crew of twenty-seven lost their lives.

There was a further loss to mines just after the Armistice. The patrol yacht *Goissa* had already made her mark by ramming a battlecruiser; unfortunately, it was a British one. On 25 April 1916, HMS *Invincible*, flagship of the 3rd Battle Cruiser Squadron, was returning in company from a fruitless sortie in response to the German bombardment of Yarmouth and Lowestoft on the 24th and 25th. At 2307 in thick fog off the Farne Islands, she was impaled by *Goissa*, whose bow was embedded in *Invincible*'s side, stoving it

Rona/Goissa moored on the River Dart, with Kingswear in the background. *(Alice Wood Collection)*

in. The battlecruiser's speed was reduced to 12 knots through flooding and she was forced to haul out of line and proceed independently to Rosyth for repairs, which lasted until 22 May. Four of the yacht's crew were killed in the smash and she had to be towed home.

HMY *Goissa* had started life as *Rona* (1893), 882grt, designed by G L Watson and built by D and W Henderson for 21-year-old Arthur Herbert Edward Wood. Wood had inherited a fortune at 16, as the great grandson of the Stoke Potteries' giant Enoch Wood. She was the last word in luxury at the time. The yacht had an impressive 9ft of headroom in the saloons and eleven staterooms, the largest five of which had their own baths under the floors and running hot and cold water in every room. The main saloon could seat forty, and boasted a piano and writing desks. The dining room had a large domed skylight of stained glass, the boudoir had its own fire-place and a second piano. Officers and engineers had their own cabins and mess, crew berthed in a spacious fo'csle, while fireman berthed amidships by the engine room and even had their own bath.

Rona had electric lighting and ventilation, piped central heating through-out, a refrigerated chamber for longer voyages and distilling apparatus. She also had an electric launch and a 28ft steam one, two racing yachts and various other boats, all of which were carried on deck or on davits. She made 15.5 knots in her trials.

Around the same time that *Rona* was launched, Wood married. Perhaps this was why he sold her after only two years. In 1895, Baron Ferdinand J A de Rothschild owned her, then Arthur Dupree of London. The Duke of Bedford had her for two years from 1910 and renamed her *Sapphire*, and then Noel Pemberton Billing. He registered her for less than a year. Camper and Nicholson then tried to sell her. Next came a period in Greece in the ownership of the Embiricos family from 1913, and from there she joined the navy as *Goissa* in February 1916.

By November 1918, *Goissa* had been despatched to the Dardanelles to assist in the process of mine clearance to open the way to Constantinople and the Black Sea. On the 15th, she was steaming north towards Chanak Kalessi when a large explosion occurred under the vessel, which broke up and sank in less than three minutes. It was later decided that she had strayed out of the cleared channel and had indeed being steering along its edge. No blame was attached to the yacht's commander, Arnold Octavius Morgan RNR, as it seemed that the instructions detailing the correct route were unclear. Five men were killed, all bar one in the engine room.[9]

Only a single armed yacht was torpedoed (some were fairly fast and therefore made a difficult target). On 26 September 1916, the armed trawler *Sarah Alice*, under Lieutenant Hugh McVey Lovett RNR, was in company with the yacht *Conqueror II* (1889), under 47-year-old Commander Thomas Roland Agassiz RNR. They were patrolling to the north-west of the Fair Isle, hunting for submarines but also looking for vessels carrying contraband as part of a blockade patrol.

Conqueror II, built by Russell and Co. in 1889, 407grt, had been firstly owned by Hull-based fishing trawler owner Walter S Bailey, a serial steam yacht owner. The Admiralty took her up in February 1915 from the spendthrift Duke of Manchester, William Angus Drogo Montague; before the duke, she had belonged to F W Vanderbilt. At 1630 the patrol stopped the steamship *St Gothard* (2,788grt, 1903)* on passage from Shetland to the Firth of Forth, inspected her manifest and confirmed her identity before letting her go. Little did they know that all three ships, stationary as they completed the task in hand, were being stalked by *U-52* and *Kapitänleutnant* Hans Walther.

The German fired a single torpedo at *Sarah Alice*, which hit home and the ex-Fleetwood trawler sank quickly. Unhesitatingly, the merchant vessel lowered its boats and went to pick up the survivors, but five minutes after firing on the *Sarah Alice*, *U-52* loosed another torpedo that hit *Conqueror II*. Agassiz should have been at full speed by then, hunting the U-boat; perhaps his compassion as a merchant sailor for his fellow amateur war warriors kept him from action. Walther then sank the *St Gothard* too, completing a full sweep of the stationary ships. Perhaps a regular Royal Navy officer would have taken greater precautions, but they were on the bigger, pukka, warships.

Whatever the reasoning, sixteen men from the trawler, including Lovett, and seventeen from the yacht were killed, including Commander Agassiz. The dead give a good indication of the make-up of yacht crews at the time. Apart from Agassiz, the list comprised two other RNR officers; four wireless and signalmen, two RNR and two RNVR; two RNR seaman and eight MMR. These latter men would have been members of her original crew, signed onto T-124Y documents. The survivors were picked up from their Carley floats by the destroyer HMS *Sylvia* a day later.

Collision

Operating in crowded coastal waters as escorts to large merchant ships or patrolling the routes that such vessels followed was often fraught with the risk of accidental collision, encounters that a yacht was ill-equipped to survive.

The yacht *Clementina* has already been met in Chapter 1. Built in 1887 by Ramage & Ferguson for the Italian entrepreneur and politician Giuseppe Caravita, Principe di Sirignano, she does not appear to have ever passed to his ownership but was instead chartered to Leopold II, king of the Belgians, for two years before going rapidly through a number of owners, culminating in her acquisition by Frederick James Harrison, director of the shipping company T and J Harrison of Liverpool, in 1903.

Of 469grt, *Clementina* was a three-masted schooner with a single steam-powered screw that could take her to around 13 knots. Harrison, a member of the Royal Yacht Squadron, seems to have kept her at Cowes, where in July 1913 she was in collision with the new destroyer HMS *Lynch*, itself under tow.

* She transpired to be an Admiralty stores carrier.

The navy took her into service on 22 September 1914, fitted her with two 6pdr guns, and sent her to patrol around the Orkney Islands and then in the Larne area. It was here that she suffered her second, and ultimately fatal, collision on 8 August 1915, when as an examination vessel she closed SS *Adam Smith* (299grt).

Badly damaged, *Clementina* was beached in Cushendun Bay, County Antrim, but the attempt to salvage her was abandoned. The wreck was eventually sold to Murray Brothers of Waterford, who part salved her, leaving the remains to rot.

Marcella, previously *Marchesa*, was an old stream yacht that under the latter name achieved a degree of fame when she was chartered by the fabulously rich Earl of Dudley* to take him on a round the world cruise in 1885 and 1886. By December 1886 he had reached Melbourne, from whence the newspapers reported that 'the yacht, which is magnificently appointed, and has a crew of twenty-seven men all told, has put in here to refit, and her stay will probably extend over a couple of months'.[10] At the time, she was wearing the burgee of the Royal Thames Yacht Club.

The yacht was taken up by the Admiralty in July 1915 and put to work as an armed boarding vessel in the Downs Patrol, stopping and inspecting traffic in the English Channel. Her life in the role was to be short for on 24 March the following year she sank in the Downs after a collision. Fortunately, no lives were lost.

Collision was also the fate of the steam yacht *Kethailes*. *Kethailes* had been built for the Liverpool-based Northern Ireland-born ship owner William Johnston† by Richardson, Duck and Company at Thornaby-on-Tees in 1903. Her designer was the much sought after St Clare John Byrne. She was a large craft at 625grt and was named for Johnston's four daughters – Kathleen, ETHel, AILeen and EStele.

On 24 September 1914, Johnston voluntarily handed her over for the war effort (he was later compensated); she was armed with two 6pdr guns and sent to patrol in the North and Irish Seas.

Kethailes achieved some measure of fame when, on 28 September 1917, the Dublin-ported cargo ship SS *William Middleton*, bound for Falmouth carrying hay, was mined in a field laid by *UC-75*. *Kethailes* and her CO, Lieutenant Commander Sidney Reginald Lane RNR,‡ were first on scene and managed to secure the ship and its valuable freight from sinking. Lane and his crew received a commendation from the Admiralty for their efforts.

But her own fate was sealed just twelve days later. On 11 October 1917, the ex-Bibby Lines troop ship SS *Leicestershire*, on passage to Liverpool, accidentally rammed *Kethailes* near the Blackwater Lightship, which marks the Blackwater Bank off the east coast of County Wexford. Seventeen of the yacht's crew were lost in the incident with only eleven survivors (including Lane), nine of whom were picked up by the P-boat *P-44*. The dead included her peacetime captain, George Clark, aged 25 and a now lieutenant in the RNR.

* William Humble Ward, 2nd Earl of Dudley. His father died in 1885 and he inherited nearly 30,000 acres in Staffordshire and Worcestershire, two hundred coal and iron mines, several iron works and a substantial fortune, as well as the Earldom.

† Johnston was a considerable philanthropist. In the year his yacht was built, he helped to establish at Liverpool University the Johnston Laboratories and the Johnston Chair of Biochemistry (the first chair in biochemistry to be established in the UK). He funded the chair as part of a £25,000 gift.

‡ Who had previously commanded another yacht, *Evening Star*, until 28 June 1916. (ADM 340/81/32, NA)

Hersilia *and* Iolaire

Weather, mines and torpedoes can all sink a ship. But the biggest threat is often incompetence.

Hersilia was a 330grt steam yacht built in 1895 by Ramage & Ferguson at Leith for the Reverend John Hutchison and was acquired in 1902 by the wealthy stockbroker (and President of the Shire Horse Society) Sir Walpole Lloyd Greenwell, 1st Baronet, a member of the Royal Yacht Squadron.

On the outbreak of war, she was requisitioned, fitted with two 6pdr guns and sent to Stornoway as a patrol vessel. Here, at 0015 on 6 January 1916, she was ordered to the Isle of Ornsay in Sleat Sound where the SS *Rondo* had run aground with a cargo of valuable coal. Apart from her crew, Rear Admiral Reginald Tupper, commanding Patrol Area Number One with his flag flown on shore at Stornoway, was on board; this would, one might think, ensure that some attention was paid by officers and men to the detail of naval life.

Hersilia's captain was 45-year-old Lieutenant Commander Hugh Henry MacLean RNR. Maclean was an experienced sailor who went to sea at an early age and rounded Cape Horn four times in the barque *Iron Crag*, and once in the barque *Valalta*. On the death of his older brother in 1908 he succeeded to the estate of Lazenby Hall, in North Yorkshire. His love of sailing, however, continued, and yachting was his abiding passion.* His navigating officer was another RNR officer, Lieutenant Frank Randall Carter.

Course was set at S ¼ W to pass east of South Rona Light and through the Inner Sound. The night was very dark with rain squalls and gale force winds blowing from the south-west. *Hersilia* sailed through the night until just before 0500, when she hit the rocks between Rudha ona Fearna and Rudha Chuaig. After striking, the engines were kept ahead to hold her against the rocky shore and at dawn the drifter *Budding Rose* came alongside and took off most crew and some stores. But the water was gaining and the yacht took a severe list. At 1015 all crew left the doomed vessel and she rolled over and started to break up.

The Court of Enquiry found that Carter had altered course during the night without informing anyone and failed to take bearings on visible lights. Sub Lieutenant Henry Fosbrooke, who had complained that he was never given any responsibility and was always having his work checked, had been allowed to plot the subsequent course unsupervised. The Admiralty held that the loss of *Hersilia* was entirely due to the negligent navigation of the steam yacht by Commander MacLean and his Navigating Officer Lieutenant Carter.[11] MacLean was discharged from the navy and the other two officers incurred 'Their Lordship's Displeasure'. As Friedrich Schiller wrote, 'against stupidity the very gods themselves contend in vain'.[12]

Quite the worst wreck was shortly after the end of the war. The steam yacht *Iolanthe* had been built in 1881 by Ramage & Ferguson for T J Waller, who had made his fortune in railway construction. She was of 415grt and powered by engines made in Beccles by Elliott and Garrood. In 1906,

* On the death of Maclean's two cousins, in 1930 and 1932, he became the eldest living male representative of the house, branch and family of the Macleans of Ardgour, and was therefore acknowledged by the Clan Maclean Association in Glasgow in October 1934 as the eighteenth Hereditary Chieftain of Ardgour.

Iolanthe became *Amalthaea* when she was sold to the Liverpool and Hamburg Steam Ship Company (owned by Donald Currie of Currie Lines) and she was taken up into the navy under that name in March 1915. Fitted with two 3in guns, *Amalthaea** joined the Auxiliary patrol.

In November 1918, the Admiralty changed her name to *Iolaire*, Gaelic for 'eagle', and continued to utilise her post-Armistice.

On 31 December 1918, *Iolaire* was detailed to take a large number of demobbed or on-leave servicemen, mainly RNR or RNVR, back to their homes in the Western Isles, primarily the islands of Lewis and Harris. She had not originally been intended for this service, as the mailboat *Shelia* was supposed to carry the men homeward, but there were way too many men who wanted to be back for Hogmanay and *Iolaire* and her crew of twenty-four men were drafted in to carry an extra 254 returnees.

Iolaire arrived at the Kyle of Lochalsh at 1600 but it was an inauspicious beginning to her task as she collided with the pier. As a result, some of the intended passengers refused to board her. Nevertheless, in total 280 crew and men were crammed on board, under Commander Richard Gordon William Mason RNR. Forty-four years old, an experienced mercantile mariner, Mason had been in the RNR since 1897 and as a lieutenant had gained a first-class pass in gunnery in 1899.[13]

The weather was poor and getting worse. But the yacht sailed as planned and at 0155 on 1 January 1919 was approaching Stornoway harbour in conditions that were now appalling, with gale force winds and a heavy sea running. Some on board could dimly make out the lights of the harbour in the distance, about 2 or 3 miles away. They were nearly home.

She made an alteration of course, which placed the sea on her beam instead of astern, as it had been during the whole of the passage hitherto. And then she struck something and all the lights went out. *Iolaire* had run

* Amalthaea, in Greek (originally Cretan) mythology, was the foster mother of Zeus, king of the gods. She is sometimes represented as the goat that suckled the infant god in a cave in Crete, sometimes as a nymph who fed him the milk of a goat.

Iolaire, whose tragic loss in 1918 blighted many Isle of Lewis families. *(Author's collection)*

onto the 'Beasts of Holm', rocks lying to the south of Holm Point, to the north-east of the entrance to Stornoway Harbour, 2 miles south-east of the town. No orders of any kind were given from the bridge, or by any of the officers or crew, but the siren was blown three or four times and signal rockets were fired. There seemed to be a paralysis of command for no instructions were issued about donning lifebelts or launching the lifeboats. The guns were not fired to gain attention nor were any flares burned.

In the light of the rockets, Carpenter John Finlay MacLeod RNR could perceive the layout of the coast. He found a heaving line and gave the end of it to an islander on the deck beside him. Together they made it fast to one of the stanchions of the depth charge chute. Putting the other end of the line round his left hand, MacLeod dropped into the sea to try to swim for land.

His first attempt failed as the surge of the waves carried him away from the shore; fortunately, he managed to get back to the ship. But the islanders lived with the sea all their lives; it had meaning for them. MacLeod was aware enough to notice that in the storm's rhythm seven smaller waves were followed by three large waves. He dived back into the water and was able to swim for a while and then be carried by the larger waves towards the land. Using the heaving line, a hawser was pulled ashore and men began to clamber along it to safety; some were washed off and drowned, but about forty were successful. Within forty-five minutes after the yacht had struck, *Iolaire* had slipped off the rocks, was driven to the shore by the storm stern first and then broadside on, broke up in the surf and became a wreck.

Only seventy-nine men survived. Twenty of the crew died, including Commander Mason and his officers; in total 205 were lost. Some bodies were washed ashore within sight of their homes and many were never recovered. The islands of Lewis and Harris had already lost more than 1,000 men in wartime action and this was a devasting final blow. Two hundred children were left fatherless; and many women left to grieve. Among the dead was Seaman Norman MacLeod, aged 20, the last of four brothers to die in the war. There were thirty-six men named MacLeod (and four surnamed McLeod) killed, twenty-seven MacDonalds, thirteen MacKenzies and twelve Morrisons. Extended families had been decimated.

An Admiralty court of enquiry found no satisfactory explanation for the disaster. Drunkenness among the crew was discounted by the enquiry. The vessel was sailing at night, in poor visibility and in deteriorating weather. The entrance to Stornoway harbour is not the most straightforward; the enquiry supposed that it was possible navigational error was to blame. This point appeared to be supported by evidence given by Leading Seaman Kenneth MacLeod, who was watching the lights of a fishing boat entering harbour. He saw their relative position change not long before the impact. Certainly, this was the view of the Admiralty's Director of Navigation, who suggested that the most likely cause of the loss was the ship being slightly to the east of the expected track.[14]

A civil accident enquiry was also convened that placed the blame on the officers of *Iolaire*, who had 'failed to exercise sufficient prudence' and 'did not slow down when approaching the harbour'.[15] The Admiralty dismissed this verdict out of hand.

But whatever the cause, the wreck generated much hostility among the islanders, who thought their tragic loss was being whitewashed. The war was over, but the dying was not.

In January 1919, the Admiralty sold the wreck to a salvage contractor. This too raised very considerable concerns among the islanders. Dr Donald Murray, Liberal MP for the Western Isles, raised the issue with Dr Thomas Macnamara, Parliamentary and Financial Secretary to the Admiralty, on 12 March, asking 'whether he is aware that among the friends of the large number of victims of the disaster whose bodies have not been recovered there exists a strong feeling against disturbing the wreck, and especially against, any blasting operations thereon; and whether he can see his way to respect the local sentiment in this matter?'

Macnamara responded positively: 'Representations were received that operations for the salvage of the wreck should not be proceeded with so long as any bodies remained unrecovered. My Hon Friend will be glad to know that the purchaser was approached, and has consented to suspend operations until further notice.'[16]

Altogether, a total of seventeen of the war yachts were sunk during the conflict and its immediate aftermath, of which seven were mined, indicating their usage in busy coastal waters. The full list can be seen at Appendix 2.

Damaged Goods

The light frames of steam yachts made them susceptible to injury. But some yachts were attacked, badly damaged and yet survived. One such example was HMY *Ombra*, built in 1902 and of 236grt, which had been designed by G L Watson and constructed by D and W Henderson and Co. Before the war, she was owned by the Anglo-German bankers Baron John Henry William Schroder and Baron Bruno Schroder of the eponymous banking firm. She was taken up immediately war broke out, fitted with two 3pdr guns, and served in the Dover Patrol, guarding the drifters that maintained the Dover barrage. *Ombra* was bombed while at Ramsgate when part of her stern was blown off and one crew member was killed. She was repaired and eventually returned to civilian life in March 1919.

If damaged, yachts had to take their turn in the wait for repair. Shipyards up and down the country were occupied with cargo vessels, warships, armed trawlers and conversions; and fixing a luxury yacht was not a skill present everywhere.

Opposite: An unknown patrol yacht showing damage at the J Readhead and Sons Dock Depot, South Shields, in April 1916. *(©IWM Q 65838)*

HMY *Ombra*, owned by the Schroder banking dynasty. She was returned to civilian life in March 1919. *(Author's collection)*

And some vessels were simply not up to the task demanded of them. The steam yacht *Thistle*, launched in 1881 at Port Glasgow by Blackwood and Gordon, had been constructed for the 12th Duke of Hamilton, William Alexander Louis Stephen Douglas-Hamilton. Nearly 187ft long and of 369grt, she passed through various hands after Hamilton sold her in 1892 and when the war came was owned by Her Imperial Majesty the Empress Eugénie of France, widow of Napoleon III, who lived in Farnborough, Hants.

The Admiralty took *Thistle* into the navy on 10 October 1914 and she was 'navalised' during the next eight weeks, with guns fitted and 'dockyard men on W/T, fitting heating apparatus in cabins and cutting scupper channels in gun platforms' on 6 November. That same day, the 88-year-old Empress visited her vessel; according to the log book the 'ship's company [was] drawn up to receive HIM the Empress Eugenie … Accompanied by the C-in-C and suite to inspect ship'.[17]

This would very much have suited her captain, Captain Bryan Godfrey-Faussett RN, who had been an aide-de-camp to George V when the latter was Duke of Cornwall and York and retired from the navy in 1906 to serve as a full-time equerry to the man who became king in 1910. On the outbreak of war, Godfrey-Faussett offered his services to the Admiralty and with the king's approval was given command of HMS *Thistle* in the Auxiliary Patrol.

On 14 November, *Thistle* began her naval career patrolling in the North Sea, but by February it had become clear she was ill-suited to the role. On 6 February, she was in the Whitby Roads, heading for the Humber. At 0400 her log recorded that 'vessel rolling heavily when swinging to ebb and shipping water aft'. Later, at 1159, 'Filey Pt abeam. Gale force 8, high sea, vessel rolling violently and shipping heavy seas fore and aft'; 1600 saw her 'shipping heavy seas and rolling violently'. And a minute before midnight 'Force 9, rough sea, shipping water'.[18]

In fact, she nearly foundered. After that experience, one of several, she returned to Portsmouth, where her armament, standard compass, chart table and all other naval equipment was removed; *Thistle* was handed back to her owner on 11 June.

Unfit, Unwanted and Repurposed

Some of the requisitioned yachts were simply too old, fragile and unable to undertake the duties required, and eventually the navy gave up on them or put them to other duties. *Aster*, launched in 1883, was a 201grt vessel owned by Austin Mackenzie, Laird of Carradale, in Argyll. Armed with two 3pdrs, she was sent to the west coast of Ireland on patrol and examination duties, renamed *Aster II* in June 1915, and paid off in May 1916. Likewise, *Vanadis*, 207grt, dating to 1880 was taken up in June 1915 and paid off in January 1918, by which time her owner, Edward Whitwell, had sold her on.

Branwen was a small schooner rigged steam yacht that once belonged to Lord Howard de Walden, who was also the unfortunate owner of *Rhiannon* (see above). Constructed by J I Thornycroft and Co. at Southampton (she was the first vessel to be built at the company's Woolston yard) and launched in 1906, she was 135ft long and 131grt. Powered by a triple-expansion, three-cylinder engine of Thornycroft's own design, she could achieve speeds of up to 11.5 knots. By 1914, she belonged to one Captain Alwyn Foster, a member of the Royal Yacht Squadron. Foster was a good example of the middling yacht-owning landed gentry. Born in 1873, he was an amateur soldier and gentleman of leisure. He had been a lieutenant in the 7th King's Royal Rifles in the Boer War (where he was awarded the South Africa Medal with clasps for Tugola Heights and the Relief of Ladysmith) and after the formation of the British Territorial Force in 1908, he served in the rank of captain in the same unit as Winston Churchill.* Married in 1907 to the daughter of a Cheshire landowner and squire, he lived in Mersham, Kent.

* The Henley on Thames squadron of the Queen's Own Oxfordshire Hussars.

The drawing room of the steam yacht *Branwen*. Note how it is top lit. *(Author's collection)*

Captain Alwyn Foster (back row, left) and his wife Muriel (seated, right) on his yacht *Branwen* in 1911. The other lady is possibly a governess to their young daughter. The skipper stands to Foster's left. *(Author's collection)*

In January 1915, Foster hired *Branwen* to the Admiralty but by March 1917 they had returned her as too small.

Then there was *Calista*, another vessel owned by Captain Foster. She was built by Charles Connell and Company of Scotstoun in 1902, with a power plant by McKie and Baxter of Govan. The navy armed her with two 3pdrs and *Calista* served in the Rosyth, Granton and Orkney and Shetland patrol areas until December 1917, when she too was paid off for the final time.

Some of the yachts were repurposed. *Corycia*, built as *Christine* by David J Dunlop of Port Glasgow in 1896, had been commissioned by Borders Baronet Sir William Scott of Ancrum Castle, Roxburghshire. In 1913, in new ownership, she was renamed *Corycia* and was hired by the Admiralty on 24 September 1914. Under the command of a retired RN lieutenant, Alexander Lyon, she soon made her mark when in December near Fraserburgh she salved a Danish steamer, *Kentucky*. No salvage money was paid, which led to questions in the House of Commons after the war (see also Chapter 10).

Corycia now began an interesting second career. On 24 November 1917 she was purchased by the Admiralty for use as a salvage vessel. In this guise she hosted several attempts to gain intelligence from sunken U-boats. In June 1918 she was deployed off Portland to salvage or otherwise obtain intelligence from the German Submarine *UB-74*, which had been sunk on 26 May 1918 by the yacht *Lorna* (see Chapter 4). Then, on 4 October, *Corycia* took on board Lieutenant Commander Guybon Chesney Castell Damant RN* and his 'Special Section' and tried to obtain information from *UC-70*, which had been sunk off Whitby on 28 August 1918 by the destroyer HMS *Ouse*.

Damant and his men next took her to Scapa Flow and the wreck of *UB-116*, damaged off Hoxa Gate by a remotely controlled minefield and subsequently depth charged while attempting to enter the empty fleet anchorage on 28 October 1918. This proved successful for, on 9 November, divers found and recovered this U-boat's code books and cyphers. These were sent ashore and their contents immediately transmitted by telegraph to Naval Intelligence in London. Diving operations didn't stop until the 14th.

In 1919, on 26 June *Corycia* was joined at Buncrana, County Donegal, by RFA *Racer* to effect the salvage of the bullion from the armed merchant cruiser HMS *Laurentic* (1908), sunk by mines in 1917. On 12 August, *The Scotsman* newspaper reported that: 'Last week it is estimated that a quarter of a million bullion was recovered and during the weekend they had another fine haul of gold.'

On 13 September *Corycia* berthed at Liverpool and discharged 1.75 tons of salved gold, which was conveyed to Lime Street Railway Station under Military Guard, consigned to Euston, and thence to the Bank of England. That was the end of her service. *Corycia* was removed from the Lloyd's Yacht Registry in 1920.

Finally, we might consider *St George*, encountered in Chapter 1, and still owned by E J Wythes, now an enthusiastic and well-known horse breeder from his stud at Copped Hall, near Epping. She was taken into service in March 1915 and renamed *Oriflamme*. Armed with just a single 3pdr, she was assigned to the Director of the Naval Intelligence Division and based on the Humber. *St George/Oriflamme* ceased active service in June 1918, and after being renamed *Wallington* was used as a base ship, remaining on the Humber.

* Damant was known for his scientific research on preventing decompression illness (with John Scott Haldane). Under Damant's leadership, a team of divers salvaged a total of 44 tons of gold bullion from the wreck of HMS *Laurentic* between 1917 and 1924.

CHAPTER SEVEN

AMERICA JOINS THE WAR

AMERICAN PRESIDENT WOODROW WILSON had gained the White House in 1912. When the European war broke out two years later, Wilson had committed to keep America out of the conflict. He, and many Americans such as his Secretary of State William Jennings Bryan, felt that his country should adopt a studied neutrality. Additionally, Wilson was up for re-election in 1916, and thought that war would damage his chances of successfully retaining the presidency.

But some in high office felt differently. US Ambassador to Britain Walter Hines Page urged intervention and the prevention of German hegemony. And another who was alarmed by the situation was Assistant Secretary of the Navy Franklin Delano Roosevelt, who had held the post in the Wilson Administration since 1913. Unlike his boss, Secretary of the Navy Josephus Daniels, Roosevelt was a supporter of the Preparedness Movement* and helped establish the United States Navy Reserve Force before America joined the fighting.

Roosevelt and others recognised that U-boats presented a clear and present danger to the US and that the means to defend against them was lacking. Moreover, the evidence of sinkings around the coast of Britain and in the Mediterranean demonstrated that the whole Allied supply chain could be severely disrupted by submarine activity. Roosevelt tried to bring a degree of pre-planning to bear; when in 1916 the American Motor Boat Club assembled at New York for a cruise, Roosevelt sent a team of naval officers to inspect and register craft for potential military service. Then owners with suitable vessels took their craft to Brooklyn Navy Yard, or to Charlestown Naval Yard in Boston, for registration and by June 1917 there were 799 vessels listed. 'Section Patrol' (SP) numbers were assigned to such craft in a series beginning with SP-1 and which ultimately extended to well beyond 4000.

Wilson won re-election in 1916 on the platform of 'the man who kept us out of the war'. But the rape of Belgium, the savagery of the Western Front, the depredations U-boats wrought on neutral shipping, loss of American lives and shifting public opinion, gradually made neutrality untenable. The United States finally declared war on Germany on

* The Preparedness Movement was a campaign led by former Chief of Staff of the US Army Leonard Wood and ex-President Theodore Roosevelt to strengthen the US armed forces after the outbreak of war in 1914.

W K Vanderbilt's *Tarantula II*, seen pre-war and dressed with flags for a regatta. *(US Naval History and Heritage Command NH 102255)*

6 April 1917.* Like Britain in 1914, the US Navy was unprepared in terms of numbers of small craft. Battleships they had; convoy escorts, anti-submarine craft, minesweepers they had not, at least in any great numbers. British First Sea Lord Admiral Jellicoe wrote that 'according to our knowledge at the time the United States Navy, in April 1917, possessed twenty-three large and about twenty-four small destroyers, some of which were unfit to cross the Atlantic; there were about twelve submarines capable of working overseas, but not well suited for anti-submarine work, and only three light cruisers of the *Chester* class'.[1]

As a result, on the declaration of war by America 'the Navy Department ... solicited the co-operation of the yachtsmen of the country'[2] and started to take up yachts for naval duty.

American Concerns

Rear Admiral William Sims USN† had been despatched to Britain in secret, before the USA had joined the conflict, to liaise with the British Admiralty and report on the naval situation obtaining. His role, if war was to break out between the USA and Germany, was to command all US naval forces in Europe.

Arriving at Liverpool on 27 April 1917 after war had been declared (and in a vessel that was torpedoed just off the Liverpool Bar), Sims sent a message to President Wilson via Ambassador Page that bleakly addressed the problem:

> There is reason for the greatest alarm about the issue of the war caused by the increasing success of the German submarines. I have it from official sources that during the week ending 22nd April, eighty-eight ships of 237,000 tons Allied and neutral were lost. The number of vessels unsuccessfully attacked indicated a great increase in the number of submarines in action.
>
> This means practically a million tons lost every month till the shorter days of autumn come. By that time the sea will be about clear of shipping.

* On 2 April 1917 President Wilson appeared before a joint session of Congress to request a declaration of war against Germany. On the 4th the US Senate voted in support of war on Germany. The House concurred two days later. The United States later declared war on Germany's ally Austria-Hungary on 7 December.

† Vice Admiral from 25 May 1917.

> Most of the ships are sunk to the westward and southward of Ireland. The British have in that area every available anti-submarine craft, but their force is so insufficient that they hardly discourage the submarines.
>
> The British transport of troops and supplies is already strained to the utmost, and the maintenance of the armies in the field is threatened …
>
> Whatever help the United States may render at any time in the future, or in any theatre of the war, our help is now more seriously needed in this submarine area for the sake of all the Allies than it can ever be needed again, or anywhere else … There is no time to be lost.[3]

Admiral Jellicoe concurred with the analysis Sims put forwards:

> Admiral Sims, from the first moment of his arrival in this country, was in the closest touch with the Admiralty in general and with myself in particular. His earliest question to me was as to the direction in which the United States Navy could afford assistance to the Allied cause. My reply was that the first essential was the dispatch to European waters of every available destroyer, trawler, yacht, tug and other small craft of sufficient speed to deal with submarines, other vessels of these classes following as fast as they could be produced; further that submarines and light cruisers would also be of great value as they became available. Admiral Sims responded wholeheartedly to my requests. He urged the Navy Department with all his force to send these vessels and send them quickly. He frequently telegraphed to the United States figures showing the tonnage of merchant ships being sunk week by week in order to impress on the Navy Department and Government the great urgency of the situation.[4]

But Wilson and Secretary of the Navy Daniels had an overarching concern on their minds. Sims was told that his 'paramount duty' was to ensure that American troop transports to Europe were protected from U-boat attack; everything else should be subjugated to that. Neither politician wanted the inevitable public fallout from a major US troop loss through sinking. They were vulnerable in the Western Approaches and in the English Channel as they headed for British or French ports. Without the necessary escort craft, how was Sims to protect them? Once again, yachts came to the rescue.

Rallying Round

Of the twenty-eight steam yachts acquired by the USN for the war with Spain, thirteen were still in service and two more that had returned to civilian life were immediately brought back to the fold. By July 1917, *International Marine Engineering* magazine was reporting that: 'In connection with the quiet campaign of preparedness which is being carried on under the orders of Franklin D Roosevelt, Assistant Secretary of the Navy, and about which there has been no previous public announcement, an active effort has been under way during the last month to procure seagoing yachts for immediate war duty.

'The Government will employ a large number of such vessels as auxiliaries to the other fighting units of the navy and the patriotic spirit of many owners who have already come forward to turn over their vessels for this valuable service is worthy of commendation.'[5]

Meanwhile, the US government promulgated an order allowing for the acquisition of private yachts: 'The Secretary of the Navy may permit the enrolment of owners and operators of yachts and motor power boats suitable for naval purposes in the naval defence of the coast; and is hereby authorised to enter into contract with the owners of such power boats and other craft suitable for war purposes to take over the same in time of war or national emergency upon payment of a reasonable indemnity.'[6]

Many were purchased from their owners on the basis that they had an option to re-purchase their yacht at the end of hostilities. Others were leased to the navy on a free lease or 'peppercorn' basis. Admiral Sims described this as a 'dollar a year' leasing agreement, 'which their owners had generously given to the national service.'[7] By a combination of such methods, the USN boasted a total of 132* armed steam yachts by November 1918.

Much work was necessary to make the yachts fit for naval service. Their lavish furnishings and decorations from peaceful days were removed and stored in Brooklyn warehouses. Grey paint was slathered over white sides and glittering brightwork. Fore and aft, guns were mounted, while machine guns were located on the upper decks. Cutlasses and rifles lined bulkheads of panelled oak or mahogany. Former smoking rooms, libraries and dining rooms became crew messes, officers' quarters, chart rooms, etc and the number to be accommodated expanded three or fourfold over their cruising days.

But not everyone in the navy was delighted by the deployment of the yachts in war. In both quality and usefulness, they were a mixed bag. Indeed, Secretary of the Navy Daniels wrote that he had accepted the yachts 'under protest', knowing 'that they had not been constructed for the purpose for which we needed them'. Daniels went on to explain that he nonetheless 'appointed a board … to inspect them and buy those that were best. It was a case of either buying them or having no ships of that character to help us until our destroyer program could enable us to send much larger [ships].'[8] And the commander of US naval forces in France, Rear Admiral Henry Braid Wilson, was distressed at the lack of homogeneity of the ships he was sent; some could make only 9 knots and would not endure heavy seas, others were more ocean-going and could attain speeds of 18 knots when pushed. This meant squadron patrolling was compromised from the start.

Indeed, it had not originally been intended that he would have yachts under his control. The plan was for them to be utilised to patrol the American Atlantic coast, but the acute need to protect US troopships arriving in France from U-boat attack saw some of them despatched to French waters. As early as 21 May, French diplomatic pressure forced Daniels to

* Thirteen still in service from 1898, plus 119 newly taken up. (Silverstone, *US Warships*, pp.169–179)

send a telegram to Commander William R. Sayles, US naval attaché in Paris, informing him that 'the Department will send ten or more yachts for service against submarines off the coast of France'.[9]

Secretary Daniels kept his word. Admiral Sims stated that there were twelve yachts based at Brest alone,[10] while another source notes that seventeen armed yachts were operating from French ports by July 1918.[11]

Manning the Yachts

How were the yachts to be crewed? Largely by the volunteers of the United States Navy Reserve Force (USNRF). On 6 April 1917, the USN could call upon 197 commissioned ships, 4,376 regular officers, 877 reserve officers, 64,118 regular enlisted men, and 12,206 reservists.[12]

But for the armed yachts, Sims noted that 'their crews were largely … young business men and college undergraduates'.[13] And yachtsmen and yacht clubs provided the more experienced sailors for officering these new auxiliary warships.

For example, ninety-three New York Yacht Club members were commissioned into the US Naval Reserve in early 1917 and 300 volunteered for either naval or army service. Ninety club members donated or leased their vessels.

As an exemplar of the volunteering yachtsman, consider Robert Elliot Tod, who had made money in railroads, banking and docks. He was sometime president of the Atlantic Yacht Club as well as the Indian Harbour and New York Yacht Clubs, owned a succession of yachts and participated in the successful defence of the America's Cup. In 1911 he launched the *Karina*, reportedly the largest private yacht afloat at the time. When war came, 50-year-old Tod joined the USNRF and served as third in command and navigating officer of J P Morgan's yacht *Corsair III*, now USS *Corsair*, SP-159.

James Aker's yacht *Florence* before he leased her to the navy and she was covered in grey paint. *(US Naval History and Heritage Command NH 101712)*

This was not an uncommon event; often the navy got the yacht and its owner, too. In April 1917, James W Aker of New York City was commissioned into the USNRF and took his 124ft yacht USS *Florence* (ex-*Quickstep*) on a free lease with him. She had been built in 1903 by Herreshoff of Rhode Island and was 104grt and 124ft in length. *Florence* served as patrol boat SP-173 in the 3rd Naval District. She sailed Long Island Sound for patrol service, guard duties and target range support, and as an escort for USN submarines. Both yacht and owner survived the war and *Florence* was decommissioned in February 1919. Lieutenant Maxwell Wyeth USNRF lent his 140ft yacht *Emerald* in July 1917 and he and his craft were assigned to the 4th Naval District. She performed as a minesweeper, convoy escort and patrol vessel. Wyeth was awarded the Navy Cross for his service in her. And William Kissam Vanderbilt's beloved *Tarantula II* went with him in it to the 3rd Naval District, again on a free lease.

John Borden was a millionaire adventurer whose fortune came from having founded the Yellow Cab company in New York. A keen yachtsman and explorer, Borden owned the steam yacht *Kanawha II* (1899), built at Morris Heights, New York, by Charles L Seabury. Capable of 21 knots, she was an obvious candidate to be taken on by the USN and on 28 April 1917, she joined the navy – and with Borden, now a Lieutenant Commander USNRF in command. Designated SP-130, and equipped with four 3in and one 6pdr guns, she was initially based around New York but after three weeks outfitted for Europe and set sail for Brest, arriving on Independence Day.

As for the yacht crews, on one they were as 'green a lot of landlubbers that ever stumbled down a gangplank for the first time. Only two were

USS *May*, rescuer of SS *Westward Ho*, her two 3in guns clearly shown. *(US Naval History and Heritage Command NH 46437)*

competent seamen. The rest varied from a farm hand to a designer of theatrical costumes, from city gangster to newspaper artist … they looked for nothing else than getting sick.'[14]

Arming the Yachts

The majority of the larger armed yachts were equipped with one or more 3in gun and a number of machine guns. Typically, the 3in was a 50-calibre weapon with a range of around 7,000yds at 15° of elevation, first introduced in 1890. These were quick-firing (QF) guns, meaning that that they used fixed ammunition, with powder case and projectile permanently attached and handled as a single unit, which weighed 34lb. The explosive projectile itself weighed 13lb.

Machine guns came from a variety of manufacturers, but were often Colt or Browning. Once on European station, Lewis guns from British or French sources might also be added. And on smaller vessels a miscellany of weapons could be fitted, including 6pdr, 3pdr and 1pdr guns.

Depth charges were also carried when on patrol. In these cases, somewhere between a minimum of two and a maximum of ten seemed to be the fit-out. These were simply rolled off the stern of the yacht. In rare instances, from the beginning of 1918 a Y-gun depth charge thrower was installed. This was a Y-shaped device, mounted on the centre line of the vessel with the arms of the Y pointing outboard. Two depth charges were slotted into the firing arms, where they rested on a cradle and expendable

The 3in gun crew of *Noma*. The one-piece shell can be seen clearly. *(US Naval History and Heritage Command NH 44872)*

A 3in gun on the armed yacht USS *Wakiva II*. *(US Naval History and Heritage Command NH 105583)*

Midships 3in guns on *Corsair III*, with sailors larking about in semaphore. *(US Naval History and Heritage Command NH 55389)*

Vedette II in dry dock at Lorient. *(US Naval History and Heritage Command NH 42430)*

'arbour'. A blank 3in shell was detonated in the vertical column of the Y-gun by pulling a lanyard, which caused the depth bombs to be launched.* At least *Alacrity* (1910), *Niagara* (1898), *Nokomis II* (1914) and *Winchester* (1916) were so equipped.

One yacht was apparently enrolled as a minelayer. This was SP-163, USS *Vedette II*, ex-*Virginia* (1900), nearly 200ft long and once the property of department store tycoon Isaac Stern and then Frederick W Vanderbilt. As *Virginia* she had famously sailed up the Amazon river in 1911. Now a warship, she carried ten mines as well as three 3in and two machine guns.

On Patrol

In May 1918, Sims warned his superiors in America that it was certain that at least one U-boat, *U-151*, was operating off the US coast; and indeed, on the 19th, the USA-flagged SS *Nayanza* sent out an SOS that she was being attacked by gunfire; she survived, battered but not sunk. Then in July, three long-range 'cruiser' U-boats were despatched to American waters. The armed yachts and other small patrol boats were placed on a high level of alert, constantly patrolling off and around major harbours and the American east coast littoral. They sank around 110,000 tons of shipping, mainly sailing vessels and small coastal steamers. New York City was blacked out for thirteen nights in June as a precaution against attack by shelling or seaplanes. And the USN introduced coastal convoys, in which the yachts participated as escorts.

German mines laid by *U-156* sank the armoured cruiser USS *San Diego* (1904) with the loss of six lives on 19 July; another mine from *U-117*

* This Y-gun device was a development of a depth charge thrower designed by Thornycroft's for the British Admiralty and was based on Thornycroft patents.

damaged the battleship USS *Minnesota* (1905) on 29 September. One U-boat even shelled the Cape Cod Canal with the aim of shutting it down so coal barges and other commercial vessels were forced to go around the Cape, where they were less well protected from torpedo attacks.

Even the yachts that were considered to be unequal to a full transatlantic trip were pressed into service as convoy escorts. As each group and merchant ships left New York or Hampton Roads, an escort screen of older destroyers and yachts accompanied them for several hundred miles before turning back. Thereafter, the convoys had a minimal escort of an armoured cruiser or two before being met by destroyers out of Queenstown or Berehaven to take them through the submarine-infested waters of the Western Approaches. Or, if France bound, they would be met by yachts from the US squadrons in French ports.

One yacht so employed was USS *May*, ordered to patrol the Atlantic seaboard. She had been built in 1891 by the Ailsa Shipbuilding Company of Troon for Edward Dennison Morgan III, a distant relative of J P Morgan. He was a successful businessman, a keen yachtsman, and rear commodore, vice commodore and eventually (post-war) commodore of the New York Yacht Club. He was also part of the winning team of the America's Cup Yacht Race in 1901 aboard the yacht *Columbia*.

Morgan sold *May* on, and she was eventually acquired by the USN in August 1917, fitted with two 3in guns, and sent on her way. *May*'s moment of fame came on 9 August 1918 when she responded to a distress call from SS *Westward Ho*, which had been torpedoed by *U-62* in the eastern Atlantic and abandoned by her crew. When *May* arrived, the merchantman was still afloat, despite a huge gash in her bow. Lieutenant Thomas Blau USNRF led a salvage party aboard and managed to start the pumps. *May*'s captain, Lieutenant Commander Charles Clifford Windsor, ordered *Westward Ho* to be taken in tow, stern first, and in this fashion *May* dragged the freighter 315 miles to Brest, bringing both ship and cargo safely home. Both officers were awarded the Navy Cross for their work.

Many of the converted steam yachts operated humdrum patrols off America's eastern seaboard. *Felicia* (1898) was constructed by J N Robins Company of Brooklyn, New York. Her deckhouses were of polished mahogany, and five guest rooms and the owner's stateroom were finished in ivory and gold. She carried an electric icemaker and a grand piano. Of 213grt and 179ft in length, *Felicia* could achieve 14 knots.

The USN purchased her on 2 June 1917, armed her with three 3pdr guns and sent her off to Newport, Rhode Island, where *Felicia* patrolled the New England coast, on duty with the 2nd Naval District. Unfortunately, for all her grace and elegance, on 30 August 1918 and in a heavy fog, she collided with a submarine off Montauk Point.

The yacht's slight frame could not withstand such a shock and she was badly damaged, so much so that she was laid up in various yards until she was sold in March 1920.

The yacht *Margaret* leaving Bermuda for the Azores in November 1917. In the opinion of her commander she was completely unsuited for naval work. Note her two 3in guns fore and aft. *(US Naval History and Heritage Command NH 46594)*

The officers of the yacht USS *Margaret* stand by her binnacle while she is at Ponta Delgada, Azores, *circa* December 1917. Lieutenant Commander Frank Jack Fletcher, her Commanding Officer, is in the centre. *(US Naval History and Heritage Command NH 46584)*

The yacht *Margaret* served as SP-527 on anti-submarine patrol around the Azores. She was constantly giving mechanical and structural trouble to her captain, Lieutenant Commander Frank Jack Fletcher, perhaps better known in the second global conflict as the operational task force commander at the crucial battles of the Coral Sea and Midway. In exasperation, Fletcher finally asked the navy to condemn her as unfit for service.

She had been built in 1899 by the Delaware River Iron Ship Building and Engine Works at Chester, Pennsylvania, as the private steam yacht *Eugenia*. Her narrow beam for her length (170ft long, but only 21ft at the

beam) made her prone to incurring damage in a seaway, and she had never been intended for oceanic sailing. Indeed, her final pre-war owner, Isaac Emerson, chief executive officer of Bromo-Seltzer, ensured that she had a fine wine cellar and an exquisite dining area and liked nothing better than to entertain people aboard in an opulent setting in a safe harbour. The navy should never have put her to the use that they did, but the exigencies of war meant that they took her anyway. She was eventually sold for scrap in 1921.

Not all yachts became patrol craft; USS *Mohican* was commissioned as a specialist kite balloon ship. She had been built in 1890 by Laird Brothers in Scotland. Designed by St Clare John Byrne, the yacht had started life as

Mohican (1890), once *Norseman*, was fitted out as a kite balloon carrier when war came. *(US Naval History and Heritage Command NH 102038)*

The magnificent steam and sail yacht *Aloha* under a full press. *(Library of Congress LC-D4-43711)*

Norseman, owned by Samuel Radcliffe Platt (see Chapter 1). She then passed through various American hands, became first *Lady Godiva* and then *Mohican* and was latterly owned by New York-based opera star Robert Perkins. Of 144ft in length, *Mohican* was armed with two 6pdrs and two machine guns, and her balloon allowed her to look over the horizon for the enemy.

And one of the best-looking USN flagships must surely have been that of Rear Admiral Cameron McRae Winslow, Inspector of Naval Districts, East Coast. This was USS *Aloha*, SP-317. Built in 1910 by Fore River Shipbuilding Company of Quincy, Massachusetts, to designs by Tams, Lemoine, and Crane, her owner was the industrialist, railroad magnate and inveterate yachtsman Arthur Curtiss James, who rejoiced in the nickname of 'Commodore' James.

She was a steel-hulled, single-screw, barque-rigged steam yacht, and was regarded by some as the 'finest thing of her kind ever built'.[15] *Aloha*, manned by a comparatively large crew of thirty-nine, was intended specifically for ocean cruising. The accommodation included six large staterooms, plus accommodation for an on-board doctor and a maid, and there were eight stewards and one stewardess.

James took his floating palace to England and Scotland on her maiden voyage in 1910; to Panama and Ireland in 1911; and to Egypt and the Near East during 1912 and 1913.

She could sail under full rig or by steam and in the former guise looked quite magnificent. But when war came, James turned over his ship to the navy under a free lease on 22 April 1917. What a billet she must have made for the fortunate Admiral Winslow.

Armed with two 3in guns (replaced by two 4in in October 1918) and carrying two depth charges, *Aloha* played no aggressive part in the war, but she did help extinguish a major town fire at Portsmouth, Virginia, in January 1918. She also sent men to guard the area after the blaze, for fear it had been caused by German spies setting off incendiaries.

An October of Collisions

The smaller yachts taken up by the USN were often assigned harbour or littoral defence duties as part of the Naval Coast Defence Reserve. One such was the USS *Mary Alice*, built in 1897 as a fast steam yacht. Originally named *Bernice*, she became *Oneta* and then *Mary Alice* in 1910, when she was owned by newspaper proprietor and businessman William J Connors of Buffalo, NY.

On 10 August 1917, the USN purchased her and assigned her the pennant number SP-397. Her naval life was quotidian. As part of the 3rd Naval District, *Mary Alice* patrolled in Long Island Sound and guarded the approaches to New York harbour.

O-13 was a brand-new US Navy submarine, built by the Lake Torpedo Boat Company in Bridgeport, Connecticut. On 5 October 1918, *O-13* was undergoing commissioning acceptance trials in Long Island Sound. *Mary Alice* had been commandeered by no less a personage than the President of the US Navy's Board of Inspection and Survey, Captain William A Gill, as his personal craft to observe this process.

Fate, however, is no respecter of rank. While conducting a submerged circular run off Bridgeport, *O-13* suddenly rammed *Mary Alice* amidships and holed her. The yacht sank in minutes, 1,800yds from Penfield Reef Light, fortunately with no loss of life. Her crew were all picked up by the erring submarine.

And this last month before the Armistice proved costly for the little patrol yachts, for another one was sunk before October was out. *Tarantula II* was, unusually, a motor yacht of 159grt, built in 1912 by George Lawley and Son of Neponset, Massachusetts, and powered by a single-screw diesel engine. As noted above, she was yet another yacht owned by the Vanderbilts, William Kissam in this case.

Tarantula too became part of the 3rd Naval District as SP-124, armed with two 6pdrs and two machine guns and operating in the coastal waters of Connecticut, New York and New Jersey. But on 28 October, her service came to a sudden end when she collided with the 7,442grt Royal Holland Lloyd Line steamship SS *Frisia* (1909). *Tarantula* went down 8 miles southwest of the Fire Island light vessel with no casualties. After the war, Vanderbilt received $75,000 to cover her loss. He had left her for a new assignment just before she sank.

CHAPTER EIGHT

US YACHTS IN FRENCH AND MEDITERRANEAN WATERS

ON 4 JUNE 1917, a collection of six rich men's toys left the New York Navy Yard and steamed slowly downstream. Collectively, they bore the official appellation of '1st US Patrol Squadron in European Waters' and they were bound for France to make good on the promise given by Secretary Daniels to send USN patrol craft to French and Mediterranean waters.

The USS *Noma* (1902), *Harvard* (1894), *Kanawha II* (1899), *Vedette* (1900), *Christabel* (1893) and *Sultana* (1889) made up the formation; they were to sail firstly to Bermuda and then the Azores, as it was not considered that they could stand up to the rigours of a direct Atlantic crossing. Two other members of the squadron, *Corsair* and *Aphrodite*, took the direct route as part of the escort for the first major troop convoy despatched from the US to France. The former had been intended for duty with the first convoy section, which was the designated 'fast' one. But she proved unequal to the task, and was unable to maintain the speed of advance; blame was apparently allocated to an 'inexperienced engine room crew'.[1] Consequently, she was relegated to the second, slower section.

J P Morgan's *Corsair II* had been taken up for the Spanish-American

USS *Aphrodite*, seen at Harwich post-war. *(US Naval History and Heritage Command NH 104493)*

War in 1898. Now his third *Corsair* joined the USN as SP-159. Of 304ft in length and armed with four 3in guns, her first mission was to be part of a twenty-two-ship escort for fourteen transports carrying the first troops of the American Expeditionary Force to France. Another yacht was *Aphrodite*, SP-135, only just shorter at 302ft. She had been built for Colonel Oliver H Payne of New York City as an ocean-going steam yacht with barque rig and capable of good speeds under sail alone. When completed she was said to be the largest American-built steam yacht at the time. Payne, who had made his fortune in oil and then tobacco and steel trusts, went on a round the world cruise in her and took the yacht to Europe every summer from 1908 until the outbreak of war. Of the others, *Noma* was constructed for William Bateman Leeds, the 'Tin Plate King', to the designs of Clinton Crane. Later, she was owned by William Vincent Astor, another who went out with his yacht for naval service. Later, Astor was joined in France by his wife Helen, who did charity work with the YMCA at the naval base in Bordeaux, while he served as Port Officer at Royan. *Noma* arrived in France with 'a graceful bowsprit', which was soon removed, and 'an accident later carried away the head of the golden figurehead on her bow. But like She of Samothrace, the headless goddess, in a coat of battle grey, braved to the end each wave that crashed over her dipping bow'.[2]

Harvard was once the pride and joy of textile industrialist William Slater, who spent $300,000 in 1894 on a three-masted, 804-ton, steam auxiliary barque that he named *Eleanor*. Tiffany and Co. designed the interior and the Colt Armoury installed three 800 rounds-per-minute electric Gatling guns on the deck for protection during his planned eighteen-month circumnavigation of the world.* When he and his family departed, they also took with them seventy-five cases of champagne. Eventually she passed to New England banker George F Blake Jnr, and on 23 April 1917 the USN leased her and commissioned her as USS *Harvard*.

* Problems of piracy existed then as now. Many of the yachts built in the heyday of the type were equipped with armaments as a provision against such trouble. Ogden Goelet's *Mayflower* was fitted with six Maxim machine guns together with rifles and revolvers, for a trip to the Far East. And A J Drexel's *Margarita I* carried two quick-firing guns forward and a pair a Gardiner guns aft.

Sultana in dry dock at Lorient. Note the depth charges on her stern. *(US Naval History and Heritage Command NH 42428)*

Vedette was yet another Vanderbilt vessel, this time owned by Frederick William Vanderbilt; and the three-masted topsail schooner *Sultana* was built by Handren and Robins at Erie Basin, New York, for Trenor Luther Park and his wife. The interiors were panelled in oak and decorated in an Italian renaissance style in cream, gold and blue. The Parks spent their honeymoon in *Sultana* and crossed the Atlantic in her some seventy-five times. After Park's death, the yacht passed to Mrs E H Harriman, who loaned her to the USN on a free lease. Now she carried sixty-two crewmen and four 3in guns.

The six yachts arrived at Brest, around and about 4 July, joined up with *Corsair* and *Aphrodite* and on the 14th began operations under squadron commander Captain W B Fletcher USN.

Corona leaving New York on 31 July 1917, destination France. *(US Naval History and Heritage Command NH 83444)*

But in fact, their introduction to the sea battle had begun before then; on 3 July, *Sultana* rescued thirty-seven survivors from SS *Orleans* (1905), inbound for Bordeaux from New York with general cargo, and sunk by *UC-71*. The merchant crew had taken to their lifeboat and asked the submarine for help to rescue those who were still swimming in the waters around their sinking ship. 'Can't help you. This is war. They've no business to be over here,' said the U-boat commander and sailed away.[3]

The 2nd Squadron arrived between 29 and 30 August, having met dreadful storms on passage. It comprised the USS *Guinevere* (1908), *Carola IV* (1885), originally Scottish-built for the Earl of Pembroke and Montgomery, *Alcedo* (1895), *Wanderer* (1897), *Remlik* (1903), constructed in Hull and owned by patent medicine manufacturer, newspaperman, horse breeder and

An example of the Mackay camouflage scheme, seen here on the steam yacht *Carola IV* (1885), built in Scotland for the Earl of Pembroke and Montgomery as *Black Pearl*, with the crew manning the rails. *(US Naval History and Heritage Command NH 89795)*

entrepreneur Willis Sharpe Kilmer, *Corona* (1905) and *Emeline* (1898). Some had badly leaking decks, damaged as they fought through the weather.

This latter grouping also bore a distinction that they might not have wished for; they were known as the 'Easter Egg Fleet', owing to the riotous patterns of colour used in creating a dazzle-type camouflage pattern on their sides and upperworks, known as the Mackay Low Visibility system. This was an idea developed in 1917 by American artist William Andrew Mackay, intended to reduce ship visibility at a distance and in varying light conditions. It also was meant to soften ship outlines to make optical range finding more difficult. *Carola IV*, for example, was painted in the Mackay scheme of stippled red, blue, green and mauve. Other designs were also used

And here is USS *Venetia*, also in Mackay camouflage, pictured off the Mare Island Navy Yard, California, in October 1917. She is about to start her long voyage to France. *(US Naval History and Heritage Command NH 47198)*

and identified by the name of the person who created them. Apart from Mackay, there were creations from Gerome Brush, Maximilian Toch, E L Warner and Lewis Herzog.

The USN forces operated in three distinct bodies of water: the north coast of France bordering on the English Channel; the west coast on the Bay of Biscay (which is really a part of the North Atlantic); and the south coast on the Mediterranean Sea. Yachts would see action in all three sectors.

The Loss of USS Alcedo

Such deception as the Mackay scheme did not save USS *Alcedo*. She was a 275ft vessel, built in Glasgow as *Veglia* in 1895 by D and W Henderson and Company for Baron Nathaniel de Rothschild, who registered her at Trieste.

In 1910, *Veglia* passed to newspaper proprietor George William Childs Drexel of Philadelphia and became *Alcedo*, and it was in that name that she was purchased by the USN on 1 June 1917. They fitted her with four 3in and two machine guns and sent her to France under the command of Lieutenant Commander William T Conn Jr.

Alcedo was swiftly into the action on anti-submarine patrol and convoy

A bow-on view of USS *Alcedo*. *(US Naval History and Heritage Command NH 57785)*

Another view of *Alcedo*. She was sunk on 5 November 1917. *(US Naval History and Heritage Command NH 105719)*

escort. But her first encounters with the pity of war involved the rescue of merchant ship crews from two vessels that had fallen victim to *Alcedo*'s intended prey. On 17 October, the yacht picked up 118 men from the troop transport steamer SS *Antilles*, which was returning to the US to embark more military men and equipment; and twelve days later she saved another eighty-five survivors from SS *Finland*. This latter action had a strong sense of *déjà vu* for *Finland* was returning most of the survivors of *Antilles* back to the US and *Alcedo* was again part of the escort. *U-93* torpedoed the *Finland* and many of the survivors from *Antilles* panicked and launched the lifeboats, being once more rescued by *Alcedo*.

The sinking of troopships, even if fortunately empty of troops, was of course just what the navy and Wilson's Democrat government did not want, and the Republicans in Congress made much of it. 'Lack of naval escort was to blame for the loss of the United States troop ship *Antilles* on October 10, it was declared today in a statement from Representative Frederick A Britten of Illinois, a member of the House Naval Affairs Subcommittee investigating the conduct of the war. The fact was ascertained in the committee meeting, which was behind closed doors, from Admiral Benson, Chief of Naval Operations. The understanding here is that the transport was too fast for the naval escort provided and had outdistanced the protecting vessel when it was torpedoed. Sixty-seven lives were lost when the ship went down. Secretary Daniel has refused to admit this fact and declined to comment on Mr Britten's statement.'[4] The heterogenic and extemporised nature of the escort could equally be blamed.

The following month, on the afternoon of 4 November, *Alcedo* departed Quiberon Bay with the yachts *Aphrodite*, *Noma*, and *Kanawha II* as escort for a convoy composed of three transports, all heading for Brest. At about 0145 the following morning, while the convoy was steaming some 75 miles west of Belle Isle, *Alcedo* sighted a surfaced U-boat. Lieutenant Commander William T Conn called for General Quarters and ordered right full rudder. But the pleasure boat turned warship responded with the peacetime leisure of its design, certainly not quickly enough to avoid a torpedo from *U-71*, which struck on the port bow. The yacht sank within eight minutes.

Alcedo lost one officer, Lieutenant (jg) John Melvin, and twenty sailors died from wounds or drowning. 'Due to the suddenness of the attack and the darkness of the night, the other escorting vessels were for a time ignorant of the *Alcedo*'s fate and proceeded with the convoy. Putting off from the sinking ship in two dories, three officers and twenty-five men were spotted by fishermen and towed to the vicinity of Pointe de Penmarch. The remaining survivors in a whaleboat and two dories pulled toward Penmarch, and thirteen hours later were picked up by the French torpedo boat *#275* and were taken into Brest.'[5]

And there was individual bravery shown that night. Yeoman William Ballatty from Brooklyn was commended by Secretary Daniels for his actions in rescuing Richard W Randolph, a pharmacist's mate, from drowning, and supporting him for an hour in the water before being rescued. Fireman George Collier was also recognised for stopping the engines and raising the safety valve on the boilers after the torpedo struck, although the water in the engine room had risen above his knees. Irish-born Patrick J Quinn, the coxswain, found Ensign William Harrison unconscious after the explosion and carried him to safety on the life raft.[6] And 24-year-old John von der Wall came back from the dead. His mother had been informed that he had gone down with the ship; imagine her surprise and joy when she received a letter from him, sent from France and saying he had been picked up and was safe.[7]

To USS *Alcedo* went the dubious honour of being the first USN vessel to be lost in the war.*

The J Beavor-Webb designed *Corsair* (III) in harbour, her truncated bowsprit in evidence. Next to her is *Harvard* (1904). *(US Naval History and Heritage Command NH 85734)*

Corsair III

One of the hardest-worked yachts on the French coast was *Corsair*. Armed with three 4in guns and depth charges, her 19-knot speed made her well suited for faster coastal convoy and patrol work. Starting her duties in June 1917, she undertook many and varied missions but perhaps stood out when, on 22 June 1918, she took off the crew of the USS *Californian* (1900), a 5,658grt freighter. Carrying coal and oil to France, the cargo vessel struck a mine in the Bay of Biscay but *Corsair* was able to stand by her and effect a rescue before the ship went under.

Then on 12 September, *Corsair* raced several hundred miles down the

* The destroyer USS *Cousins* had been torpedoed off the Irish coast on 15 October 1917, with loss of life, but was subsequently salvaged.

French coast to assist the Norwegian ship *Dagfin* (1902, 1,442grt), which had broken down 600 miles west of France and was drifting uncontrollably in heavy seas. *Corsair* towed the merchantman all the way to port.

The Wreck of the Guinevere

In legend, Guinevere was the wife of King Arthur. In America she was a three-masted, 488grt, steam and sail schooner built in 1908 by George Lawley and Son at Neponset, Massachusetts, for the zinc magnate and property developer Edgar Palmer, a well-known yachtsman who had served as Commodore of the American Yacht Club in Rye, NY.

On 10 June 1917 the navy acquired her, and she was commissioned as USS *Guinevere* (SP-512) on 20 July 1917 with Lieutenant Guy Davis in command. Together with her sisters, she was part of the second wave of yachts sent to France and after arrival in Brest at the end of August, she commenced patrols off the French coast and began escorting convoys to Quiberon, Ushant, Lorient and Saint-Nazaire, before becoming the command ship of a minesweeping force in December.

But her life in French waters would not end well. On 26 January 1918, *Guinevere* was cruising at about 9 knots in dense fog, returning to base from Quiberon with both her commander and a French pilot on the bridge. Around a mile east of Pointe du Taut and 5 miles from Lorient, she struck a low-lying reef. It tore the bottom out of the vessel such that within two hours her deck was under water and the tide was pounding *Guinevere* against the reef, causing the yacht to break up. Luckily there were no casualties. She could not be saved and was abandoned; so was lost the second USN armed yacht of the conflict in French waters. Post-war *Guinevere*'s wreck was sold to the French firm *Société Americaine de Sauvetage* for scrap.*

The Adventures of USS Venetia

Venetia was a single-screw, steel-hulled steam yacht built in 1904 at Leith by Hawthorn and Co. to plans drawn up by designers Cox and King, and was acquired by the USN on 4 August 1917 from John Diedrich Spreckels. Spreckels had made his fortune in transportation and real estate and was credited as the 'founder' of San Diego.

Designated SP-431, *Venetia* was fitted out at the Mare Island Navy Yard, Vallejo, California, and was commissioned at Mare Island on 15 October 1917, with 38-year-old, Alabama-born, Commander Lewis B Porterfield as her captain. Of 589grt and 226ft long, she was armed with four 3in guns.

Before she could enter the war, *Venetia* had to transit the Panama Canal, reaching Philadelphia on 15 November to be fitted with new radio equipment. She was also painted up in the Mackay pattern camouflage of red, green, blue and mauve. Minor repairs at New York followed and it wasn't until 21 December that she finally departed for the Mediterranean, sailing via Bermuda, the Azores and Portugal with a submarine chaser destined for the French Navy in tow. Arriving at Gibraltar on 18 February, she needed

* Palmer commissioned a second yacht, also named *Guinevere*, which served in the USN in the Second World War.

repair to damage sustained on passage and received a new depth charge rack and releasing gear.

Venetia's progress shows something of the difficulty that the USN had in getting its escorts to a war station and footing; she had been acquired in August 1917 and five months later had still not joined the fight.

But now she set to, escorting merchant ships to Bizerte, Tunis, and other Mediterranean ports. Her first contact with the enemy came on 11 May. *Venetia* was steaming off the port quarter of a 7-knot convoy bound for Gibraltar when a torpedo streaked past her bow, some 150 to 200yds ahead. Lookouts on the armed yacht then sighted water shooting into the air over the bow of SS *Susette Fraisinette*, a French steamship about 100yds away. The merchantman had been torpedoed by *UB-52* and later sank at 0412. Thirty-four of her crew were picked up by the French trawler *Isole*.

Venetia, meanwhile, cruised in ever-widening circles until 0520, carrying out a search for the attacker. At 0527, the yacht's maintop lookout sighted *UB-52* 8 or 9 miles away, standing well off the convoy's track and on a course between west and south-west.

Porterfield sounded general quarters and headed for *UB-52* at full speed, keeping the submarine bearing one point to starboard as it continued standing off to westward.

As *Venetia* bore down on the enemy, Commander Porterfield articulated his plan; keep the U-boat one point on the starboard bow, open up with 3in gunfire at about 6,500yds, machine guns at 2,000yds and, if necessary, ram it.

But the U-boat's commander, *Oberleutnant zur See* Launburg, now aware of the threat to his ship, ordered a dive. By the time Porterfield got *Venetia* over the spot where he had disappeared there was no sign of the submarine.

Venetia steamed in the vicinity, within a five-mile circle, probing until 0738. During that time, she dropped thirteen depth bombs and subsequently set a course to keep between her enemy and the convoy.

Twelve days later, *UB-52* was sunk by the submarine HMS *H-4* in the Otranto Strait. Her two survivors reported that *Venetia*'s efforts had not only prevented further attacks on the convoy but had driven off *UB-52*. Since Porterfield's action in tirelessly pursuing the U-boat had probably saved the rest of the convoy, he received commendations from the British Senior Naval Officer, Gibraltar (Rear Admiral Heathcoat S Grant); from the Commander in Chief, Mediterranean (Admiral the Hon Sir Somerset A Gough-Calthorpe); and from the American Patrol Force commander, Rear Admiral Wilson.

Six days later, *Venetia* had another enemy contact. She was part of the escort of a convoy outbound from Gibraltar. The composition of the escort shows how stretched resources were. Apart from the yacht there was USS *Wheeling*, a 990-ton gunboat launched in 1897; USS *Surveyor*, built as a Coast and Geodetic Survey vessel; two French sub chasers and two trawlers, one British, one French.

Just before dusk, one of the merchant ships, SS *Sculptor*, suddenly

A US propaganda sheet, boosting the efforts on the steam yacht USS *Venetia* in the war. *(Author's collection)*

exploded, hit by a torpedo from *U-39*. *Venetia*, about 1,300yds away, sounded general quarters and rang down emergency full speed ahead.

As the yacht passed astern of *Sculptor*, Porterfield assumed that, after making her attack, the submarine had turned aft on the starboard side of the convoy. *Venetia* depth charged that area at 1901. Then the yacht's foretop lookout reported that he could see the wake of a submarine moving through the water.

Venetia altered course and dropped depth charges ahead of the wake at 1906, 1908, 1909, 1911, and 1913. Meanwhile, *Surveyor* stood by the damaged merchantman, and *Venetia* radioed Oran to send a tug.

Wheeling, meanwhile, concentrated on collecting the ships of the convoy, all of which had scattered in panic. At about 1915, her lookout reported a submarine off the starboard bow, and *Wheeling* moved in to attack. She steamed to the spot at which the supposed U-boat had last been seen and marked the location with a calcium light. From there, she circled outward dropping a total of six depth charges – two of which failed to detonate.

U-39 was not deterred. Twice more her commander, Heinrich Metzger, closed the convoy, sinking the British steamer SS *Mavisbrook* at 2028 and then damaging SS *Elswick Grange* at 2320. The latter eventually reached port under tow.

However, the next day, a badly damaged *U-39* put into Cartagena and was interned for the duration. She had been attacked by French aircraft with two men killed. The U-boat was out of the war, even if not sunk.

Venetia's adventures continued until she had a refit and change of commander in August. But her story was the same; convoy escort, U-boats sometimes successful, sometimes not. But no enemy submarine sunk. *Venetia* survived the war and was reunited with Spreckels in April 1919. He was, however, not best pleased with her condition and claimed it would cost $100,000 to restore the yacht to its original condition. The navy counter-offered $76,331. Spreckels took the yacht but reserved the right to sue for damages. But in the end, he accepted the government's money.

Lydonia

The yacht *Lydonia* came nearer to success against a U-boat.

William A Lydon was the co-founder of the Great Lakes Dredge and Dock Company in Chicago in 1890. This made him very rich and, like all wealthy Americans of the time, he felt in need of a steam yacht to display his good fortune. In 1912 he commissioned a 181ft, 497grt vessel from Pusey and Jones of Wilmington, Delaware, and to make sure people got the point, named it *Lydonia*. She was built with a steel hull that incorporated five watertight bulkheads and three non-watertight bulkheads, the latter extending from keel to the main deck. She carried 125 tons of coal (loaded through four scuttles with watertight openings on the main deck) and could achieve 12 knots, but most importantly *Lydonia* was the height of luxury. Her fittings included an observation window for viewing the machinery from the starboard deck passage, a large library equipped with bookcases and with a domed skylight above for illumination and, further astern, a music room through which the main mast passed. This latter room was furnished with comfortable seating and boasted the stairs to the guest

Lydonia in peacetime. *(US Naval History and Heritage Command NH 1928)*

staterooms in the aft starboard corner. Throughout *Lydonia* was panelled with African mahogany and gilt-covered ceilings. She was popularly known as the finest yacht on the Great Lakes, as befitted a man who was Commodore of the Chicago Yacht Club.

Five years later, Lydon's yacht was purchased for the war effort and commissioned into the USN on 27 October 1917 as patrol vessel SP-700, armed with four 3in guns and a couple of machine guns. Just before Christmas 1917, *Lydonia* arrived at Gibraltar to join the USN patrol squadron protecting Mediterranean convoys on either side of the Straits of Gibraltar.

In the early months of 1918, she and her consorts maintained a constant watch for U-boats and *Lydonia* had two encounters with the underwater enemy in February without apparent success.

Better fortune attended her in the May, however. On the 8th, *Lydonia* was steaming as convoy escort from Bizerte to Gibraltar when the merchant ship SS *Ingleside* was attacked and sunk by a U-boat, 80 miles off Algiers. Together with the British destroyer HMS *Basilisk* (1910), the yacht made a depth charge attack at 1735 but eventually had to break off in heavy seas to rescue survivors from the stricken freighter, eleven of whose sailors died nonetheless.

Despite an apparent lack of hard evidence, both *Lydonia* and *Basilisk* were credited with sinking the submarine, said to be *UB-70*, which was blamed at the time for the sinking of *Ingleside*. This may or may not be the case. *UB-70* had sailed on 16 April from Germany for Cattaro and vanished during the crossing. Her last contact was on 5 May, when she reported from east of Gibraltar, and modern scholarship credits her with only one sinking, on 2 May. Nothing was heard from the submarine and her thirty-two crewmen again.

As for *Lydonia*, she continued escort operations and was finally decommissioned at Norfolk, Virginia, on 7 August 1919, transferring to the Coast and Geodetic Survey Service the same day.

Christabel *Claims a U-boat*

By mid-1918, the USN had seventeen converted yachts operating off the French coast. By far the smallest and oldest of these was *Christabel* (1893). She had been built for wealthy iron master Arthur C Kennard, who owned the Falkirk Iron Works in Stirlingshire, by D and W Henderson to the designs of G L Watson. *Christabel* was sold on to the USA in 1910 and she eventually came into the ownership of Irving Ter Bush, son of Rufus T Bush, who had made a fortune in oil and industry; Rufus was also a keen yachtsman, a passion his son inherited. Irving became the founder of the Bush Terminal Company, responsible for the construction of the massive Bush Terminal transportation, warehousing and manufacturing facility, commissioned Manhattan's landmark Bush Tower skyscraper on 42nd Street near New York City's Times Square and funded the construction of Bush

Christabel, the supposed U-boat killer. *(US Naval History and Heritage Command NH 300)*

House in London. Purchased by the USN for $55,000 in April 1917, she was just 248grt, 164ft long and armed with two 3in and two machine guns.

Despite her age and relatively slow speed, *Christabel* had an interesting

The star that was painted on *Christabel*'s funnel as proof of her 'success'. *(US Naval History and Heritage Command NH 55162)*

Ensign Daniel Sullivan of *Christabel*, who saved his ship from destruction. *(US Naval History and Heritage Command NH 44173)*

career as a naval unit. For example, on the night of 17 April 1918, the US-flagged cargo ship SS *Florence H* (3,820grt) suddenly erupted in a brilliant fireball while at anchor in Quiberon Bay. Her cargo of 2,200 tons of smokeless powder had spontaneously exploded. Several vessels in the harbour rushed to her aid, including *Christabel*. Forty-five of the freighter's complement of Naval Armed Guard died in the blast and another seventy-eight men were rescued, of which about half were extensively burned and injured. For the rescue, one of *Christabel*'s crew earned a Distinguished Service Cross. He was Chief Pharmacist Mate Louis Zeller, who dived into water filled with burning exploding powder boxes from the *Florence H* to rescue severely burned seamen.

The following month, on 21 May, *Christabel* was on escort duty, standing by SS *Danae*, a laggard about 8 miles adrift of her coastal convoy out of La Pallice to Quiberon Bay. Two miles outside the Île d'Yeu, a lookout on the American ship spotted an oil slick to port. The yacht investigated it and saw nothing, but then at 1720, the wake of a periscope was sighted, 600yds off the port quarter. The yacht headed for it at her best speed of 10.5 knots, whereupon the wake disappeared amidst a number of oil slicks.

Commanding Officer Lieutenant Millington B McComb went up to the foretop to con his ship and, believing he had arrived over the U-boat's position, dropped a depth charge. At 2052, still lagging the convoy, *Christabel* again sighted a periscope about 200yds off the starboard beam. Manoeuvring to where it had been seen, at 2055 she dropped another depth charge and then a second one moments later. Nothing followed the explosion of the first charge, but the second occasioned a third and violent explosion that shot skyward between *Christabel*'s stern and the water column raised by the second bomb. The detonation was such that 'the officers thought at first that the ship had been seriously damaged, and a couple of men were knocked sprawling on the deck'.[8] *Christabel* turned, cruised in the vicinity and observed a quantity of heavy black oil and splintered pieces of wood, with very large oil bubbles rising to the surface. 'In a few minutes the sea, for a space many hundred yards in diameter, was covered with dead fish – about ten times as many, the officers reported, as could have been killed by the usual depth charge.'[9]

While this was taking place, some of the yacht's depth charges had come loose and began to roll around the deck. Ensign Daniel A J Sullivan USNRF flung himself on them and secured the bombs, for which he later received the Medal of Honor [*sic*]. The citation noted that the award was 'for extraordinary heroism as an officer of the USS *Christabel* in conflict with an enemy submarine on 21 May 1918. As a result of the explosion of a depth bomb dropped near the submarine, the *Christabel* was so badly shaken that a number of depth charges which had been set for firing were thrown about the deck and there was imminent danger that they would explode. Ensign Sullivan immediately fell on the depth charges and succeeded in securing them, thus saving the ship from disaster, which would inevitably have caused great loss of life.'[10]

UC-56 interned at Santander after surviving an attack by USS *Christabel*. *(Author's collection)*

Christabel claimed a U-boat sunk and on 12 September 1918, Admiral Henry Wilson, Commander, US Naval Forces in France, wrote to McComb that: 'You are authorized to paint a white star on the smokestack of the vessel under your command as a mark to denote the fact that the USS *Christabel* has successfully engaged and put out of action an enemy submarine.'[11]

But in fact, the U-boat she had attacked, the minelayer *UC-56*, although badly damaged, escaped and made a difficult three-day voyage to Santander in neutral Spain where she was interned, as were her crew. Not sunk, but still put out of the war by a rich man's yacht.*

Wakiva II

May 1918 had seen *Venetia*, *Lydonia* and *Christabel* in action against U-boats. The final act of that busy month involved another converted yacht, *Wakiva II*.

She was a steel-hulled steam yacht built at Leith in 1907 by Ramage & Ferguson for Lamon Vanderburgh Harkness, an American businessman and one of the largest shareholders in Standard Oil. In *Wakiva II*, the Harkness family had sailed as far afield as the Dutch East Indies and the North Sea, before the USN acquired her on 20 July 1917 and commissioned the yacht on 6 August at the Boston Navy Yard, Lieutenant Commander Thomas R Kurtz commanding. Of 853grt, capable of 15 knots and armed with four 3in and two machine guns, she sailed for France as the command ship of Squadron Four of the Patrol Force and arrived at Brest on 18 September. There, Captain Thomas Magruder, who had hoisted his pennant on board for the voyage, disembarked to establish his headquarters ashore.†

From that point *Wakiva II* was involved in patrol and escort work. On 28 October 1917, she assisted *Alcedo* at the rescue of survivors from the

* Some sources suggest that *Christabel* attacked *UB-74*, later sunk by *Lorna*. It remains a moot point.

† From 13 December 1917 Magruder commanded a minesweeping detachment of ten converted trawlers, with his command pennant in *Guinevere*.

torpedoed SS *Finland* (see above). On 23 November, there was a flurry of excitement when the yacht's lookouts sighted an object 500yds distant that seemed initially like a submarine's conning tower. Kurtz went to general quarters and conned his vessel towards the contact at full speed, opening fire with the forward guns. After seven shots, a closer examination revealed that their enemy was a convincingly painted target. But they had, at least, destroyed it.

The real thing came a week later. On the 28th, *Wakiva II* departed Saint-Nazaire to join a west-bound convoy, now under the command of Lieutenant Commander Guy Davis, previously of *Guinevere* (Kurtz having joined Admiral Wilson's staff). After an uneventful passage, *Kanawha II*, under Lieutenant Commander John Borden (met in Chapter 7), fired off two Very pistol flares and sounded a loud blast on her siren, the signal that a submarine has been sighted. *Wakiva II* went to general quarters and Kurtz rang down for full speed ahead, while another yacht, *Noma*, closed the tanker to screen the vulnerable oiler's starboard side, Kurtz taking position to port.

However, a thirty-minute search found nothing and all three ships re-joined the main convoy. No sooner had they done so than *Noma* sounded another alarm and dropped depth charges on what her lookouts took for a submarine. *Wakiva II* sped to her assistance and at 1902, while still 1½ miles from *Noma*, sighted a periscope 100yds away. Going hard to port, Kurtz commenced fire with the after guns and with her third salvo claimed to have sheared a periscope. As the yacht passed over the suspected U-boat for a second time, she dropped a depth charge barrage, all of which exploded and sent oil and debris to the surface. Two hits on the wreckage, fired from number one gun, added to the attack and during a third pass three men were reported to be clinging to wreckage, which now covered a wide area of the surface, mixed in with floating patches of fuel oil.

Wakiva II received credit for at least damaging a U-boat and was praised by both Rear Admiral Wilson and Admiral Sims. Davis received the Navy Distinguished Service Medal. The citation read: 'On 28 November 1917, as Commanding Officer of the USS *Wakiva*, Commander Davis engaged and destroyed an enemy submarine which attempted to attack the convoy escorted by the *Wakiva*.'[12] But no U-boat was recorded as sunk that day.

Wakiva's career as a submarine hunter drew to a close in May 1918. On the 21st, she was steaming in convoy with a group of eight ships, positioned on the port flank and sailing through the Bay of Biscay. Fog came down after dark and the convoy reduced speed, with *Wakiva II* taking station on the freighter *Wabash*, a German cargo ship of 5,586grt, impounded in the neutral USA when war commenced and turned over to the US Navy for wartime use on American entry into the conflict.

In view of the conditions, protective zigzagging had been abandoned. Fog continued into the following day and by 0310 all the ships in the convoy

Opposite: Wakiva II displaying her searchlight platform and a magnificent bowsprit, in Boston Harbour, 1917. *(US Naval History and Heritage Command NH 579)*

were sounding their sirens to indicate their positions. Those on watch in *Wakiva II* distinctly heard *Wabash*'s hooter but could not see the ship. As another blast from the cargo vessel seemed nearer than before, Lieutenant Commander E G Allen, who had replaced Davis in command, ordered the helm put over one point to port and had the whistle sounded once more. Ten seconds later, *Wabash* made another blast, which appeared even closer to the yacht.

Suddenly, the massive shape of the freighter loomed out of the murk, bearing straight for *Wakiva II*. Allen rang for full speed ahead and a full turn to port but before the helm could be put over, *Wabash*'s stem smashed into the yacht's starboard quarter, just abaft the mainmast and forward of the after guns, ripping a huge gash in the ship's side from the main deck down to the propeller shaft.

The collision, which threw both ships briefly on parallel courses, also carried away *Wakiva*'s starboard boats. The two ships briefly remained alongside each other and then *Wabash* slowly went astern of the doomed yacht.

Two crewmen died in the immediate aftermath of the smash, but three reservists demonstrated the sort of heroism that is surprising only after the event. Chief Gunner's Mate Oliver P Cooper USNRF ran aft to the fantail where the depth charges were secured, withdrew the bursting pins from some British mines stored there, and set the American depth charges to 'safe'. He was able to report that the charges were secure within five minutes of the hit.

Meanwhile, Electrician Second Class Charles E Kirkpatrick UNSRF, on duty in the ship's radio room, remained at his post and sent out the SOS, staying on board until abandoning at the last possible moment. And another reservist, Chief Boatswain's Mate Thomas Olson, rigged out the motor whaleboat and rounded up the men from below decks. He then accompanied Lieutenant Commander Allen in checking that everyone was off the stricken yacht.

Wakiva II sank by the stern and disappeared under the waves at 0336, 20 miles south of the Île d'Yeu. The fog of war indeed.

Piqua I *(aka* Kanawha II*)*

Kanawha II was renamed *Piqua I* in March 1918, and it was in this guise that John Borden's moment of high drama came. On 16 July 1918, while steaming as convoy escort, he sighted the conning tower of a U-boat, on a heading almost parallel with the course of the convoy. Lieutenant Commander Borden closed and at 11,000yds opened fire. The gun crew, unable to see their target, aimed according to ranges and bearings calculated and yelled down to them from the bridge. Regrettably she scored no hits, but her shells forced the U-boat to abandon her intended victims. And Borden's service was recognised by the award of the Navy Cross at the end of the war: 'For distinguished service in the line of his profession as Commanding Officer of the USS *Piqua*, engaged in the important, exacting and hazardous duty

John Borden's yacht *Kanawha II*, renamed *Piqua I* in 1918, seen in peacetime. *(US Naval History and Heritage Command NH 102128)*

of transporting and escorting troops and supplies to European ports through waters infested with enemy submarines and mines during World War I.'[13]

The yacht was decommissioned in July 1919 and Borden went on to become an explorer, sailing through the Bering Strait to Siberia.

Bravery and Depth Charges

Depth charges seemed to be a constant threat, not so much to the enemy as to the yachts themselves. Two examples of conspicuous courage in dealing with them occurred at the turn of the year 1917.

Pusey and Jones of Delaware had built the 243ft-long *Nokomis II* in 1914 for automobile pioneer Horace E Dodge. In June 1917 she was purchased by the USN and sent to France to be part of the Breton Patrol Squadron.

On 11 January 1918, while at sea in heavy weather, a wave rolled on board and smashed the depth charge Y-launcher, causing the bomb in the firing chamber to break loose and roll across the deck. Chief Carpenter's Mate E Artimas Chastain threw himself at it and hung on for grim death, to stop the bomb hitting the other depth charges stored nearby, until help arrived. He received the Navy Cross for his bravery.

And USS *Remlik*, ex-*Candace*, had earlier had a depth charge problem, too. On 17 December 1917, in the middle of a raging storm in the Bay of Biscay, she spotted a surfaced U-boat. Lieutenant Commander I C Johnson, her captain, rang for her full speed of 14 knots but the U-boat submerged before he could engage it. But now the storm increased in ferocity, which both prevented further prosecution of the enemy and caused a wave to smash into the fantail and break open the depth charge store, sending an armed bomb rolling across the deck. Chief Boatswain's Mate John McKenzie leapt on it and, for want of any other method, sat on the weapon until it could be secured. He was recognised with the Medal of Honor [*sic*].

By mid-1918, sufficient destroyers became available for them to take the responsibility for troopship escort. The yachts were relegated to escorting stores ships and coal convoys. Worn and battered by constant use and with seemingly perpetually leaking decks and seams, the old ladies of leisure still kept at their work.

USS *Rambler* was the renamed *Dreamer* (met in Chapter 1), once thought the most luxurious yacht in the world. Her task now was to escort convoys composed of British, French, a few American and even Spanish ships carrying coal traffic from England to the Gironde or Brest. *Rambler* lost only one vessel under her care, the British-flagged *Philomel* (3,050grt), sunk by *UB-88* on 16 September. The yacht attacked with depth charges to no avail, but the whole of the stricken ship's company was saved.

In total, the USN deployed twenty armed yachts in the French and Western Mediterranean theatres (see Appendix 3). Three were lost there. None sank a U-boat, but the hard-worked yachts patrolled and escorted unceasingly, and surely their efforts kept the enemy away from attacking positions that they might otherwise have exploited.

This achievement came despite their relative lack of manoeuvrability, compared to – say – a destroyer, which placed them at greater risk of torpedo, or even mine, strike. And, as an official report by Admiral Wilson put it: 'In many ways, the service of these vessels on the coast of France may be considered the most difficult of any performed by vessels operating in the war. Nearly all of them were lightly built, intended for fair weather cruising only, and designed more for comfort than for seagoing qualities. Nevertheless, from the time of their arrival in France until the time of the Armistice, they were worked without rest, and it was very seldom that any of them were not ready for any service required, whether of a routine or of an extraordinary nature.'[14]

Rambler's fantail, showing her after 3in gun and depth charges on racks and in a Y-gun thrower, taken at Brest, France, 1918. USS *Bridgeport* (a destroyer tender) is in the background, with two destroyers tied alongside. The litter of depth charges on her deck illustrates what a problem they could be breaking loose in rough seas. *(US Naval History and Heritage Command NH 73255)*

CHAPTER NINE

NAVAL STEAM YACHTS AROUND THE WORLD

Canada

Prior to 1905, the Royal Navy had two Canadian bases, Esquimalt (established 1842) and Halifax (1759), both of which boasted dockyards. Protection of Canadian waters was provided from these ports by RN squadrons.

But the navy withdrew from these commitments in 1904–05, leaving the Canadian coast with scant security. After much debate, a Royal Canadian Navy was formed in 1910, and Britain provided two vessels, the cruisers *Rainbow* (1891) and *Niobe* (1898), which served on the west and east coasts respectively.

HMCS *Niobe* (1895), one of only two warships in the Canadian Navy at the start of the war. She was a *Diadem*-class protected cruiser armed with sixteen 6in QF and fourteen 12pdrs. Her active service in Canadian waters was brief. *Niobe* patrolled the approaches to the St Lawrence River and then joined the Royal Navy's 4th Cruiser Squadron to cruise off New York City. She returned to Halifax, Nova Scotia, on 17 July 1915 and never put to sea again. *(US Library of Congress ggbain08665)*

Both of these ships were gifted to Canada* and as the nation also possessed two fine ports and dockyards – Halifax and Esquimalt – abandoned by the Royal Navy and which had cost the country virtually nothing, Prime Minister Sir Wilfred Laurier wanted to use the navy's budget to launch a shipbuilding programme and provide the new navy with four cruisers and six destroyers. These were to be built in Canada and manned by Canadians. However, Laurier lost the 1911 election to his rival Robert Borden, who was against the programme, and the ships were never built.

Thus when war came, Canada had just two old cruisers for coastal and shipping defence. And more, the Royal Navy could spare no resource from its other pressing needs to assist. So, as with the RN and USN, the Canadian Navy turned to armed yachts as patrol vessels.

But where to get them from? The obvious country to turn to was the USA but there was a sensitivity in the US government about selling American arms to combatant nations. The USA was officially neutral in the war. But, in fact, large parts of American commerce were doing very nicely thank you selling goods to all sides, including food and other supplies to Germany. However, the official position, set out very clearly by US President Woodrow Wilson in 1914, was that: 'The United States must be neutral in fact as well as in name during these days that are to try men's souls. We must be impartial in thought as well as in action, must put a curb upon our sentiments as well as upon every transaction that might be construed as a preference of one party to the struggle before another.'[1]

Nonetheless, a purchasing mission was sent to the USA in July 1915 and two vessels were acquired via Cox and Stevens (shipbrokers), but the sales were blocked by the US government. It required the intervention of legendary champion yachtsman Commodore Aemilius Jarvis,† who had headed the purchasing mission, and who sailed the ships with civilian crews from the USA to Canada under false pretences.

One of the yachts was the *Waturus*, acquired at a cost of $80,000. *Waturus* had been built by Hawthorn and Company at Leith and launched in 1900. Her first owner was the Habsburg Archduke, Charles Stephen Eugene Viktor Felix Maria of Austria, *Grossadmiral* in the Austrian Navy.

The archduke was also a keen yachtsman. He was a flag officer of the Austrian Imperial and Royal Yacht Squadron and visited England on several occasions to compete or sail his craft, including in 1879 for the Royal Yacht Squadron Regatta, in 1900 and 1911. Indeed, Charles had been made a member of the British Yacht Racing Association in 1892. *Waturus* was not his only vessel; in 1892, he had bought *Valkyrie* from the Earl of Dunraven and *Ul* direct from Ramage & Ferguson in 1911.

Archduke Charles had sold *Waturus* to Randal Morgan, an American millionaire, in 1902, and after refitting the yacht he too raced her along the eastern coastline of the United States before putting her up for sale.

The Royal Canadian Navy renamed her as HMCS *Hochelaga* in August and she sailed to Montreal for conversion to an armed yacht,

* The Royal Canadian Navy (RCN) was proclaimed as such by King George V on 16 August 1911. The anniversary is marked, however, on 4 May 1910, the date the Naval Service Act became law and established the Canadian Naval Service.

† President of the Trader's Bank of Canada, Jarvis founded the Steel Company of Canada. He built Toronto's iconic King Edward Hotel and created the British Columbia Salmon Canning Industry.

Two views of HMCS *Hochelaga*, ex-*Waturus*, with her yacht bowsprit and forward 12pdr evident. *(Author's collection)*

which included fitting a 12pdr gun in her bows and another at the stern.

Apart from two incidents, she had an uneventful career, but both of these were memorable. As part of the East Coast Patrol, she was present in Halifax harbour on 6 December 1917 at the time of the great Halifax explosion,* when she suffered damage and six casualties.

The second event brought shame to the ship. On 21 August 1918, *Hochelaga* was on anti-submarine patrol with a small group of four ships off the coast of Nova Scotia. Here, when detached from the flotilla, she sighted *U-156*, armed with torpedoes and two 105mm (4.1in) guns, in the process of boarding and sinking four Canadian fishing schooners.† *Hochelaga*'s commanding officer, Lieutenant R D Legate, for some reason did not engage the enemy but instead turned about to re-join his flotilla, a decision that looked much like cowardice. That was certainly the view of

* The blast was the largest human-made explosion at the time, releasing the equivalent energy of roughly 2.9 kilotons of TNT.

† The U-boat's commander, Richard Feldt, also captured the Grimsby-built trawler *Triumph* (1907) and used her to sink a further seven sailing fishing vessels.

his superiors, for on return to port, Legate was arrested and court martialled in Halifax that October for his failure to confront the enemy. He was found guilty and dismissed from the service with the forfeiture of his commission, war service gratuity, medals and other benefits.

Hochelaga remained in the service until late 1920, when she was sold on. But she had one last brief moment of fame. Renamed *HaChayal Ha'Ivri*, she was used in an attempt to carry Jewish immigrants to Palestine in breach of British (who held the Mandate for the country at the time) orders. She left Antwerp on 14 July 1946 carrying some 550 passengers but was seized off Haifa by the destroyer HMS *Saumarez* and taken instead to Cyprus.

The other yacht acquired by Jarvis was HMCS *Stadacona*. She had been constructed in 1899 as the American steam yacht *Columbia*, the second yacht of that name built for J Harvey Ladew of New York, a wealthy leather merchant and noted yachtsman.

Two views of *Stadacona*, her 4in forward and 12pdr aft guns visible. *(Author's collection)*

Florence seen in peacetime.
(Author's collection)

In August 1915, she was sent to the Canadian Vickers shipyard in Montreal, Quebec, to fit out. Here she gained one 4in gun forward (a 12pdr was added aft later in the war) and sailed to Sydney, Nova Scotia, to begin her career as a patrol vessel and where she became the flagship of the East Coast fleet in 1916. After the war, *Stadacona* was decommissioned on 31 March 1920, transferred to government service and used for hydrographic surveys and occasionally for fisheries patrol along the west coast until sold off in 1924.

The 262-ton HMCS *Florence* was originally launched in 1903 as *Czarina*, then renamed *Emeline*. American-built, she was named *Florence* by her new owner, retail millionaire John Craig Eaton. He brought her to Toronto in

Florence in her warpaint.
(Author's collection)

1910 and after the onset of war presented her to the Royal Canadian Navy. She was commissioned on 19 July 1915, armed with a single 3pdr, and served as a guard ship at Saint John, New Brunswick, and as a patrol vessel in the Bay of Fundy. However, *Florence* was paid off in August 1916 as not suitable for naval duty. Many such American yachts had been designed for leisure cruising on the USA's broad rivers; they were much less suitable in oceanic waters.

Another yacht acquired by the RCN in 1915 was HMCS *Grilse*. As *Winchester*, she had been constructed for Peter Rouss, who inherited a retail fortune, in 1912 at Yarrow and Company of Scotstoun, and was the third of Rouss' vessels to be named *Winchester*.* (The USN took another, the oil-fired *Winchester* of 1916, purchased for $300,000 in 1917 and which was used for paravane testing; she had a top speed of 31.65 knots.) *Winchester III* was powered by two oil-fired Parsons turbines driving two screws and could achieve speeds of at least 32 knots.†

She joined the Canadian forces through the agency of Canadian industrialist, millionaire and playboy John Kenneth Leveson 'Jack' Ross,‡ another emissary sent to the United States to acquire ships for the RCN. Ross purchased *Winchester* for $100,000 of his own money. Again, the American government discovered the sale and attempted to block the transaction, but Ross managed to get out of the country with the ship and sailed her to Halifax. On arrival, she too was despatched to Canadian Vickers in Montreal, where she was armed with two 12pdr guns, one placed on the forecastle and one aft, on the quarterdeck. A 14in torpedo tube was sited amidships and the aft deckhouse was removed to make room for it and the three torpedoes that were to be carried on deck. The mast was moved forward to directly behind the bridge and a second mast was installed to give the vessel a horizontal antenna to improve radio communications. Thus, she became a torpedo boat; 'almost alone among the tinpot fleet of the Canadian Navy, she bore at least some resemblance to a modern warship'.[2]

Grilse was commissioned as such on 15 July 1915, with Ross as her commander,§ and operated off Canada's east coast for much of the war. Spending the better part of her service with the Halifax patrol, she was loaned to the Gulf patrol in September 1915 and operated as a ship escort in the Gulf of St Lawrence.

However, once more the suitability of vessels designed for civilian leisure purposes for naval usage came to be questioned, and *Grilse* proved unsuitable for winter operations in Canadian waters.

Instead, she was sent to the Caribbean Sea for the winter and then in December 1916 to the North America and West Indies Station. On passage, she met a heavy storm and nearly sank. Indeed, it was believed that she was lost, for her antenna had been washed away in the storm and she was out of communication. *Grilse* was then towed to Halifax for a refit, re-entering service on 10 May 1917 for duty as a patrol vessel, in which role she saw out the war, and was paid off on 10 December 1918.

* He commissioned four *Winchesters* in total, always seeking after speed; his other love was fast horses.

† The *Winchesters* were particularly fast, deliberately so. It had become evident to some owners that comfort and seaworthiness were incompatible with high speed, so a group of destroyer-like high-speed yachts evolved. These yachts carried their owners along the coast in comfort, if not in complete luxury. Allegedly Matthew Chaloner Durfee Borden, the 'Calico King', returning to New York in his steam yacht *Little Sovereign*, was overhauled and passed by one of the *Winchesters*. Turning to his captain, he said, 'Don't stop at the Yacht Club landing, but continue on to Seabury's yard so I can order a faster yacht.' (Hofman, The Steam Yachts, p.16)

‡ A keen yachtsman, he was the second Canadian to be made a member of the Royal Yacht Squadron. The first had been his father.

§ Ross commanded until July 1916, when Lieutenant Walter Wingate RNR took over.

A drawing by official war artist Arthur Lismer of HMCS *Grilse* on convoy escort duty. *(Author's collection)*

Jack Ross also managed to acquire the yacht *Tarantula* for the RCN, where she became HMCS *Tuna* (1902). Again built by Yarrow, initially for W K Vanderbilt Jr, *Tarantula** was among the first turbine-powered private yachts. Her hull was similar to the torpedo boats that Yarrow Shipbuilders had constructed for the Royal Navy and the ship was partly modelled on *Turbinia*, the first turbine-powered ship, and – most unusually – had nine propellors on three shafts. Again, the US government tried to block the sale, so Ross arranged for her to be fitted out in the United States in secret and she arrived at Halifax, Nova Scotia, on 10 September 1914, after sailing with her civilian crew. Ross sold the ship to the RCN for $1 and offered to repurchase it if still functional at war's end.

She was commissioned as *Tuna* in December 1914 as a torpedo boat (small wonder, given her pedigree) and fitted with two 14in torpedo tubes and a 3pdr gun, sailing under Ross's command out of Halifax. In May 1917, however, she was paid off due to an irreparable engine mount fracture.

On Patrol

All five of these yachts filled valuable roles in the protection of Canadian waters.

Early 1915 saw a steady increase in the tonnage of Allied and neutral

* One of two of that name in Vanderbilt ownership.

Grilse in 1916. *(Author's collection)*

merchant shipping lost to U-boats and other enemy predation; 47,981grt in January, 59,921 in February, 80,775 in March.[3] Even the great liners were not safe, as the sinking of the *Lusitania* on 7 May proved. And U-boats were operating out into the Atlantic.

Concern grew that German agents in the USA might attempt to establish U-boat supply bases along the more remote stretches of the Newfoundland and Canadian coastlines. Accordingly, in late June the Canadian Navy's chief of staff, Commander Richard M Stephens, proposed a scheme for ten patrol vessels to watch the waters of the Gulf and the coast of Nova Scotia between Halifax, Cape Race and the Strait of Belle Isle. Making the best of the limited resources available to him, Stephens deployed five auxiliary patrol vessels: *Canada*, *Margaret*, *Sable I*, *Premier*, and the yacht *Tuna*. The first two were fisheries patrol vessels that had at least been built along naval lines, while *Premier* and *Sable I* were civilian vessels chartered by the navy. *Tuna* was the only one among them capable of any great speed.

Such dispositions show the poverty of Canadian naval resources; the addition of some trawlers and drifters being built in Canada for the Royal Navy, and around two dozen converted civilian steamers, eased the situation but another constraint was a lack of men to man them. Even when the

Tuna with a bone between her teeth. *(Author's collection)*

Canadian Navy reached its peak size of sixty-six vessels in 1918, it 'would be very hard-pressed to find qualified seamen for [them]'.[4]

In 1917 the danger of submarine attack remained in the eastern Atlantic but that changed in 1918. During the winter the British Admiralty warned that new types of large, long-range submarines would almost certainly begin to strike in Canadian and US waters in the coming spring. Moreover, since mid-1917, sailings of merchant ships from Canada to Britain and vice-versa were in convoy.

Such developments meant the designation of a new convoy port, Sydney, previously a small outstation of Halifax. 'Sydney, with its large harbour, abundant coal supplies, and strategic location on both the St. Lawrence route and the Great Circle route to Europe, became the assembly port for slow-speed shipping from Canadian and US ports. As many as fifty to sixty vessels appeared for each convoy, which sailed at eight-day intervals.'[5]

To defend the departure points of the convoys, a new 'Mobile Patrol Flotilla' was formed. This comprised a fisheries patrol vessel (*Canada*), a customs cutter (*Margaret*), the post office steamer *Lady Evelyn*; and two yachts, *Stadacona* and *Hochelaga*.

The flotilla was organised into divisions that each included one or two of the larger ships and a pair of trawlers. The task of these divisions was to roam the Gulf of St Lawrence and waters south of Newfoundland ready to respond to any reports of submarines, or to assist the convoys funnelling out of Halifax and Sydney.

By September, convoys began to assemble at Quebec. Convoy HC-16 was the first (with a separate section sailing from New York to rendezvous east of Newfoundland). The next Quebec sailing, HC-17, departed on 13 September and the Canadian Navy sent three vessels from Sydney, which included the yacht *Stadacona*, to meet it. They escorted the merchant ships through the Strait of Belle Isle, a voyage of nearly 400 miles, before turning back for home.

Meanwhile, the yacht *Hochelaga* was assigned to escorting the slow HS convoys from Sydney, together with two or three trawlers.

And so, in Canada as in Britain and America, steam yachts had a key role in the defence of the nation and its seaways.

Australia

To the north of Australia, German New Guinea (*Deutsch-Neuguinea*) was an Imperial German protectorate from 1884 and comprised the territories of the north-eastern part of New Guinea (*Kaiser-Wilhelmsland*) and the near-by Bismarck Archipelago, consisting of New Britain and New Ireland.

Concerned about potential raids by Admiral von Spee's East Asia Squadron on British and Empire shipping, the British government requested that Australia destroy the German wireless stations and coaling facilities in the Pacific, including those of New Guinea. An Australian Naval and Military Expeditionary Force (ANMEF) was hastily raised, and tasked with the capture of the Imperial German Pacific Protectorates within six months. This included seizing or destroying the radio and coal stations supporting the East Asia Squadron.

The naval component of the force was soon in action when on 14 September the destroyer HMAS *Warrego* (1911) captured the official steam yacht of the German Imperial administration at Kavieng, New Ireland. This was the *Nusa*, a 74ft 6in-long wooden vessel armed with two 3pdr guns.

She was taken to Rabaul, commissioned as HMAS *Nusa*, armed with a 12pdr gun and manned by a scratch crew drawn from the armed merchant cruiser HMAS *Berrima*, ex P&O.

Under 31-year-old Lieutenant John Metcalf Jackson,* a Royal Navy officer and son of the vicar of Moulton, Lincs, who had been attached to *Warrego*, *Nusa* was soon in action. On 11 October 1914, she was on patrol at Komethafen, on the north-west coast of New Britain, when her crew and an embarked infantry detachment captured the German government steam yacht *Komet*. A week later, Jackson had further success, when he apprehended the 450-ton steamer *Siar* and the motor schooners *Matupi* and *Senata*. *Komet* would later commission in the RAN as HMAS *Una*, while the other three prizes were put to use by the Australian occupying forces in German New Guinea. It was a heady haul for such a little vessel. As for Jackson, he was given command of *Una*, now fitted with three 4in and two 12pdr guns.

The Australian Navy also came to possess one of the more unusual steam yachts to take part in the First World War, SY *Ena*. She was a rarity at the time for she was designed (by Walter Reeks) and built (by W M Ford boat-builders) in Sydney around 1900, a time when most steam yachts seen in

* Promoted to commander in November the following year.

Antipodean waters had been imported or constructed locally to international designs.

Ena had been commissioned by Thomas Dibbs, Commodore of the Royal Sydney Yacht Squadron, at a cost of £5,800 and was constructed largely of Australian timber, the exception being the choice of lighter New Zealand kauri wood* for the topsides planking. It was considered a light but strong hull at the time. The steam machinery was also Australian built and the vessel was named after Dibbs's wife Tryphena. While construction was under way, another Sydney yard was cutting down the former HMVS *Nelson* (1814), which, with 126 guns, had once been the Royal Navy's largest first-rate ship of the line. Some of her timbers were used for *Ena*'s interior fittings.

Ena was originally designed for day trips and entertaining guests, and the layout provided for two cabins below the decks, fore and aft, a galley aft of the helm position, and a large open but covered deck area, ideal for parties. A few years after it was launched, an enclosed saloon cabin was added to the aft end of the superstructure.

Dibbs used her for hospitality and overnight cruising in Sydney harbour or up the Hawkesbury River. But in 1917, he sold her to the Royal Australian Navy (for just £1,000). Renamed HMAS *Sleuth*, painted black and fitted with a Hotchkiss 3pdr gun on the foredeck, the ship was used to patrol in the Torres Strait (between Australia and New Guinea), around Thursday Island and along the east coast during the final days of the war, searching for German raiders. Apparently, 'the crew were ever fearful of firing the gun because it shook the entire ship'.[6]

However, in September 1917, her skipper, Lieutenant James Capstick-Dale, signalled his superiors that his men were refusing to proceed to sea because 'the ship is totally unsafe'. By that stage, *Sleuth* had run aground twice, inspiring the local humourists on Thursday Island to remark that she

* *Agathis australis*, it produces very long, clear lengths, ideal for boat building.

Ena, as HMAS *Sleuth*, her 3pdr gun visible under the forward awning. *(Australian Maritime Museum)*

was a fine survey ship because, on almost every voyage, she discovered uncharted rocks and reefs. Eventually, the Naval Board conceded that she was 'ill-suited' for duty as an ocean-going patrol vessel.[7] She returned to Sydney to finish the war as a tender to the training ship *Tingira*.*

Austria and Italy

Both the Austrian and Italian navies pressed steam yachts into service as they contested the Adriatic and Ionian Seas.

The Austrian imperial yacht *Miramar* (1872) was an 1,830-ton paddle steamer with a design speed of 17 knots. When war came, she was fitted with two 3pdr and two 1pdr guns and with her 159 crew was put to work as a patrol vessel. A second, much smaller, yacht, *Dalmat* (1896, 260 tons), also served in the *kaiserliche und königliche Kriegsmarine*, fitted with one or two small quick-firers and a machine gun.

* *Ena* continued to sail until 1981, when she sank. The vessel was salved and restored and is now in the possession of the Australian Maritime Museum.

The Austrian royal yacht *Miramar*, seen her at Medolino in 1902, with the emperor embarked. *(US Naval History and Heritage Command NH 87790)*

In 1906, the Austro-Hungarian government had acquired *Nirvana* (1904) from France, for whom she had served as the official yacht of the French ambassador to the Ottoman empire. Built by D and W Henderson and designed by G L Watson as *Taurus*, originally for the Comtesse de Bearn, she was put to use by the Austrians as a government yacht. In 1915, she was repurposed as a harbour patrol boat and naval accommodation vessel, and at the war's end was stricken before being allocated to Italy as war reparations.

The Austrian line of battle also boasted a 'fleet yacht' in August 1914. This was SMS *Lacroma* (1887), built as the torpedo cruiser *Tiger* in Austrian yards and armed with domestically produced 35cm torpedo tubes. In 1905–06 she was converted to a yacht and renamed, and by 1916 had become a depot ship for German U-boat crews at Pola.

The Italians too took their royal yacht into naval service, although to call her a yacht might be a misnomer, as she had been launched in 1883 as the

SMS *Tiger* (1887), later *Lacroma*, seen at Pola soon after completion. Two covered shipbuilding ways are in the right background, located on Oliven Island where naval shipbuilding was concentrated. *(US Naval History and Heritage Command NH 88919)*

5,528grt British passenger liner *America* for the National Steam Ship Co. Ltd of Liverpool. In 1887, *America* was purchased by Italy for King Umberto I and became *Trinacria*. Built by James and George Thomson of Clydebank, she was 442ft in length and her single screw could drive her at 15 knots. In 1915, when Italy joined the global conflict, *Trinacria* gained four 6pdr and two 1pdr weapons and served as an auxiliary cruiser until the war's conclusion.

And at the end of 1901, the Italians had converted the armoured cruiser *Carlo Alberto* (1896) into a 'yacht' for King Victor Emmanuel III. He sailed to the Coronation and Fleet Review of Edward VII in her, accompanied by Guglielmo Marconi, who conducted radio experiments on board. But, unlike *Trinacria*, she saw no war service and was converted into a troop transport in 1917.

Then there is the mystery of the gunboat *Misurata*. She started life as another of trawler mogul Walter S Bailey's steam yachts called *Sargitta* (see also Chapter 4). Built in 1894 by William Hamilton and Co. of Port Glasgow she was of 402grt and capable of 12 knots from a single screw. By 1901, Bailey had sold her and in 1907 she was registered with Camper and Nicholson, presumably for sale.

In 1912, she turned up in the Italian Navy, fitted out as a gunboat and named *Misurata* after the Italian for the port of Misrata in Libya. Presumably, she was so designated in honour of the Battle of Misrata, part of the Italian–Turco war. It seems she served in this struggle and also in the coming world war. What is certain is that *Misurata* survived both wars, for in 1927 she was converted back to a yacht and assumed her original name, *Sagitta*.

The Italian *Trinacria*. *(US Naval History and Heritage Command NH* 47657)

The Italians also took up Ninian Ballantyne Stewart's yacht *Maria* (1893),* also in 1912, for use as a gunboat. She had already gone through one name change, in 1896 to *Rhouma*, and then became *Giuliana*.

Apart from *Misurata* (1894, two 14pdr, 12.5 knots), the *Regia Marina* also took up five other smaller yachts, all requiring crews of around thirty to forty men, single screw only, and variously armed with 14pdr or 6pdr guns. These were *Tobruk* (1894, two 14pdr, 11.5 knots); *Giuliana* (1893, four 6pdr, 11.9 knots); and *Archimede* (four 6pdr, 13 knots). This later vessel was seized by the Germans at Odessa in June 1918 and recovered after the Armistice. There were also two yachts captured from the Turks during the war between Turkey and Italy of 1911–12: *Cunfida* (ex-*Shipka*, 1892, two 14pdrs, 12.9 knots) and *Capitano Verri* (three 6pdrs, 10.5 knots).

Russia

Several steam yachts with colourful backgrounds entered Russian service. One was the G L Watson-designed *Surprise*. She had been built in 1896 by the Ailsa Shipbuilding Company of Troon. Of 1,144grt and powered by two four-cylinder, 448nhp engines, which drove two screws, this large vessel was named *Alberta* in 1899 when she became the royal yacht of King Leopold II of Belgium. She was registered in Britain, however, and managed on the king's behalf by Little and Johnson of London.

When Leopold died in 1909, *Alberta* was sold on and in 1915 came into the ownership of American businessman Frederick G Bourne, President of

* Named after his wife.

the Singer Manufacturing Company. Bourne was the original owner of Singer Castle on Dark Island in the Thousand Islands of the USA, which lie on the border of northern New York State (USA) and south-eastern Ontario (Canada). Bourne was an avid yachtsman and owned boats of all types and sizes, from small speedboats to large steam yachts. He was a member of several yacht clubs in the area, including the New York Yacht Club and the Seawanhaka-Corinthian Yacht Club, and in 1903 he was made Commodore of the NYYC, a position he would hold until 1905. His steam yacht *Delaware* was the flagship of the yacht club during most of his term as its commodore. She was 350ft long and had a crew of more than 100 men!

However, *Alberta* lasted only a year in his ownership before she appeared in naval guise as part of the Russian Arctic Ocean Flotilla under the name *Razsvet*. From here, she was seized by the Royal Navy in September 1918 and put to work as a despatch vessel, based at Dover and named HMY *Surprise*. The navy retained her until 1923, when she was sold to a private owner, before being taken up again in 1939.

Another G L Watson-designed yacht that found itself in the Russian Arctic Ocean Flotilla was *Lysistrata*. She had been built in 1901 by William Denny and Sons in Dumbarton as a 1,943grt, quadruple-expansion-engined steam yacht for James Gordon Bennet Jnr. Bennett was the publisher of the *New York Herald* (founded by his father) and a major league socialite, especially in the field of sports. *Inter alia* he organised both the first polo match and the first tennis match in the United States, created the

A model of James Gordon Bennett's yacht *Lysistrata* (1901) showing her beauty and the unusual squared bow of the G L Watson design. Atypically she had a single mast, stepped aft. *(© National Maritime Museum LO456)*

Gordon Bennett cup for international yachting, and personally won the first trans-oceanic yacht race. He sponsored explorers, including Henry Morton Stanley's trip to Africa to find Livingstone, and the ill-fated USS *Jeannette* attempt on the North Pole. Unstinting in his self-gratification, Bennett owned yachts, opulent private railroad cars, and lavish mansions. And he was the youngest commodore ever of the New York Yacht Club, taking office in 1870, aged 29.

Lysistrata (the heroine of a play by Aristophanes) had every luxury, was 314ft long and was fitted with twin screws for speed (she could make 19.5 knots) and manoeuvrability. Her crew numbered 100 and they were paid by Bennett to remain unshaven. For a figurehead, *Lysistrata* had a giant owl (Bennett's personal symbol), which concealed two searchlights behind

The owl figurehead for *Lysistrata*, which had searchlights behind the eyes. *(© National Maritime Museum P45224)*

its eyes. Among the yacht's many 'extras' were a Turkish bath and a full-time masseur (to ease the publisher's hangovers, perhaps). But the most eccentric feature was a soft padded cell with special seagoing fittings for the ship's cow, an Alderney, which supplied the sybarite's butter and the ingredients for his brandy milk punches at breakfast. *Lysistrata* cost Bennett £125,000.* He sold her in 1914, and she became part of the Imperial Russian Navy under the name of *Lyzystrada* (possibly also *Yaraslavna*), on patrol in the frozen north and armed with two 4in guns.

She briefly joined the RN in 1918, for just two weeks after being seized on 14 August 1918, before she was returned to the Russians and by 1920 she was employed in the Soviet Navy under the name *Vorovsky*, later becoming a fisheries protection vessel.

The Imperial Russian state yacht *Standart* was named after a famous frigate of Peter the Great. She was constructed in Copenhagen in 1895 by the Danish firm Burmeister-Wain and was a magnificent, black-hulled 5,557-ton yacht, measuring 401ft in length and 50ft beam, making her the largest private ship in the world at the time. *Standart* was also one of the fastest, with a design speed of 21 knots.

As large as a small cruiser, she combined elegance and comfort, a sort of floating palace. A large bowsprit, covered with gold leaf, projected forward from her bow and three masts towered over two white funnels. In summer, white canvas awnings stretched over the decks to shield the passengers from

* More than £12 million in 2022 money.

Russian royal yacht *Standart* at Yalta. *(Author's collection)*

the sun, and on the main deck was a huge dining saloon that could seat up to seventy-two guests at one long table. Below deck was a formal reception salon and drawing rooms panelled in mahogany, polished floors, brass and elegantly hung crystal chandeliers and velvet drapes. The yacht even had its own chapel for the private use of the Imperial Family.

When the Tsar was aboard, a large household staff attended to his needs, and her crew in such instances numbered around 275, with the sailors drawn from the Russian Imperial Navy. There was also a platoon of marines, a brass band and a balalaika orchestra.

And in case of trouble, although *Standart* always sailed in company with Russian naval units, she was armed with eight 47mm Hotchkiss guns.

When war came, she was laid up in a dry dock but with the demise of the Romanov dynasty in 1917 – and now renamed *Vosemnadtsate Martza* – she was in the hands of the Bolshevik forces. After another period laid up, in 1936 she was converted to a minelayer, *Marti*, in which guise she served in the Second World War. It was not until 1963 that *Standart* was finally scrapped.

In 1907, *Standart* had hit a rock and was damaged enough to require dock repairs. Her replacement for most of 1908 was a strange beast, *Almaz*, officially classified as an unprotected second-class cruiser but built as the official yacht of the Viceroy of the Russian Far East, Yevgeni Alekseyev. Launched in 1902, she was armed with four 3in and eight 2in guns and could make 19 knots. *Almaz* was at the Battle of Tsushima in 1905, as part

The peculiar interim Tsar's yacht *Almaz*. *(Author's collection)*

of the scout division, when the Russian Baltic Fleet was destroyed by Admiral Togo Heihachiro and his Japanese naval forces. *Almaz* was one of only three survivors to reach their intended destination, Vladivostok. Successfully evading Japanese patrols, she arrived at the port on 29 May, two days after the battle had commenced.

After her brief imperial career, she served as a despatch vessel and in 1915 was converted to a seaplane carrier, with seven 4.7in and four 3in weapons and four floatplanes carried on board. Was she ever a yacht? Well, she had that designation for a while and *Jane's Fighting Ships* so described her in 1919.

Portugal

Another royal yacht that also served a naval purpose was the Portuguese *Amélia IV*. She had been built as *Banshee* for Colonel Harry McCalmont by Ramage & Ferguson to designs by Cox and King. McCalmont was a British army officer, racehorse owner, yachtsman, member of the Royal Yacht Squadron and Conservative party member of parliament.

Launched in July 1900 by a 'Miss Lawson of London', she was sold to King Carlos I of Portugal in September the following year for service as a royal yacht. When not in royal use, she served as an oceanographic research vessel for the Portuguese Navy.

When the monarchy of Portugal was overthrown in 1910, *Amélia IV* transported the young king, Manuel II, to safety in Gibraltar and was subsequently named *Cinco de Outubro* by the new republic.

During the First World War, she was fitted with two 3pdrs and four 1pdr guns, used as an *aviso* (despatch vessel or scout) and remained in naval service until she was sold on in 1937.

France

France too operated several armed steam yachts. *Ibis* (1883) was a vessel of 254 tons built at Rochefort and used initially as a coastguard vessel. She carried two 2pdr guns and during the war was utilised as a second-class *aviso*.

Then there was *Jeanne Blanche*, an 820hp steel schooner of 420 tons. She was commissioned by Monsieur Rodolphe Faulquier, variously described as being a resident of Marseilles and Montpellier, built at La Seyne sur Mer and launched in 1894. The yacht carried 660 square metres of canvas, forty crewmen and was decorated internally with various exotic woods.

In November 1905, Faulquier bequeathed her to the state, intending that she be used as a presidential yacht, but instead *Jeanne Blanche* was sent to Constantinople for the use of the French ambassador there. Sometime in 1908 she became the *stationnaire** vessel at Constantinople, joining the iron screw yacht HMS *Imogene* (1882), originally the civilian *Strathendrick*, for the British, the armed yacht USS *Scorpion* (1896)† for the USA and *Loreley* (1885) of Germany.

* In Ottoman times ambassadors and their attached diplomatic staff were not immune from arbitrary arrest and imprisonment. When war broke out the diplomats of the warring country would put out to sea in their *stationnaire* yachts; the other use for them was as an entertainment centre for important guests and local dignitaries. The usual anchorage for these yachts was the bay of Therapia, halfway up the Bosphorus, facing the shore where the summer embassies of various European powers were sited.

† Upon America's entry into the First World War, *Scorpion* was interned at Constantinople from 15 November 1917 until 9 November 1918, despite the fact that the USA did not declare war on Turkey.

In 1913, *Jeanne Blanche* was rebuilt and converted into a patrol boat, classified as a second-class *aviso*. In this new guise she carried four 1pdr guns, could achieve 12 knots, and served in the Mediterranean for the duration of the war.

And then there was *Bacchante II*. Built as *Zaria* by Ramage & Ferguson in 1891, she was a 759grt vessel commissioned by Count Pavel Sergeyevich Stroganov. Described as a single-screw steam schooner, she had a three-cylinder, 165hp engine. Stroganov died in 1911 and she passed into the ownership of the French chocolate makers Menier. In February 1915, *Zaria* was taken over by the Admiralty, armed with two 12pdrs and renamed *Bacchante II*. Apparently, 'she is a box of electronic contrivances. When a line hanging by the bedstead is pulled, a bell rings continuously and the bed swings violently sideways. There is a bath on board that … does wonderful things but nobody so far has dared to have a bath in it.'[8] However, almost twelve months to the day after taking her up, the Royal Navy transferred her to the French and she disappeared from the record.

Another British yacht that ended up in the French Navy was *Medea* (1904). She was a 112grt steam yacht built by Alexander Stephen and Co. of Govan for William Macalister Hall, who owned Torrisdale Castle and estate near Campbeltown, in Scotland. By all accounts she was an attractive vessel, constructed in steel and with teak and quarter sawn oak woodwork and a two-cylinder compound engine that generated 30nhp, driving her at up to 10.5 knots. As such she was ideally suited for social and hunting trips around the isles and lochs of the western Scottish coast.

She seems briefly to have passed through the hands of aviation pioneer Claude Grahame-White but by 1915 was back at the Stephen's yard. However, in 1917 the French Navy purchased *Medea*, classified her as a gunboat, renamed her *Corneille* (crow), and fitted her with a 75mm (~3in) gun, depth charges and an observation balloon. In this guise, she operated as an escort for slow, often sail-only, convoys until the end of the war, when she reverted to her original name and British registry.*

Ninian B Stewart's second yacht of the name, *Maria II* (1896), was designed by Watson's, 217ft long with electric lights, four boats, two steam launches and, *inter alia*, an oak-panelled dining room. Purchased in 1902 by American Frederick Gilbert Bourne, fifth president of the Singer Manufacturing Company, she acted as the flagship of the New York Yacht Club between 1903 and 1905 as *Delaware* and again 1911–12 as *Diana*. However, she was sold to the Russian Navy and served on the side of the White Russians from 1918 as Russia collapsed into civil war. The French seized her to prevent the vessel falling into the hands of the Bolsheviks and she then became the flagship of the French Navy's admiral commanding in the Levant, surviving to fight again in the 1939–40 war.

Additionally, the RN also passed over to France HMY *Ariane* (1898), as will be related in the next chapter.

Across the warring nations, steam yachts played their part.

* In the Second World War, *Medea* was again pressed into use with a balloon, this time as a barrage balloon vessel in the mouth of the Thames. She survived the conflict, went to the USA, and was eventually restored and presented to the San Diego Maritime Museum.

CHAPTER TEN

SERVICE ABOARD

WHAT WAS IT LIKE to serve on the steam yachts at war?

First of all, the vessels had to be 'navalised' and armed before they could enter service. Commander Ernest George Henry Brady RNR collected *Rosabelle* at Wivenhoe in February 1915 (see Chapter 4) and immediately sailed her to Marrim's Yard at Cowes on the Isle of Wight. He reported to his brother Noel that 'the Portsmouth dockyard is so busy that all the arrived yachts are having alterations etc done by contract at the various big yacht yards. I am in clover over here but can get little work done as we are the last comer and earlier arrivals are getting attention first. Also labour is so scarce.' One of the reasons for his 'being in clover' was perhaps the fact that: 'I have received a card from the Committee of the Royal Yacht Squadron today making me an honorary member of the club during my stay at Cowes. As the club is about the most exclusive in the world I feel honoured.'[1] Additionally, his wife had come to stay with him on the yacht while it was worked on.

Rosabelle eventually received her guns at Portsmouth but having commissioned her, Brady was transferred to another steam yacht, *Ariane*. She had been built as *Sheelah** in 1898 by Clydebank Engineering and Shipbuilding Co. Ltd. Of 447grt, she had a three-cylinder compound engine of 63nhp driving a single screw and had been ordered by William A Donaldson of Duntocher, Dumbartonshire, who was a director of the iron merchants James Watson and Co.

In 1901, the yacht was acquired by a Frenchman, Gaston Menier (inheritee of his father's chocolate and industrial empire), who registered her in Rouen and by some route she came into the hands of the Admiralty in February 1915. Brady felt both were good patrol vessels: 'I don't know yet which ship I will have on patrol, but it will be *Ariane* or *Rosabelle*. They are equally good. The *Rosabelle* is the faster but the *Ariane* is the better gunned and has a good searchlight too. As I have fitted out (and will have commissioned both) I am about equally attached to both, and whichever I have will be content. I feel and believe I am going to have my chance.'[2]

In fact, Brady went back to *Rosabelle* and patrol duty around the Scillies and the Cornish coast, and *Ariane* was returned to France on 25 February the following year. As winter approached, *Rosabelle* moved to a punishing routine of four days out on patrol followed by two in port. In October

* Not to be confused with Admiral Beatty's yacht of the same name.

1915, there was a refit at Falmouth during which *Rosabelle*'s three Hotchkiss 6pdrs were to be replaced by heavier guns. Brady was 'quite satisfied with the old armament but have to accept the new arrangement'.[3]

And in December, Brady received a missive from *Rosabelle*'s owner, Theodore Pim, who had paid a visit to his yacht while Brady was away; Pim wrote: 'I hope that they make you comfortable on board my little ship; we are very fond of the *Rosabelle* and have done many thousand miles in her, and hope if you bring her home not too much gone to pieces, that we may yet get another cruise in her, but all this depends on the war, which I am sorry to say shows no sign of ending.'[4] How Brady felt about such pleading is not recorded.

Commanding a patrol yacht in a British winter required a great deal of stamina. Leonard Charles Cockrell was a 50-year-old master mariner who was skipper of the steam yacht *Vanessa* when war broke out.

Vanessa had been designed by G L Watson and built by Ramage & Ferguson in 1899 as *Golden Eagle* of 356grt. Her first owner was Sir Samuel E Scott Bt, Conservative MP for Marylebone West. In 1907, he sold her to Arthur Salvin Bowlby of Knoydart in Scotland and Gilston Park near Harlow, quondam High Sheriff of Hertfordshire, who renamed her *Vanessa*. Bowlby was still her owner when hostilities commenced.

Vanessa (1899) in her initial guise of *Golden Eagle*, photographed in 1900. *(Author's collection)*

On 15 October 1914 she was requisitioned by the Admiralty and nine days later Cockrell joined the RNR as a sub lieutenant and second in command of his old vessel and the whole crew volunteered to sail in her. She was fitted with two 6pdr guns, an amount of armour plate and, with a new captain, retired Rear Admiral Evelyn Robert Le Marchant, sailed to Stornoway. Fifty-eight-year-old Le Marchant had retired from the navy in 1913 but immediately volunteered to become yet another dug out.

On 21 January 1915, Cockrell was promoted to lieutenant commander and the following day took over from Le Marchant, once again captain of his own ship. He was not only responsible for the yacht but also for a number of trawlers and drifters, variously used for examination purposes, anti-submarine work or net barrier management. It was a demanding role, and occasionally exasperating, as his personal log entry for 25 July shows: 'Proceeded patrol with *Lily Melling*. *Noogana* standing by net drifters all nets out one drifter hanging on lee end. Disposition *Vanessa*, *Lizzie Melling*, *Noogana*, *Champion*, *Vonemara*, *W J R* at Flannans. *Princess Alice*, *Bush*, at Butt. *Calliope* and *Caldy* at St Kilda. *Cardiff Castle* – Carloway. *Celandine* don't know where.'[5*] *Celandine* was an armed drifter, which seemed to have drifted.

In the six-month period from taking command to the end of July, Cockrell had just one ten-day period of home leave, despite the awful weather conditions that continually battered his ships. His was obviously a very tough character.

Tedium and Fear

The quotidian nature of the daily patrols can be seen by the following extract from the log of HMY *Atalanta*. In 1915, she was based at Milford Haven, patrolling in the Irish Sea. Her log for three days in August reveals the non-stop but dull nature of her routine:

26 August 1915
0400: Gentle breeze, moderate sea and swell, fine, clear and dry
0800: Fine
0925: Altered course to escort SS *Comanchee* [oil tanker steamer, from Texas to Manchester. It was common at this stage in the war for individual ships to be escorted through dangerous areas by a single escort.]
Noon: Passed Norwegian steamship outward
1600: Moderate breeze and sea, misty and fine
1700: Crew exercised at torpedo attack, boat stations and fire
2000: Fine, hazy
2130: Passed three trawlers
Midnight: Fine and clear

27 August 1915
0200: Passed three trawlers
0400: Fresh breeze, moderate sea and swell, fine and clear

* There was no such vessel as *Vonemara*, which must be a spelling mistake. The author has corrected two other errors in the original.

0800: Fine
0930: Passed SS *Sotero*, Palermo to Liverpool
1055: Altered course to signal steamer
Noon: Fine and clear
1500: Passed tramp steamer 1600: Gentle breeze, slight sea, fine, clear and dry
1635: Cleared steamer *Kilnsea*, gave reports
2000: Two trawler patrol steering SSE. Fine, hazy, sea smooth
Midnight: Fine and clear

28 August 1915
0130: SS *Beacon* sighted, passed and hailed [presumably to ask where bound and where from]
0350: Reduced to ½ speed to pass ships
0400: Light wind, slight sea, overcast, fine and clear
0500: Hailed SS *Vasconia* Swedish steamer [presumably to ask where bound and where from]
0800: Fine, cloudy
1000: Passed three trawlers
Noon: Fine and clear
1340: Liner American Line passed bearing NNE
1440: Passed two armed trawlers bearing south
1600: Light wind, slight sea, overcast
1710: Passed HMY *Valiant*
1830: Passed fleet of trawlers mine sweeping
1900: Passed patrol trawler
1945: Passed two trawler patrols
2000: Fine, hazy
2140: Passed two trawlers
Midnight: Overcast and hazy.[6]

But, of course, danger always lurked. A U-boat might suddenly spring to the surface, or a floating mine might bob into view.

Or consider *Hersilia*, which was part of a patrol group comprising four yachts and four armed trawlers. Sub Lieutenant Charles Evans later recalled that their standard operating method was: 'We are well spread out in a line from Triumpan Head to Ru Steer, right across the Minch and thus we wearily patrol night and day, yachts and trawlers at their respective stations.'[7]

Harry Chadwick-Smith in *Zoraide* thought that the routine of patrolling the North Sea was generally 'a tedious job'. *Zoraide* operated in a 200 square mile stretch of water that had been mined by both the British and the German navies. 'Our job was to patrol along the edge of one of the mine fields and keep a sharp look out for trouble,' he later recalled. 'These mines … would come popping up like corks especially after stormy weather.'[8] When this happened, things became a little less tedious. Before destroying the mine, the crew were required to note the type and number. This meant sending a boat's crew to look at it, armed with boat hooks to sweep away the sea detritus that covered the necessary information. As Chadwick-Smith recalled: 'It was no joke prodding a mine … with boat hooks in an attempt to remove the seaweed or scrape away the barnacles, for the least touch … would have meant curtains for the boat crew.'[9]

On one occasion it was decided to despatch a mine by gunfire from the vessel's main armament, and to ensure a good hit the Gunnery Petty Officer decided on a close-range engagement. But his shell only hit the horn of the German mine and it went off spectacularly, showering the crew with shrapnel, dead fish, seaweed and other fruits of the sea. Chadwick-Smith felt that the GPO was not a popular figure after that.

'By Construction Entirely Unfitted for the Service'

Like their companions in the auxiliary forces of the various navies with which they served, the steam yachts had not been designed for war. Those who sailed in them in time of conflict must have pictured them beforehand as graceful pleasure craft, immaculate with white paint and gleaming brightwork, spotless decks and awnings and pillowed wicker chairs on the after deck. They were the province of the rich and aristocratic and they frequented upper-class social gatherings. Steam yachts bejewelled the summer seas, in sparkling harbours or at regattas bright with flags, where wealth and fashion met.

War changed all this. Ensign Joseph Husband USNRF, a reservist volunteer like so many who sailed in these makeshift warships, noted the transformation that took place. 'As the months passed there was soon a noticeable change of aspect, soft white decks became torn and dented by hobnailed boots and the heavy gear which was hauled over them. Long rows of depth charges, ash-can-like cylinders charged each with three hundred pounds of high explosive filled the graceful curve of their fantails. Squat Y-guns, heavy mortars to discharge simultaneously two depth charges, one on either side of the vessel, crowded the hand steering gear on the after deck. Saloon windows repeatedly shattered by heavy seas, or the detonation of the guns and depth charges, were boarded up. Below decks similar changes appeared in worn and battered furnishings repeatedly stained by sea water straining through leaking decks.'[10]

It should be borne in mind that the steam yachts requisitioned by any navy were originally designed for the comfort of their owners. They were, by and large, elegant floating palaces and not necessarily equipped and constructed to meet naval demands. If, for example, the weather on a particular routing was unpleasant, the owner or skipper could choose not to sail or to travel by a different course. This was not an option for the yachts in naval service. They had to go where they were ordered and required, regardless of the sea state.

They were also 'by construction entirely unfitted for the service'[11] and

USS *Lydonia*, rolling in a heavy sea; the scant protection offered to her crew is obvious. *(US Naval History and Heritage Command NH 46887)*

uncomfortable to serve in. For Ensign Husband, sailing in them required 'clinging to an open bridge in seas so heavy that they were constantly drenched with bucketfuls of spray' while 'the officers of the escorting yachts watched their plunging charges wallow in the sliding seas, now lost to sight behind a cresting wave, now pitched high against the sky, half-bared propellers churning the sea. There were interminable nights of anxiety when the convoy scattered in the blackness and four thousand-ton freighters were running wild in a wilder sea; invisible, ungovernable leviathans, careening far out of their courses, liable without warning to loom out of the darkness high above the bridge of a yacht reeling on the flank or in the rear of the convoy.'[12]

For Charles Evans, patrol work in the Minch was difficult given the prevailing sea condition in the area. The Minch 'is a troubled sea,' thought Evans, 'O this Minch, I am sick of it.'[13] He rather despaired of the ceaseless patrolling; 'I fancy that the rest of my service will be just patrolling and so I shall be heartily glad when the war is over and I can return to my peaceful avocations.'[14] On 27 December 1914, he and *Hersilia* were caught in a terrible storm, the vessel could make no headway against the wind and two big waves broke into the aft saloon, causing the yacht to ship 'tons of water'.[15] He had to sleep under a rubber sheet as the deck above his head leaked and pools of water would develop on his recumbent form.

Then on 6 January the following year, *Hersilia* made a 90-mile run from Oban to Stornoway with a tearing south-easterly wind behind and foresail and trysails set: 'She was rolling like the pigs in the home pond,' Evans remembered.[16]

The perils of weather are evidenced by the travails of the large yacht *Atalanta* (see also Chapter 3 and above). She was a 1,303grt steam yacht of 1903, designed by Cox and King and built by Ramage & Ferguson at Leith, 269ft in length with a 33ft beam. Driven by three Parsons steam turbines producing 650nhp, *Atalanta* could cruise at 18 knots and was one of the largest and fastest steam yachts of her era.

In June 1915 she was taken up by the Royal Navy, fitted with two 3in guns and sent for patrol duty at Milford Haven under the command of Captain Robert Stevenson Dalton Cuming RNR.* But in November she was allocated to the Gibraltar station and on the 12th was on passage and crossing the Bay of Biscay when she ran into a heavy storm, one that in peacetime her crew would probably have tried to avoid.

At 0400, *Atalanta*'s log recorded 'wind and sea increasing, lurching and shipping water fore and aft', which by 0730 had reached 'Strong gale. Heavy confused sea, shipping water'. By 1130 her captain turned her head into the wind but some two hours later the log noted that she had 'shipped sea and smashed deck house on starboard side. Stave in port lifeboat, injured three men, cuts. A door and six shutters, starboard and alley, smashed in and other damage. Electric circuit for navigation and engine room lights failed, oil lamps in inaccessible room on account of seas. Brought ship to wind and reduced pressure.' This was a vessel that had problems.

The storm continued. At 1700 she was rolling her heart out; 'extreme roll: 50° port, 39° starboard', and between 1700 and 2030 'more damage done to port alley. Captain's bath turned over. Room pretty well wrecked. Two windows smashed. Wheel gear jammed, put into hand gear.' Then

* Sixty-three-year-old Cuming had retired from the navy in 1907 with the rank of rear admiral and had advanced to admiral on the retired list before he was reactivated and given a commission in the RNR.

Noma in bad weather. The precarious position of the depth charges perched on her stern can be seen clearly. *(US Naval History and Heritage Command NH 44876)*

SUBJECT: NUMBER AU
165-WW 335C22
Central News Photo Ser.
PHOTOGRAPHER
July 1, 1918 REC'D
1918 TAKEN
P.N. 9228
DESCRIPTION:
AM AMERICAN AUXILLARY WAR vessel weathering an Atlantic "blow". The vessel is the converted steam yacht "Christobel" and is representative of a type of ship that is performing heroic service.
ISSUED:
NOTES:

An American Central News Service press release and photo of *Christabel* in an Atlantic storm. *(Author's collection)*

'tremendous seas and confused with hard rain and hail squalls, wind hauling to northward in same'.

She was being smashed up, the bridge steering was out of order and at midnight she was still 'shipping heavy water'. The next day brought no respite; among the log entries were '0130, port lifeboat washed away. Davits bent down flush with deck. Aft boxes smashed. 0400, hard squalls with hail and rain. Heavy and high confused sea. Shipping much water.' At 0600, 'aft lazarette* covers washed adrift. Place full with water, also cabins and saloon, great damage. Crew pumping out the same.'[17]

The storm did not ease until 0800, by which time her crew had endured over twenty-four hours of fear and destruction and the yacht was badly damaged in all areas. That they survived at all is a tribute to their seamanship and resilience.

This was not an uncommon experience. Out in the waters of the White Sea, Able Seaman J G 'Happy' Sadd of *Sagitta* told his diary 'about 0200 she dived into an exceptionally heavy sea and broke one of the bow windows in the smoke room. These are three eighths inch plate glass. Rocky says he thought the bridge and all were going. The smoke room was inundated. The hands rigging the weather screen received violent electric shocks. The whole time we have been shipping heavy water over the counter which she dips frequently.'[18]

* A lazarette is usually a storage locker used for gear or equipment.

And always in the background was the threatening menace of the invisible U-boat, although many sailors came to consider them a secondary concern when on routine escort duty, especially coastal convoys. One USN yacht sailor confided to his diary that: 'We have long since learned that our most dangerous enemy is not the submarine. First it is the fog. Secondly rocks and perhaps mines.'[19]

Stress and Strain

Such service in the patrol yachts was very demanding, especially on the officers. Forty-seven-year-old Commander Ernest Brady in *Rosabelle* was feeling the strain by October 1915, writing to his brother that: 'I am … having an acute attack of sciatica and rheumatism, which is annoying and has upset our plans.'[20] By January the next year, Brady was worn out and his eyesight was deteriorating. He requested a quieter posting but was instead sent as second in command of the trawler forces of the Dover Patrol, in the rank of acting captain from 1917. He never recovered from the strain and died in 1929 a defeated man. His local paper reported at the time that 'the Armistice found him sadly strained and broken in health and with increasing eye trouble. He returned to Weston to take up his old work, and he entered with enthusiasm into the work of reorganisation at the Pier. But his eyesight grew worse, and notwithstanding all that medical science could do, he felt constrained to relinquish his post in 1925. He then moved to Henfield, Sussex, to be near his family, where he has since lived.'[21]

Commander John Jackson, last noted in Chapter 9 in command of the steam yacht HMAS *Una*, went down with malaria in late 1916 and became seriously ill, so much so that he was taken into hospital and discharged from *Una* on 30 November. It was not until March 1917 that he was well enough to return to Britain and in July he took command of a surveying trawler, *Daisy*, based at Dover.

However, on several occasions when back in port, Jackson called on a local doctor to seek help for recurring bouts of depression and dizziness, a function of his severe malarial fever. Each time he returned to his ship when he felt able to continue.

On 7 March 1918, while *Daisy* was at sea, Jackson seemed to be particularly depressed. Turning to his second in command, he told him to carry on and went below. About two hours later a shot rang out and Jackson's body was found with a wound to the head. He died within a few minutes in the chart room, brought down by depression and the fear that he would never recover from the dreadful tropical disease he carried around with him. John Metcalf Jackson was buried at St James' Cemetery, Dover, another brave man shattered by the war.

'Disrated Admirals'

As has been noted, many commanders of the armed yachts were retired RN officers and not a few were quondam admirals. This could lead to some testy encounters, such as that described in *The Spectator* magazine in 1916. 'As everyone knows, some of our most sporting admirals without employment have become captains RNR so as not to be out of the scrap, and may be seen, in command of patrol yachts and other ships, wearing the twisted stripes of the Reserve. One of these sportsmen came into a certain port with his yacht, and wished to see the Senior Naval Officer, a captain RN. He called at his office and was received by an old three-badge [Royal] Marine, messenger and general factotum to the SNO. This worthy, having put the whilom Admiral in the waiting-room, leisurely announced to the SNO, who was very busy, that an RNR officer wished to see him. He then went back and watched that same RNR getting more and more restless. (We do not, as a rule, keep Admirals waiting overmuch in this Service.) After a bit the fuming and blowing of his guest seem to have impressed him, and he returned to the SNO, and, standing in front of his table, solemnly got this remark off his chest "If you please, Sir, would yer see that there RNR, as I surmises 'e's one of them disrated admirals!"'[22]

As illustrated in Chapter 5, a considerable number of retired naval officers came forward for service, much advanced in age. Officers were retired at age 60 (or before). Median age at death for males in the UK was 60 in 1914. So many of these retirees were – quite literally – living on borrowed time. But their integrity, bravery and patriotism shone through nonetheless.

Visitors

The first large American troopships 'reached the coast of France on 10 November 1917'[23] and Brest soon became the major terminal for disembarkment of the incoming American soldiery and the headquarters of the US naval command. And it wasn't long before the troopships began to deliver special 'visiting firemen' as well. 'There were cabinet members on official missions. There were committees of the Senate and of House of Representatives. There were government officials and diplomats of the various Allied countries as well as those of our own land. There were agents of every branch of war work connected with the transportation of a vast army from American to French soil.'[24]

President Wilson's confrere Colonel House arrived on 7 December, in company with Admiral W S Benson, Chief of Naval Operations, and General Tasker H Bliss, Chief of Staff of the Army. On 10 March, Newton D Baker, Secretary of War, visited and Franklin D Roosevelt, Assistant Secretary of the Navy, came in the summer of 1918. Various other secretaries and assistant secretaries made landfall, as did a number of senators and congressmen. Two such gained a deeply personal insight into the dangers of the voyage. Senator J Hamilton Lewis and Congressman Thomas D Schall were returning from Brest to the USA on board USS *Mount Vernon* when, on 5 September 1918, she was torpedoed by *U-82*. 'Senator Lewis hastened on deck and distinguished himself by helping to care for the sick and wounded who were on board … [and] a special tribute was paid to the pluck and courage displayed by Mrs. Schall, the only woman on the ship at the time of the attack. She remained perfectly calm, her one thought being for the safety of her husband who is entirely blind.'[25] The ship survived and returned to Brest for dry dock and repair.

In August 1918, French President Poincaré, accompanied by the Minister of Marine, the Chief of Staff of the French Army, and a number of officers of the French Army and Navy, came to Brest on a special train to the Headquarters of the United States Navy in France.

Bishop McCormick, of the Episcopal Church of Western Michigan, delivered an address to naval men at the Carola Barracks. Among other religious leaders who came to Brest were Bishop Wilson of the Methodist Episcopal Church, Bishop Perry, Bishop Brest and Rabbi Wise. And in the long list of visitors, there were two women; the redoubtable Miss Kathleen Burke, the British-American philanthropist and war worker, and Irene Franklin, American actress of stage and screen, vaudeville comedian and singer.

No doubt all these travellers felt they were doing good; and equally, they were probably resented by those trying to do an already difficult job with limited time to spare.

A Different Sort of Visitor

The presence of so many young men, alone and far from home, often sexually naïve, brought with it another visitor, but a most unwelcome one – venereal disease,* an affliction for which, if of the syphilitic variety, there was at the time no reliable cure with madness the likely end result (*dementia paralytica*).

At the USN bases of Saint-Nazaire, and later Brest, a certain sort of French woman became a clear source of trouble. Prostitution was rife and rates of venereal disease skyrocketed: 'To the Americans it was innocence defiled. By mid-Autumn 1917, the costs of vice had become so pronounced that both the US Army and US Navy forbade their people from openly consorting with French women on pain of non-judiciary punishment or worse.'[26]

Nor were the British immune from this problem. At Le Havre, the brothels were concentrated in the Rue de Galions, first class for officers, second class for other ranks. Lieutenant Dennis Wheatley RFA, estimated that 'hundreds of French women plied the most ancient of all trades' there from midday onwards.[27] Personnel reporting with VD would have their home leave stopped; nonetheless, the British Army treated 153,531 cases on the Western Front alone.[28]

The problem had reached such epidemic levels that in 1918 an Inter-Allied Conference on venereal disease was convened at the behest of the Dominion governments, and Sir George Sydenham Clarke, Lord Sydenham, was appointed as Chairman of a Royal Committee on Venereal Disease 1918. In both the US and British forces, the navy and army's

* Nowadays more generally known as STDs.

concern was not one based on morality but, as General Sir Henry Rawlinson, commander of the Fourth Army of the British Expeditionary Force, put it, because 'venereal disease removes men from the firing line'.[29]

Prizes and Salvage

There were some perquisites to serving in the Royal Navy, and one of them was prize and salvage monies.

During the First World War, and for centuries beforehand, Royal Navy warships received prize bounty money for the sinking or capture of enemy ships (until August 1918). Warships and auxiliaries also received salvage money for saving ships, cargoes and ships' boats. Fifteen Royal Navy yachts gained salvage money, some multiple times and one, *Lorna*, was given prize money for sinking a U-boat (see Appendix 4 for a full list). For a U-boat the Admiralty adopted the practice of paying firstly £500, then later £1,000 to be divided among the crew. Such largesse continued until August 1918, when the Naval Prize Act changed the system such that the prize money was paid into a common fund from which a payment was made to all naval personnel whether or not they were involved in an action.

Salvage payment was a less clear-cut position. Technically, it had not been the practice to pay salvage awards to the 'servants of the Crown for services rendered in that capacity in connection with the salvage of His Majesty's ships or of ships at the risk of His Majesty's Government or of an Allied Government'.[30] However, there were exceptions to this rule, more generously applied in wartime, and where a salvage award was 'made to the Admiralty on behalf of the Crown, for services rendered by the Admiralty, and their servants, in connection with the salvage of vessels ... the Admiralty in turn make awards to their servants'.[31]

But the amount of money passed on to the crews varied and led to questions as to the fairness of such awards being asked in the House of Commons, such as in April 1919. The answer given on behalf of the Admiralty was that 'the proportion of the award made to the Admiralty on behalf of the Crown which is retained by the Admiralty does not, in general, exceed three-fourths, and varies according to the extent to which the personal efforts of the salvors have contributed to the success of the salvage'.[32]

The case of the non-payment of salvage money to the yacht *Corycia* for her salvage of SS *Kentucky* was noted in Chapter 6. On 6 June 1919, this issue was raised in parliament by Gershom Stewart, MP for The Wirral. He 'asked the First Lord of the Admiralty whether the Danish steamer *Kentucky* was salved near Fraserburgh by naval ratings in December 1914; whether the ship and cargo were valued on leaving New York at £180,000; whether any salvage money was earned by the salvors'.[33]

Dr Thomas Macnamara, Parliamentary Secretary for the Admiralty, patiently replied that 'the Danish steamer *Kentucky* was salved by a party from His Majesty's yacht *Corycia*. The value was reported to be as stated. The Admiralty did not allow a claim to be made, as the *Kentucky* at the time was being sent to Leith under the charge of a naval armed guard for her cargo to be examined. In these circumstances, it was considered undesirable to add a naval claim for salvage.' On the more general point of the Admiralty's desire or otherwise to pay, he noted that 'the matter is by Statute one for the discretion of the Admiralty, but in general claims by the crews of naval vessels are allowed if the salvors are considered to have rendered any special service over and above their ordinary duty of assisting ships in distress and their special duty of protecting the property of the Crown'.[34]

So it would appear that it was the Admiralty that stood to gain most from its servants' efforts.

Nonetheless, any such award must have been most welcome and a prize distribution of £1,000 was a windfall to crews, even if the proportion that ratings were allotted was less than that retained by the ship's officers. Such a sum would equate to between £40,000 and £70,000 today.*

* Depending on which measure of inflation is used.

CHAPTER ELEVEN

AFTER THE ARMISTICE

WAS THE DEPLOYMENT of armed steam yachts in both the 1898 and the 1914–18 wars a successful naval gambit or a flawed piece of strategy?

In 1898, it is debatable whether the USN could have mounted the blockade of Cuba without the purchased yachts. As Milan Vego has noted: 'A US landing on Cuba was possible only if command of the Caribbean and Western Atlantic was obtained by the US Navy. A naval blockade of the island was eventually to starve out the Spanish garrison and a US invasion … [would] greatly speed up the collapse of Spanish power … [but] the US Navy was able to obtain command of the sea only by destroying or immobilising the Spanish naval forces. Until that was achieved, it was too risky for the US to send its transports to sea at all.'[1] The steam yachts allowed this to happen, and the pleasure boat warships distinguished themselves in action, taking part in coastal raids, shelling of land targets and engaging with Spanish warships. They acquitted themselves well.

The primary adversary of the patrol yachts in the First World War was the submarine. Only one RN yacht – *Lorna* – sunk a U-boat, although one – *Diane* – was given a share of a sinking. No USN yacht probably destroyed one, although several claims were made. But this is to ignore the fact that the presence of the yachts, whether escorting convoys later in the war, leading auxiliary patrol groups of trawlers or on single- or multi-ship patrols, would have had a deterrent effect and forced U-boats to remain under water, exhausting the batteries and time on station. We cannot really know the cumulative impact of the yachts' presence.

Further, at the beginning of the war, and in 1917 when the Americans joined in, neither the RN or the USN had a sufficient number of patrol or escort vessels. Yachts <u>had</u> to suffice, despite their manifold imperfections as related in this book. And they were still being pressed into service as convoy escorts at the end of the war.

For the USN, defence of the American coastline was a domestic priority. US and foreign ships were sunk by U-boats off the United States' eastern seaboard. But only one so-called assault on US territory took place when, on 21 July 1918, *U-156* 'attacked' Orleans, Massachusetts. Two people were taken to hospital, a tugboat was damaged and a schooner and three barges were sunk. But in fact, the incident had never been intended as a territorial raid. The submarine had fired on a small convoy of barges led by the tug off the coast of the Cape Cod peninsula. Several shells missed their intended targets and fell instead around Orleans, giving the impression of a deliberate attack on the town. Otherwise, the coastal patrols, in which the yachts were prominent, played a major role in keeping the littoral safe from raiding.

The majority of crews in both RN and USN yachts were reservists or volunteers. Their translation from peace to war, on vessels not intended for that purpose, was often an abrupt one. But they performed well, in the main, endured their privations and – for the original yacht crews – the misfortune of seeing their beautiful, well-cared for, craft reduced to near ruin by the war's end.

Their service, and that of the other sailors in the Auxiliary Patrol's vessels, was recognised in the House of Lords when in late 1917, Earl Curzon, Lord President of the Council, spoke: 'Equally wonderful is the record of the auxiliary naval services, which have been expanded to an extraordinary degree to meet the changes that have occurred in maritime warfare by the development of the mine and the submarine. I allude more especially to the mine-sweepers and the patrol vessels … They are out in all weathers, day and night … patrolling the coastal routes, escorting merchant traffic, hunting the enemy submarines. It is impossible to imagine a more arduous or a more dangerous duty.'[2]

If the yachts and their sailors were not a total success, they were certainly not a failure.

Royal Navy Yachts from November 1918

The Royal Navy quickly disposed of its 159 steam yachts; by the end of 1919 there were very few left in service; *Caerolite*, hired in 1918, carried on with miscellaneous duties until 1920. *Corycia* (see Chapter 6) continued as a salvage vessel until she was sold in June 1920. And *Assegai* (1876), a small (78grt) vessel, was purchased by the Admiralty in 1915 and used as a tug at Portsmouth from March 1918 until her sale in November 1921.

Another yacht that ended the war as a tug was *Mairi* (1911). A smaller type of gentleman's yacht (65grt, 80ft long), she had been taken up in in August 1914 and fitted with a single 3pdr. At some point the Admiralty purchased her and from March 1918 *Mairi* was operated as a naval tug.

Her story is distinctive for two reasons. Firstly, her commanding officer from December 1918 to March 1919 was Lieutenant James Courtenay Keith Wright RNVR DSC, known as 'Shiner'. He had been second in command to Lieutenant Percy Dean in the motor launch *ML-282* during the Zeebrugge raid of 23 April 1918, in which Dean won the Victoria Cross and Wright distinguished himself for his bravery under fire.

During the action 'Shiner' had been wounded in the stomach. Taken to a hospital ship, the steam yacht *Liberty*, the doctors pronounced that he would not live. In an action that demonstrated the better side of raid commander Vice Admiral Roger Keyes' nature, he phoned First Sea Lord 'Rosy' Wemyss and asked him to request of the king an immediate grant of a DSC to Wright, so that he could be decorated before his death. This was done. But Wright refused to die and made a full recovery. *Mairi* was his first command following his discharge from medical care.

Secondly, *Mairi* carried within her the seeds that would help sound the death knell of the steam yacht as a class. She had been built by Ritchie, Graham and Milne of Glasgow for the Marquis of Graham, Commodore James Graham, later 6th Duke of Montrose. Graham had been instrumental in founding the Royal Navy Volunteer Reserve (RNVR) in 1903, and served in the Auxiliary Naval Service during the conflict. But he was also a talented engineer and a director of William Beardmore and Company of Dalmuir. And the power plant fitted to his yacht was a 130bhp semi-diesel* manufactured by Beardmores. She was not a steam yacht in the historical sense; the internal combustion engine was becoming more useful for marine purposes – and here it was in a yacht. Or as she was in 1918, a tug. She was sold out of the service in August 1919.

Adele (1906), 228grt, was purchased in 1915 by the Australia Government for £21,500, from the estate of Henry Dutton of Kapunda, South Australia. Dutton was a wealthy farmer and landowner and a member of the Royal Australian Yacht Club. *Adele* had bulwarks of steel, neatly panelled with teak and so arranged that they could be taken down when the yacht was laid up. She was fitted with steam and hand-steering gear, teak and brass mounted. The masts and bowsprit were of Oregon pine and the yacht was rigged as a schooner. There were eight cabins neatly lined with polished hard woods, each containing lockers and drawers, dressing tables and wardrobes; the wash basins had a hot and cold water supply. Built by Hawthorn, Leslie and Co., *Adele* had a guaranteed speed of 11.5 knots on a measured mile, and 11 knots for six hours.

On 14 September 1915 she was commissioned into the RAN as HMAS *Franklin* and served as a tender to the Royal Australian Naval College until 1921, when she was gifted to the Administrator of Papua New Guinea, serving there until 1929. She continued to operate in various roles until sunk in 1943.

* The semi-diesel engine is not a true diesel, as it does not rely on high compression. In such engines, a bulb in the combustion chamber is heated to near red heat, usually with a kerosene torch. The engine has a manual pump that sprays fuel through a nozzle in the combustion chamber against the heated area. As the engine is turned against compression, the pump is activated, and the sprayed fuel ignites. This in turn creates pressure in the combustion chamber against the piston, thus starting the engine.

Dotterel, aka HMY *Dotter*, as painted by Antonio de Simone. *(Author's collection)*

Dotterel as photographed immediately pre-war. *(Author's collection)*

Then there was the hired yacht *Ironsides*, which lasted to March 1920, and *Triad* (met in Chapter 4), which carried on until May 1933.

Dotterel was an iron screw steam yacht designed and built by Ramage & Ferguson at Leith in 1887. Registered at 165grt, she measured 119½ft in length with a 20ft beam and was powered by one of Ramage's own three-cylinder engines. *Dotterel* had been ordered by one Charles Combe, but in 1908 she was purchased by Sir Richard Garton of Lyth Hill, Haslemere, Surrey, a wealthy philanthropist and owner of Mambré and Garton, sugar refiners to the brewing industry. Garton, who in 1912 had established the Garton Foundation for the study of international relations, also founded the British Empire Cancer Campaign and donated large sums of money to their work, and he was a member of the Royal Thames Yacht Club.

He was still *Dotterel*'s owner when war broke out but it was not until 1918 that the Admiralty hired his yacht as a tender, renamed her *Dotter*, and subsequently purchased her in 1919, disposing of her three years later, in June 1922.

And finally, there was *Mlada*. She was originally launched as *Margarita II* in 1900, a large (1,780grt) vessel designed by G L Watson and built by Scott and Co. of Greenock for Anthony Joseph Drexel Junior (see Chapter 1) and named after his wife. In 1910 she was acquired by Charles Henry Alexander Paget, 6th Marquess of Anglesey, and became *Semiramis*, and three years later by Russian Princess Eugenie Schahovskoy-Gleboff-Strechneff and registered in Petrograd.

In 1917, *Semiramis* was somehow transferred to the Russian government, for use as a despatch vessel for the Russian Navy's Arctic Ocean Flotilla, based at St Petersburg. Due to the revolution she sought refuge in Britain, where in August 1918 she was taken over by the Royal Navy and renamed *Mlada*. She saw brief service as an armed boarding vessel before recommissioning in mid-1919 as HMS *Alacrity*, the yacht and despatch vessel of the Commander in Chief Far East, based in Hong Kong, thus providing

Margarita II as *Semiramis*, designed by G L Watson and owned from 1910 to 1913 by the Marquess of Anglesey, seen off Cowes around 1912. *(Author's collection)*

luxurious accommodation for both Vice Admiral Sir Frederick C T Tudor and Admiral Sir Alexander L Duff.

There she served until 1922, when she was paid off in the UK and returned to Princess Schahovskoy-Gleboff-Strechneff (noted in Lloyd's Register, 1923), but remained laid up. In the 1930s she became a floating club house for some London members' clubs, moored in Poole Harbour and later Chatham Dockyard.

Thus ended the Royal Navy's remaining yachts.

The US Naval Yachts After Two Wars

Of the 1898 war's USN yachts, five gave exemplary service well into the twentieth century.

Two of them became presidential yachts. *Sylph* commissioned on 18 August 1898 at Norfolk Navy Yard, too late to participate in the conflict. Instead, she was based at the Washington Navy Yard to serve as personal yacht for President McKinley and other high-ranking officials. By 1902 she

The American presidential yacht *Mayflower* in 1912. *(Author's collection)*

The reception room of the US Presidential Yacht *Mayflower*, seen in 1909, demonstrating the level of internal décor and comfort typical of the steam yachts of the time. *(Library of Congress LC-USZ62-97437)*

was alternating in this duty with two other vessels, *Dolphin* and *Mayflower*, and was used by both the Secretary of the Navy and America's great reforming president, Theodore Roosevelt, who liked to sail her to and from his house at Oyster Bay, NY. Roosevelt's successor, William Howard Taft, also enjoyed *Sylph* and took excursions along the New England coast in her in the summer months of his term. She was finally decommissioned in 1929 but not scrapped until 1959.

Mayflower served as a presidential yacht until 1929, hosting many and various diplomatic and social events, among which was the lovesick courtship of Edith Bolling Galt by President Woodrow Wilson. However, her days of glory were ended by Herbert Hoover when he took office. He dispensed with her as an economy measure and she was decommissioned in March 1929.*

After service in 1917–18, *Hawk* was recommissioned in April 1922 and assigned to the 9th Naval District, operating on the Great Lakes until she was scrapped in 1940.

USS *Yankton* also continued to serve after the war's end. In February 1919 she became the flagship of Rear Admiral N A Cully, commanding US naval forces fighting the Bolsheviks in Murmansk.

And *Scorpion*, freed from internment (see Chapter 9) when the war ended, became the flagship of Rear Admiral Mark Lambert Bristol, US High Commissioner to the Ottoman Empire and Senior US Naval Officer in Turkish Waters. She acted as a despatch vessel, took part in relief work and was once again the *stationnaire*. It was not until 1927 that she returned to the USA, and in March 1929 *Scorpion* was stricken.

Of the other yachts, *Aphrodite* (see Chapter 8) was sent to Harwich as the USN official presence and station ship at the surrender of the German U-boat fleet to Rear Admiral Reginald Tyrwhitt and the Harwich Force on 20 November 1918. She also later served as station ship at Portland and

* When America joined the Second World War, *Mayflower* was repurchased and served with the coastguard service as a patrol vessel.

MAY

Mayflower, here on duty for President Taft in the North River, by 42nd Street, New York, during the 1909 Hudson-Fulton celebration that memorialised the tri-centenary of Henry Hudson's discovery of the Hudson River and the 100th anniversary of Robert Fulton's first successful paddle steamer. *(US Library of Congress LC-DIG-det-4a16108)*

USS *Scorpion* serving out her captivity at Constantinople. *(Author's collection)*

Hamburg before decommissioning on 12 July 1919. Colonel Payne had by this time died and her new owner was Harry Payne Whitney, who had inherited the majority of his uncle's estate. By one of those circularities that attend the life of the super-rich, his sister Pauline was married to Almeric Hugh Paget, younger brother of Arthur Henry Fitzroy Paget, last met in Chapter 3 as the British Observer in the American–Spanish war of 1898.

Just eleven of the armed yachts that had fought in the war continued in their service beyond 1919. These gained new pennant numbers in 1920, when the USN instituted an alphanumeric hull classification system. PY (patrol yacht) replaced the old SP designation and the remaining yachts became PY-1 to PY-11. Of these, *Mayflower* was PY-1, *Scorpion* PY-3 and *Sylph* PY-5.

By 1935, only *Nokomis* (PY-6) and *Isabel* (PY-10) were still in commission. Indeed, *Isabel* would prove to be the longest lasting of the yachts;

Another view of *Scorpion*. *(Author's collection)*

A post-war view of *Isabel* (PY-10) at Hankow, China, on 14 May 1937. She is dressed overall in honour of the coronation of King George VI and flies the four-star flag of Commander in Chief, US Asiatic Fleet. *(US Naval History and Heritage Command NH 83530)*

originally intended for the automobile manufacturer John North Willys, and armed with four 3in and two torpedo tubes, she remained in service until 1946, the last of a noble breed.

Decline and Fall

Nor did the concept of the luxurious steam yacht really survive the war. The precursors of the cause of their decline were there, if not yet completely apparent, before the conflict. For in the years prior to the struggle, it had not been all beer and skittles for the landed rich. Britain fell into a severe agricultural depression in the 1880s that lasted until Edward VII's ascension to the throne. Rental income from land holdings fell sharply, and the aristocracy had to sell land, houses and other treasures to stave off their decrease in liquid money. Corn imports from Australia and the USA, combined with more efficient bacon production in Denmark and new refrigerated ships bringing beef from South America, caused agricultural rents to drop by an average 22.6 per cent between 1878 and 1893. The price of wheat fell from 46 shillings per quarter in 1870 to 22 shillings in 1894.[3] As the Duke of Bedford commented in 1897: 'Low prices, bad seasons and a crushing weight of taxation have entirely caused rent … to disappear from the Thorney Estate.'[4]

Fortunately, American millionaires simultaneously filled their homes with the treasures of the Old World, bought into the troubled estates and married their daughters into these suddenly less wealthy aristocratic families, desperate for English status and titles for themselves and their offspring. They also provided staggeringly large dowries. But this seemed not to matter – the yachts were traded from aristos to mercantile arrivistes and back again as fortunes grew in some areas even as they declined in others.

The Great War changed all that. The components that went to make up the British Victorian–Edwardian world – a largely subservient proletariat, cheap labour, land-based wealth, respect for status and authority, the restricted place of women in the workforce and in society, chivalry as the ethical basis for behaviour, a limited electoral franchise – were all swept away in the maelstrom of the First World War. As were many of the best favoured in the land as well. By just the end of 1914, the war had killed six peers, sixteen baronets, six knights, ninety-five sons of peers, eighty-two sons of baronets and eighty-four sons of knights.[5] The cream of the aristocracy had been killed before twelve months of war had passed. By the end of the war, 'not since the Wars of the Roses had the aristocracy been so systematically slaughtered'.[6]

The scale of massacre and change brought about by the First World War altered realities and brought to an end the life and values of Victorian and Edwardian England. 'It was not just millions that died,' Mary Countess of Wemyss and March (Lady Mary Elcho until 1914) remarked, 'it changed the world, our world, for ever, shaking all things to their foundations, wasting the treasures of the past and casting a sinister influence far into the future.'[7]

What the war had done to the fortunes of the aristocracy was clear. As Lady Curzon* said: 'Truly, England lost the flower of her young men in those terrible days ... there was scarcely one of our friends who did not lose a son, a husband or a brother.'[8] And the changes brought about meant that, as historian David Cannadine observed, the aristocracy made the supreme sacrifice selflessly and stoically 'in defence of a country that was gradually but irrevocably ceasing to be theirs'.[9]

The survivors never again knew the Edenic existence that the pre-war years had bought, as death duties, income tax, increased wage bills and the demise of deference ruined their world. By 1922 in the UK, the income tax rate had risen 20 per cent since 1918 to six shillings in the pound, there was another agricultural depression and unemployment reached the one million mark. And in America, a dangerous boom was building towards the Great Crash of 1929.

However, there were some still able to operate and enjoy the steam yacht. The Admiralty returned *Liberty* (see Chapter 3) to Lord Tredegar in 1919. He had her restored to yacht condition and in 1920 sailed around the world twice in her, at the conclusion of which voyages he sold her to Sir Robert Houston, a shipping magnate.

After his marriage to the much younger Lucy, courtesan, actress and divorcee,† Houston moved to Jersey for tax avoidance purposes and lived part time on his yacht. When he died aboard *Liberty* in 1926, apart from leaving his wife the colossal sum of £5.5 million, which made her the second richest woman in Britain, he left her the yacht, too.

Lady Houston also lived on *Liberty* and became a considerable financial supporter of British aviation. But *Liberty* achieved renewed fame for different reasons. In 1932, her ladyship offered to give £200,000 to strengthen the British armed forces. The National Government of Prime Minister Ramsey MacDonald refused. She hung a huge electric sign reading DOWN WITH MACDONALD THE TRAITOR in the rigging of *Liberty* and sailed her around Great Britain, attracting much attention.

But generally, post-war and on both sides of the Atlantic, the steam yacht became an expensive, nay ruinous, possession. Crew and running costs,‡

* Grace Curzon, Marchioness Curzon of Kedleston.

† And later philanthropist, political activist, supporter of British airpower development, and suffragist.

‡ For example, the UK retail price index had doubled between 1913 and 1919.

construction and maintenance prices and – eventually – the proliferation of private and commercial aviation, ended their pomp with only a few exceptions. Chauffered limousines, personal aircraft and luxurious, fast, cruise liners took their peacetime place. Only the mega-rich could afford one and increasingly choose not to. The steam yacht era had come and gone. It lasted perhaps for only fifty years; about 1864–1914 in Britain and about 1875–1917 in the US, about the same length of time as the private American railroad car.* The golden age had passed.

A good example of the lot of the old steam yachts is given by the fate of *Ituna*, last noted in Chapter 1. Although a publicity document for the post-war G L Watson company states that *Ituna* was used on war service, this cannot be substantiated. But what is known is that she entered the American registry in 1916 under the ownership of the Vogel family. They sold her to a Los Angeles attorney (presumably a proxy), and it was reported that she would be converted from coal to oil burning, turned into a refrigerated cargo boat with passenger accommodation, and would be operated by the Mexican Navigation and Commercial Company. But this was clearly unsuccessful, for in 1918 *Ituna* passed into the hands of deep-sea trawler owner Frank E Booth, president of F E Booth Canning Company of San Francisco, CA. He converted her into a trawler. And in 1920, she was lost in a storm. From the height of luxury to a stinking fishing boat in just thirty-four years.

A Fair Reward?

The regular Royal Navy sailor was not well paid. In 1914, an able seaman with six years' service earned £2 18 shillings per month.† By 1918 this had only risen to £3 3 shillings and coppers.

By contrast, a similar position on, for example, Liverpool-based merchant ships paid £5 10 shillings per month (and an agreement was made to pay £1 a month above the port rates in the Union's book for 1913 to retain or recruit Mercantile Marine ratings as a reward for added danger and their patriotism in volunteering).

Many of the British steam yachts' crews were their pre-war sailors; these signed on to the navy in the Mercantile Marine Reserve by agreeing to the T-124 (Y) contract that placed them under naval discipline but left them on their original rates of pay. Thus they were considerably better paid than any regulars they might end up serving with. This was not always the case, however. Those original crewmen who were also members of the Royal Naval Reserve only received RN rates and thus suffered a pay cut.

At the end of the war, it was decided to pay everyone who had served in the war a war gratuity. This was calculated on the basis of a minimum for each rank for the first year of service with monthly increments for additional time served.

For ordinary soldiers and sailors this was a minimum payment varying with rank from £5 for a private (or equivalent), up to £15 for a warrant officer class I (approximately equivalent to sixty-seven days' pay). There

* In a sense, steam yachts were the private rail cars of the sea. In 1909, when Alfred Harmsworth, Lord Northcliffe, made a six-week, 9,000-mile land journey across Canada, he travelled in the Pullman car 'Independence' attached to the rear of a train. 'It was a home on wheels … there were four private cabins, a dining room, an observation room where we spent most of the day and an observation platform at the rear.' (quoted in Roberts, *The Chief*, p.171)

† An amount that had only increased by 2 pence a day since 1852.

Ituna as a fishing trawler. Note how her bowsprit has been cruelly cropped. 'How the Mighty Have Fallen'. *(San Francisco Maritime National Historical Park, P78-449A.00616gs)*

were additional payments for those who had more than twelve months' service of 10s or 5s for each month or part of a month's war service beyond the first twelve months, according to whether they had served overseas or not. The maximum number of these monthly additions was forty-eight, equivalent to a gratuity of five years' war service.

The yachtsmen were by and large excluded. As MMR T-124(Y) men, they were considered undeserving of this bonus as they had been paid at a higher rate throughout the war.

This led to many questions in the House of Commons. For example, on 25 February 1919, F C Thompson MP asked the Secretary to the Admiralty 'whether it has been decided to pay gratuities to men who served under naval discipline in auxiliary yacht patrols?' Dr Macnamara responded that 'the answer is in the negative. The naval war gratuity is issuable only to men who received naval rates of pay. Should any of the men referred to in the question have served for any period during the war at naval rates of pay, they would be eligible for a gratuity calculated on such period under the usual conditions.'[10]

And in July 1919, William Tyson Wilson (Labour MP for Westhoughton) raised the issue and with specific reference to the RNR anomaly. He asked of Macnamara 'whether men who were in the Yacht Patrol Service are entitled to the war gratuity; if so, whether he is aware that these men were not in receipt of mercantile pay, a case in point being that of a carpenter who received £2 5s per week, on which he had to keep himself and his family at home; and whether he will give instructions that these men shall receive either the mercantile rate of pay for their services or the war gratuity?'

The reply was in the negative. 'The men in the Yacht Patrol serve under a Mercantile Agreement (T-124Y). They are in receipt of rates of pay which are doubtless less in cash payment than mercantile rates, but which, in view of the fact that T-124 men are employed continuously and, as well, enjoy the benefits of full pay while sick, free uniforms, and gratuity for upkeep, leave, with pay, demobilisation benefits, and pensions on navy scale if injured or disabled, do, in fact, approximate in value to what is received by men of the Mercantile Marine. They are, therefore, regarded as ineligible for the seamen's war gratuity, which is only paid to naval ratings who received naval rates of pay.'[11]

Given that many of the crewmen were now unemployed, as their owners could no longer afford to run their yachts, the decision might seem to modern eyes a little harsh.

Clyde-Built Ships

Many steam yachts were built on the banks of the River Clyde. Ships had been built on the river since the fifteenth century but in the mid to late 1800s, the area boomed as a hub for global shipbuilding and became highly significant in the economy of Glasgow. Robert Napier (see Chapter 1), who became known as 'the father of shipbuilding on the Clyde', trained many of those who went on to establish leading shipbuilders, and these grew towards the end of the nineteenth century to become the some of the leading suppliers of the Royal Navy, as well as building liners, steamers and yachts.

The shipbuilding firms became household names both on Clydeside and around the world. These included, among many others, John Brown and Company of Clydebank, Denny of Dumbarton, Scott of Greenock, Lithgows of Port Glasgow, Simon and Lobnitz of Renfrew, Alexander Robertson & Sons of Linthouse, Fairfield of Govan, Inglis of Pointhouse, Barclay Curle of Whiteinch, Connell and Yarrow of Scotstoun.

Almost as famous were the engineering firms that supplied the machinery needed to drive these vessels, including the boilers, pumps, and steering gear, namely Rankin & Blackmore, Hastie's and Kincaid's of Greenock, Rowan's of Finnieston, Weir's of Cathcart, Howden's of Tradeston, and Babcock & Wilcox of Renfrew. And the phrase 'Clyde-built' became synonymous with quality and shipbuilding expertise. Clyde-built yachts had a reputation for excellent seakeeping and very reliable machinery; and in the early days of yacht building, they came with the Scotch boiler, in contrast to US-built vessels, which gave better fuel efficiency.

But Britain had been broken by the war, and the economy stuttered throughout the 1920s and 1930s. Shipbuilders suffered with the rest of the country, and some went to the wall; these included two yards noted for their steam yacht work: Ramage & Ferguson succumbed in 1934 and D and W Henderson in 1936. And although the Clyde limped on into the second half of the twentieth century, it was never the same force again, and the beautiful steam yachts that were built there became a distant memory.*

* Although the one-time royal yacht *Britannia* was built by John Brown on the Clyde, and launched in 1954.

ENVOI

In the late nineteenth and early twentieth centuries, steam yachts were objects of great desire; they even appeared in popular song. In 1908, Paul West and Herman Avery Wade wrote *I Want A Fine Little Steam Yacht*, in which the singer regales his beloved with the pleasures to be found: 'pleasing to my mind is a boat that goes by steam' and where 'you'll have nothing to do, dear, … but love me all day long'.

But steam yachts flourished briefly. Like butterflies, they displayed their beauty for a short period, one that concluded with many of the type finding their languid grace compromised by a terrible war, in which they would be called to serve and where so many of the families that owned them suffered all kinds of loss.

They were primarily a British and American phenomenon. From the 696 registered in 1913, 545 (78 per cent) were in those two countries (see Appendix 5 for details).

Of 272 American yachts registered, 132 (48 per cent) served in the war. And of 263 British examples, 159 (60 per cent) joined the Royal Navy. More than forty-five G L Watson-designed yachts were claimed to have taken part in the war, in the RN, USN (eight), Imperial Russian Navy (two) and one with the Austro-Hungarians (see Appendix 6).

The sheet music cover for the song *I Want A Fine Little Steam Yacht* (1908). *(Author's collection)*

A beautiful picture of the steam yacht *Venetia* in peacetime. *(Mersea Museum/ John Leather Collection)*

The crews were mainly volunteers, often the men who had manned the vessel in peacetime. The change from providing an environment of gilded leisure, and close personal attention to the owners' wishes, to naval discipline was not necessarily an easy one. John Langdon Leighton, on volunteering for the USN, noted 'we left a universe of freedom and entered a world in which hours for smoking, shore leave, uniforms to be worn, and the adjustment of our lives were prescribed by autocratic law and regulations. We chafed under our restrictions.'[1] But by and large the men gained the respect of their new naval overlords and often vice-versa.

And they also gained each other's respect; hardened seamen and civilians, regular professionals and irregular laymen worked together in harmony in their makeshift warships. Each year the crew of *Sagitta* produced their own Christmas card; one year it contained a poem, including these verses:

Does the lamb go to bed with the tiger?
Or the heat retain warmth in the snow?
If you carefully consider these questions
You will find that the answer is no.

Yet the things that are done in *Sagitta*
I am sure would surprise you no less,
For the novice and pro work together
And there's never too much of a mess.[2]

The yachts' duties were generally mundane and workaday. Routine patrols, occasional excitement when a U-boat was sighted or presumed to be present, long watches with nothing to report. And always the challenge of the sea itself. But they acquitted themselves well and generally the vessels stood up to their hard usage, although by the war's end, most were in pretty poor condition.

The amateurs – both ships and men – had proved their worth.

What of the men who owned them? Through these pages have stalked the titans of the American Gilded Age, such as Jay Gould and his fellow Robber Barons. Morgans have graced the narrative, as have Vanderbilts and other household names. In Britain, the extended Edwardian period was also the apogee of the steam yacht. Lord-This and Sir-That, various Rothschilds, dukes and barons, businessmen and gentlemen of leisure, all glided through The Season, entertained on their yachts, and then sailed off to warmer climes. And they seemingly bought and sold yachts on a whim, as most steam yachts went through multiple ownership.

But there was also a code, which these men and women had to abide by. The people who formed this privileged circle all largely subscribed to a particular view of the demeanour necessary to be considered a 'good sort', a pillar of their societies and a well-regarded member of their club, be it

An unknown but lovely steam yacht flying what appears to be the flag of the American Yacht Club, founded by Jay Gould, railroad magnate, financial speculator, and one of the 'robber barons' of the US Gilded Age. Gould helped found the club in 1883 and owned the steam yacht *Atalanta*, later sold to the Venezuelan Navy.

Gentleman's or Yachting. In Britain, the concept of gentlemanly behaviour was entwined closely with the dominant moral codes of the late Victorians and Edwardians and these in turn were derived from their association with chivalric values, the lost Avalon of Arthurian legend, Camelot, the Round Table and from their obsession with imperial England as a new Rome, both having world-girdling empires. And as a result, the system of high society, and its public schools and colleges, tended to produce a breed of men who were devoid of guile and conditioned to believe in romantic notions of honour, glory and sacrifice. 'British schoolboys might be encouraged to cultivate the stoic virtues the Roman Republic had borrowed from Sparta … They might identify the British Empire with the Roman one and, reading Macaulay's *Lays*, compare the dogged courage of his Roman heroes with that of British … officers.'[3]

And as one historian has written: 'Every public schoolboy was familiar with the *Iliad* and the *Odyssey* and the poetry – with its emphasis on honour, discipline, athleticism and courage in the face of death – spoke across the ages about what it meant to be a gentleman and a scholar at the height of empire.'[4] And the American 'gentleman' tended to follow suit, often marrying into the British aristocracy and aping its behaviours.

And so when war came, these red in tooth and claw capitalists, or aristocrats of immense pedigree (and often snobbery), responded to their country's call with little hesitation. Steam yachts and all sorts of other craft were volunteered for service and often owners put themselves forward, too. And their sons marched off to the army and suffered dreadful rates of mortality. Greed may (or may not) be good, patriotism surely is.

Twenty-one years after the Armistice, global conflict broke out again. And again, there was a desperate shortage of smaller naval ships. So, once more, yachts were called to the colours. Not all were steam yachts; the internal combustion engine, in some form or other, now drove sea vessels, too. But they were still pleasure craft and still required erstwhile civilians to man them. The Royal Navy took 155 named yachts into service.

Forty-seven were deployed in nine anti-submarine groups (the 81st to 89th), which were fitted out in the first three months of war, each of four to six vessels and comprised entirely of yachts. Many were initially armed only with depth charges, one or two 3pdr or 12pdr guns being added later.

A further nineteen were attached to minesweeping flotillas, used by the Senior Naval Officer at minesweeping bases, or as danlayers.

Seventy-seven were pressed into service on miscellaneous duties, primarily as examination ships (armed boarding vessels). Additionally, twelve were designated as accommodation ships.

And other yachts, names now unknown, were requisitioned for such purposes as harbour defence or air-sea rescue craft.

Additionally, the Royal Canadian Navy purchased seventeen yachts in the USA in 1940, to which it added two of its own and three on loan from the RN.

Some yachts were refitted after the war. Here is one of the lounges of *Sapphire*, seen in 1924. She later became *Breda* and served in the Second World War. *(Author's collection)*

Yachts were called up for service in the Second World War. Some had already served in the Great War. This is *Marynthea*, renamed *Conqueror* in 1926, on patrol in 1939, her forward gun seeking the enemy. *(© National Maritime Museum N6772)*

We can wonder that the need for yachts arose once again. But, in fairness, the criticism that the Admiralty has received for the decision to neglect smaller vessels before the First World War and again in the inter-war period could be construed as misplaced, at least to some degree. As Professor Norman Friedman has noted, 'escorts and minesweepers had little peacetime function. The battlefleet had a very real function, to deter possible attackers.'[5] So that was where the money went.

And in the USA, the navy turned to yachts when it entered the war in 1941; 120 were deployed, mostly diesel powered, in a variety of roles. A further, now unrecorded, number of smaller yachts were used as District Patrol Craft.

By 1959, the *Lloyd's Register of Yachts* showed just twenty-nine steam yachts remaining in the world, of which thirteen were either government owned or royal or presidential yachts. Of the remaining sixteen, nine were registered as being owned by companies and seven by individuals.

There are still luxurious sailing and motor-powered craft, of course, still yachts for the wealthy and the not so well endowed. Sailing yacht competitions still attract the affluent and the skilled. Races such as the Volvo Ocean race, the Vendée Globe and, of course, the America's Cup, still hold audiences and participants in their thrall.

However, in the press, the words 'super yacht' are bandied around as synonymous only with mega-rich Russian oligarchs, or self-obsessed, Silicon Valley types. The *Daily Telegraph* of 7 March 2023, for instance, reported: 'Amazon founder Jeff Bezos's £415 million superyacht *Koru*, complete with

Marynthea (1911) as she was built for one H J Mason Esq by Camper and Nicholson at their Gosport yard. In common with many of their larger vessels, the hull was constructed by J I Thornycroft at Woolston, as the Gosport facilities were too small. A large vessel at 854grt, she was taken up by the Admiralty in February 1915 and fitted with two 12pdr guns. After the war, *Marynthea* became *Emerald* and in 1926, *Conqueror*, when she was owned by H Gordon Selfridge. *(Julian Mannering)*

helipad and pool, spotted in the North Sea on a test run'. It had been built in the Netherlands. Yachts are still show-off, 'look at me' items, often portrayed as representing the worst excesses of capitalism, dictatorship, or state exploitation.

But there are many other yachts still that combine travel and glamour, whose owners love sailing and can afford a little decadence. But they are not steam yachts. Once they were the personification of elegance; then they were warriors. And now steam yachts are no more. *Sic transit gloria mundi.*

AUTHOR'S NOTES

Steam Yachts at War is my tenth book commissioned by Seaforth Publishing and I thank Managing Editor Julian Mannering for his confidence in, and support for, my work.

The book is the third in a loose trilogy that has examined the major components of the Auxiliary Patrol in the First World War. *British Naval Trawlers and Drifters in Two World Wars* (2021) looked at fishing craft converted for war purposes; *The Petrol Navy* (2023) examined motor-powered vessels; and now we have steam yachts. I still find it remarkable that the war at sea would not have been won without these auxiliary warships and their largely volunteer crews.

It is a solitary job to write a book but the research cannot be done without the help of many people. I particularly wish to thank the following for their assistance. Andrew Choong Han Lin, Curator, Historic Photographs and Ship Plans at the Brass Foundry, National Maritime Museum, gave generously of his time to help with ship plans. John Collins, archivist of the Nottage Maritime Institute, was most helpful regarding photographs and the history of yachts at Wivenhoe. And Tony Millat at Mersea Island Museum kindly assisted me with photographs and attributions. These latter two gentlemen are excellent examples of the breed of volunteer historians who, without any state assistance, do so much to sustain and improve our knowledge of local history. They are to be commended.

Mike Wells shared his knowledge of SY *Rona/Goissa*, and generously obtained permission for me to use pictures from the Alice Wood collection, for which I am most grateful. Janet Andrew produced her usual excellent index.

Research was aided by the Special Collections Unit of the Library of Leeds University, who were most helpful and, as often before, the National Archives at Kew, the Churchill Archive in Cambridge and the Imperial War Museum in London proved fertile hunting grounds.

American picture archives are both extensive and more generous than British ones; many images are provided free of charge, a benefit not granted by any British picture repository, which is a real shame. As ever, I offer heartfelt thanks to the Library of Congress in Washington DC and the US Naval History and Heritage Command at the Washington Navy Yard for access to their collections. This book could not have been produced without their munificence.

This has been a complex book to write, following the many and frequent changes of ownership of yachts through time. If an error has crept in despite my best endeavours, I should like to hear of it.

Finally, I thank Vivienne, without whose assistance and encouragement none of my books would have been written.

Steve R Dunn, Worcestershire, 2024

APPENDICES

Appendix 1: *A Typical Crew Agreement (from* Rannoch, *1913)*

The several persons whose names are hereto subscribed, and whose descriptions are contained below, and of whom – blank – are engaged as Sailors, hereby agree to serve on board the said Yacht, in the several capacities expressed against their respective Names, until the said Yacht shall be paid off. Upon a voyage or voyages to any Port or Ports in the continent of Europe, voyage not to exceed six months.

And the said Crew agree to conduct themselves in an orderly, faithful, honest and sober manner, and to be at all times diligent in their respective duties, and to be obedient to the lawful commands of the said Master, or of any person who shall lawfully succeed him, and of their Superior Officers, in everything relating to the said Yacht, and the stores thereof, whether on board, in boats, or on shore: in consideration of which Services to be duly performed, the said Master hereby agrees to pay to the said Crew as Wages the sums against their names respectively expressed. And it is hereby agreed, That any Embezzlement, or wilful or negligent destruction of any part of the Yacht's Stores, shall be made good to the Owner out of the Wages of the person guilty of the same. And it is further agreed, that if any Seaman enters himself in a capacity for which he is incompetent, he is liable to be disrated. And it is also agreed, That if any member of the Crew considers himself to be aggrieved by any breach of the Agreement or otherwise, he shall represent the same to the Master or Officer in charge of the Yacht in a quiet and orderly manner, who shall thereupon take such steps as the case may require: And it is also agreed, that any man guilty of misconduct shall be liable to be discharged by the Master at any port in Great Britain or Ireland; and that the voyage shall be considered as terminated when the Yacht is paid off. And it is also agreed, that all clothing supplied by the Owner is and shall be considered Yacht Stores and is to be worn as the Master shall direct, upon the termination of the voyage the said clothing will become the property of the individual wearers providing they have behaved themselves to the Master's satisfaction. Any member of the crew being paid off before the termination of the voyage by reason of misconduct or otherwise, shall forfeit all claim to the said clothing. No member of the crew allowed on shore without leave, and no boats belonging to the Yacht to be taken away without the permission of the Master or Officer in charge. Anchor watch to be strictly kept and relieved, the man going off watch to see his relief on deck before going below. Any member of the crew found smuggling shall be liable to instant dismissal and forfeit all wages due. Firemen and Sailors to assist each other if required. One shilling per week will be given to ABs and Firemen at the termination of the voyage provided they conduct themselves to the Master's satisfaction.

(source: gunfleet.net)

Appendix 2: *RN Armed Yachts Sunk During the First World War and Immediately Afterwards*

HMY and Date	Detail	Lives Lost
Aegusa 27/28 April 1916	Mined. Sunk after hitting a mine while looking for survivors from HMS *Nasturtium* sunk hours before. Both victims of a minefield laid off Grand Harbour, Malta, by *U-73*.	6
Aries 31 Oct 1915	Mined. Sunk by a mine from the German submarine *UC-6* off Leathercoats.	23
Brown Mouse 28 Feb 1918	Burned, total loss. Had been converted as a Q-ship.	Nil
Clementina 5 Aug 1915	Collision. In use as an Armed Boarding Vessel, closing the SS *Adam Smith* (299grt) for examination off Tor Cor Point in the early morning, in collision, holed, and flooded from the stokehold aft. To prevent her sinking, run aground and beached nearby. Unsalvageable.	Nil
Conqueror II 26 Sept 1916	Torpedoed. Sunk by the German submarine *U-52* north-west of Fair Isle. *Conqueror* was assisting HMS *Sarah Alice*, which was also torpedoed by *U-52*.	17
Goissa 15 Nov 1918	Mined. Sunk in Dardanelles, during mine clearance operations.	5
Hersilia 6 Jan 1916	Wrecked. She was caught in a bad storm hunting a U-boat and was wrecked on North Rona.	Nil
Iolaire 1 Jan 1919	Wrecked. Sunk off Stornoway on the 'The Beasts of Holm'.	204

Kethailes		
11 Oct 1917	Collision. She was sunk in the Irish Sea after a collision with SS *Leicestershire* off the Blackwater Light Vessel.	17
Marcella		
24 Mar 1916	Collision. In use as an Armed Boarding Vessel, she sank after a collision in the Downs.	Nil
Mekong		
12 Mar 1916	Wrecked. Caught in a bad storm off Scarborough. See Chapter 5.	3
Resource II		
12 Nov 1915	Burned, total loss.	Nil
Rhiannon		
20 July 1915	Mined. Sunk off Longsands in a field laid on *UC-3* on 5 July, which had not been detected in the subsequent sweeping operation.	5
Sanda		
25 Sept 1915	Shellfire.	13
Verona		
24 Feb 1917	Mined. She was sunk by a mine from the German submarine *UC-33* off Portmahomack, sinking in less than a minute.	23
Zaida		
17 Aug 1916	Mined (probably). There is confusion as to the cause of her loss. Hepper* says that she was sunk by a French mine, other sources by Turkish shellfire. The official record† says a torpedo from *U-35*.	13
Zarefah		
8 May 1917	Mined. She was sunk by a mine from *UC-31*, 1 mile north-east of Mull Head, Deerness.	16
Total yachts	**17**	

Note: *British Vessels Lost at Sea* only lists thirteen yacht losses. *Brown Mouse* is accounted in 'Special Service' and *Marcella* under 'Armed Boarding Steamers'. *Goissa* and *Iolaire* were excluded because they sank after the Armistice but are included here for completeness and because they were on war service.

* Hepper, *British Warship Losses*, pp.67–68; 'It later emerged that she had been sunk at 0845 when she struck a mine … broke up and sank within a minute.'

† *British Warships Lost at Sea*, part 1, p.14; 'Sunk by submarine in the Gulf of Alexandretta.'

Appendix 3: *USN Yachts Serving in French Coastal and Mediterranean Waters, 1917–18*

Alcedo
Aphrodite
Carola IV
Christabel
Corona
Corsair
Emeline
Guinivere
Harvard
May
Noma
Nokomis
Piqua
Rambler
Remlik
Sultana
Utowana
Vedette
Wanderer
Wakiva I

Appendix 4: *Royal Navy Armed Yachts Receiving Naval Salvage and Prize Money*

(excluding Battles of Heligoland Bight, Falklands, Dogger Bank and Jutland)

As per the *London Gazette*, issue number given in brackets

Agatha, salvage of SS *Anders*, 18 to 19 Jan 1917 (30538)
Amethyst III, salvage of casks of oil, 11 to 16 Aug 1915 (29667)
Atalanta, salvage of SS *Camlake*, 5 Oct 1916 (31180), SS *Normanby*, 17 to 19 Dec 1917 (31517)
Boadicea II, salvage of schooner *Venedocian*, 19 Nov 1916 (30353)
Goissa, salvage of Norwegian barque *Henrik Ibsen*, 21 to 23 Nov 1916 (30708)
Hecate, salvage of schooner *Edith S Cummins*, 24 Aug 1916 (30324)
Lorna, salvage of SS *Waiwera*, 17 Jan 1918 (32025)
Lorna, prize money, destruction of *UB-74*, 26 May 1918 (32169)
Maid of Honour, salvage of SS *George Pyman*, 6 Aug 1916 (30105), SS *Clan Mackenzie*, 5 to 7 Mar 1918 (31685)
Nairn, salvage of SS *Roanoke*, 11 to 14 Feb 1917 (30599)
Safa-el-Bahr, salvage of SS *Sebek*, Oct to Nov 1916 (30987)
Sapphire II, salvage of SS *Andromachis*, 18 to 20 Mar 1917 (30522)
Valiant II, salvage of SS *Ludgate*, 26 Jun 1916 (29967
Venetia II, salvage of SS *Forsvaret*, 17 to 19 Dec 1917 (30934)
Yarta, salvage of SS *Ecrudijk*, 7 to 9 Apr 1916 (30378), SS *Eemdijk*, 7 to 9 Apr 1916 (30484)
Zaza, salvage of SV *Benguela*, 27 to 28 Sep 1916 (30958), SS *Jupiter*, 8 to 11 Oct 1916 (30384)

(Fifteen yachts in total)

Appendix 5: *Numbers of Steam Yachts in 1913*

Country of Registration	Up to 449 tons TM	500–999 tons TM	1000+ tons TM	Total
USA	236	29	7	272
Canada	19	2	1	22
UK	210	41	12	263
France	34	7	2	43
Germany	8	0	1	9
Russia	5	4	3	12
Other	74	7	3	84
Total	**586**	**81**	**29**	**696**

(Source: Hoffman, *The Steam Yachts*, p.4)

Appendix 6: *G L Watson Steam Yachts on War Service, 1914–18*

Name, tonnage TM	(launch date)	[name when launched]
Lysistrata 2089	(1900)★★★	
Mayflower★ 1844	(1896)	
Nahma★ 1806	(1897)	
Margarita 1797	(1900)	
Atmah 1746	(1898)	
Liberty 1571	(1908)	
Sapphire 1421	(1912)	
Alberta★★★ 1322	(1896)	[*Surprise*]
Warrior 1266	(1904)	[*Wayfarer*]
Alcedo★ 1111	(1895)	
Zarnitza 1086	(1891)	[*Forus*]
Goissa 1023	(1899)	[*Sapphire*]
Jeannette 1023	(1911)	
Eileen 1022	(1910)	[*Doris*]
Eros 1020	(1905)	[*Honor*]
Nirvana★★ 971	(1904)	
Diana 815		
Salvator 766	(1903)	[*Katoomba*]
May★ 737	(1891)	
Mohican★ 704	(1890)	
Catania 668	(1895)	
Mingary 639	(1899)	
Vedette★ 516	(1900)	[*Virginia*]

Zara 516	(1895)	
Hecate 471	(1903)	
Emeline⋆ 469	(1898)	
Vanduara 450	(1886)	
Vanessa 445	(1899)	[*Golden Eagle*]
Monsoon 432	(1887)	[*Latharova*]
Primavera 432		
Triton⋆ 337	(1902)	
Christabel⋆ 330	(1893)	
Queen O'The May 270	(1895)	
Madinina 267		
Mavis 260	(1903)	
Minona 249	(1906)	
Zara (2)⋆ 249	(1891)	
Ituna 243	(1886)	
Mora 226	(*c*1904)	
Gael 115	(1904)	
Saevuna 70	(1901)	
Stadella 69	(pre-1912)	
Iris 68	(pre-1893)	
Ottawa 34	(1912)	
Nykr 30	(1893)	

⋆ Served in USN
⋆⋆ Served in Austro-Hungarian navy
⋆⋆⋆ Served in Russian Imperial Navy

The list of names and tonnage is as per G L Watson Ltd brochure in wartime (1915).

THE PLANS

THE PLANS depicted in this section are chosen to demonstrate a range of steam yacht designs. They range from the auxiliary steam yacht type, through the smaller 'gentleman's yachts' to the large and luxurious 'statement' craft. Most served in the First World War and feature in the body of the book.

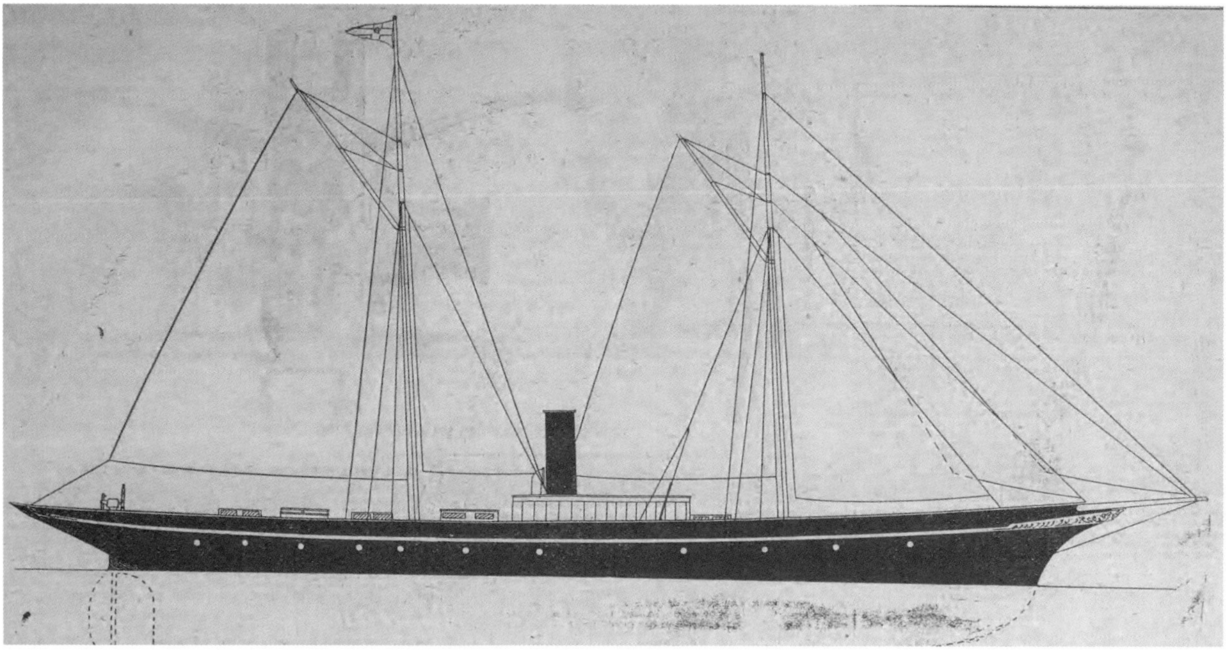

Above: A schematic of the steam yacht *Carmen* (1884) designed by John Beavor-Webb and built by John Reid and Co., Port Glasgow. She had a two-cylinder engine generating 35nhp driving a single screw and was of 142grt. *Carmen* was commissioned by one Llewellyn Llewellyn of Dartmouth but seems to have immediately passed into the ownership of Sir Richard W Bulkeley of Barron Hill, Beaumaris, whose family were the dominant Anglesey landowners of the time. The image was originally printed in *Forest and Stream* in 1886. *(Author's collection)*

Opposite, top: This is the USS *Scorpion* (1896), built as *Sovereign*, which served in the 1898 war. In that conflict she was armed with six 6pdr guns and four 5in, the mountings for which can be clearly seen. Before the First World War she was *stationnaire* at Constantinople and was interned when the USA entered the war. *(Author's collection)*

Opposite, bottom: The lightweight decks of the armed yachts had to be strengthened before they could carry a weapon. Here is a yard drawing of the necessary bed plate and wood packing for USS *Calumet* (1903) to receive a 3pdr gun. She was commissioned as SP-723 on 7 December 1917 and served as a guard ship, harbour entrance patrol craft and provided anti-submarine escort for New York area inshore convoys. *(US National Archives at College Park)*

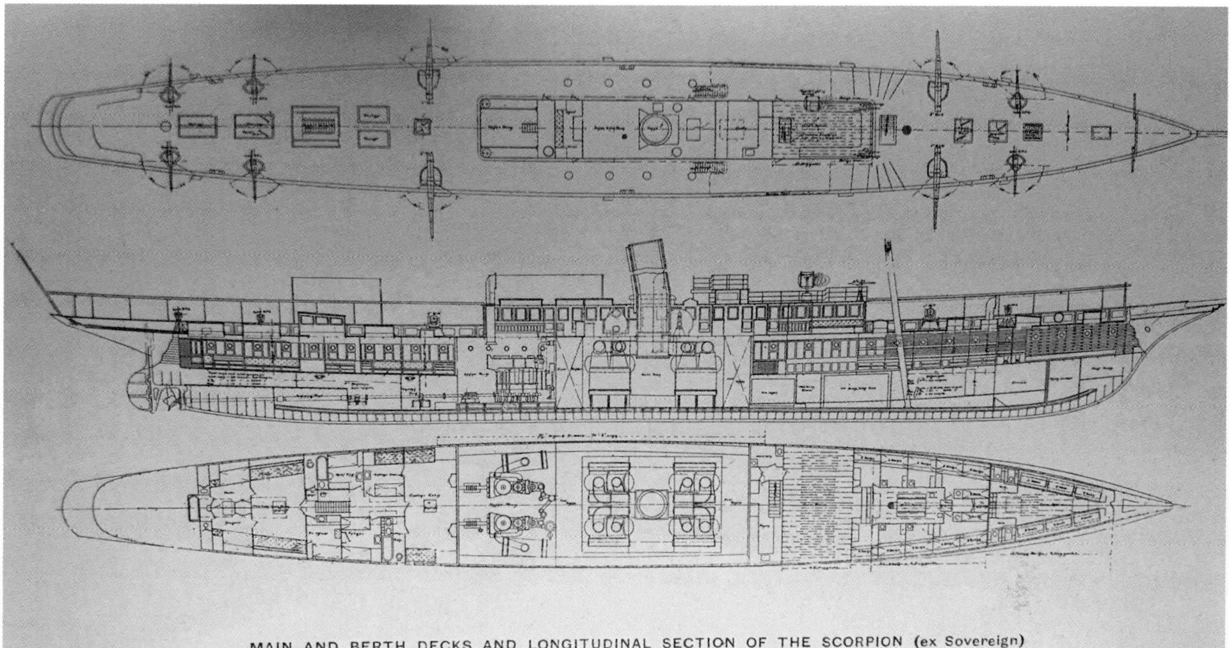

MAIN AND BERTH DECKS AND LONGITUDINAL SECTION OF THE SCORPION (ex Sovereign)

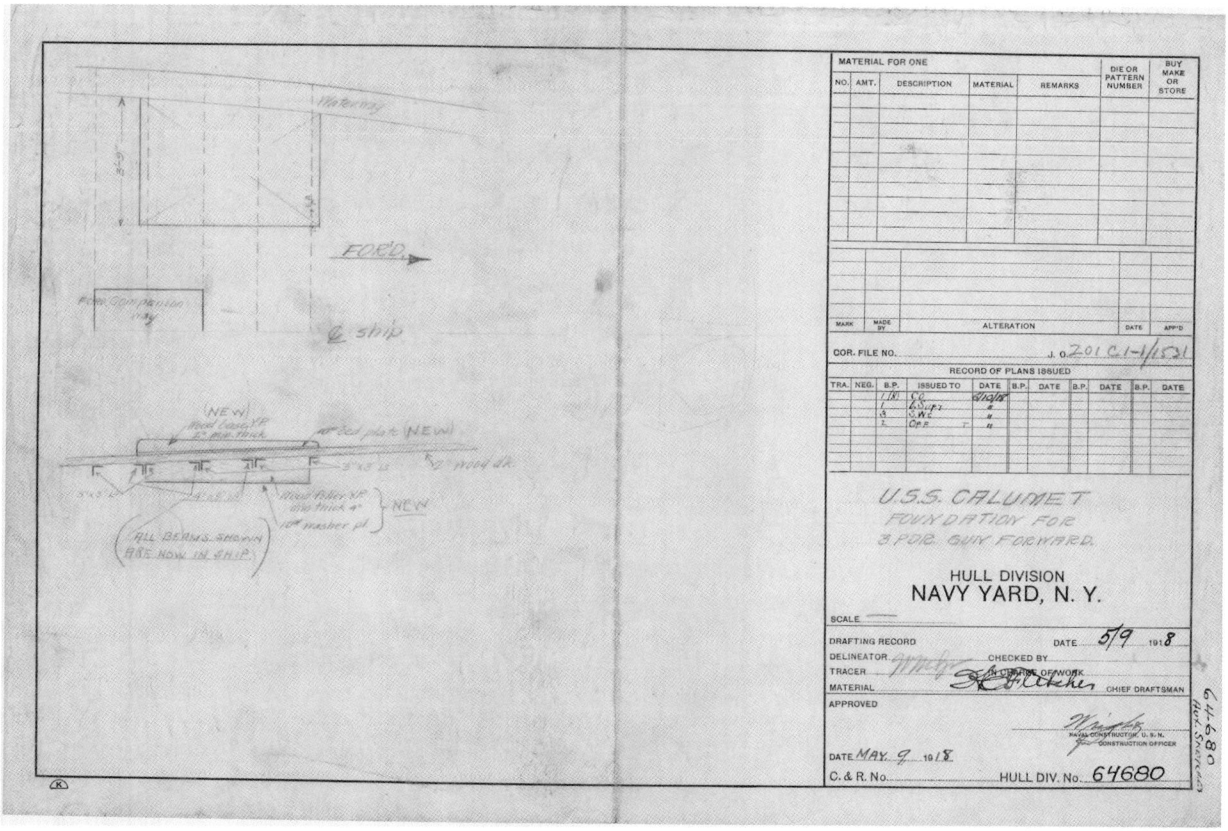

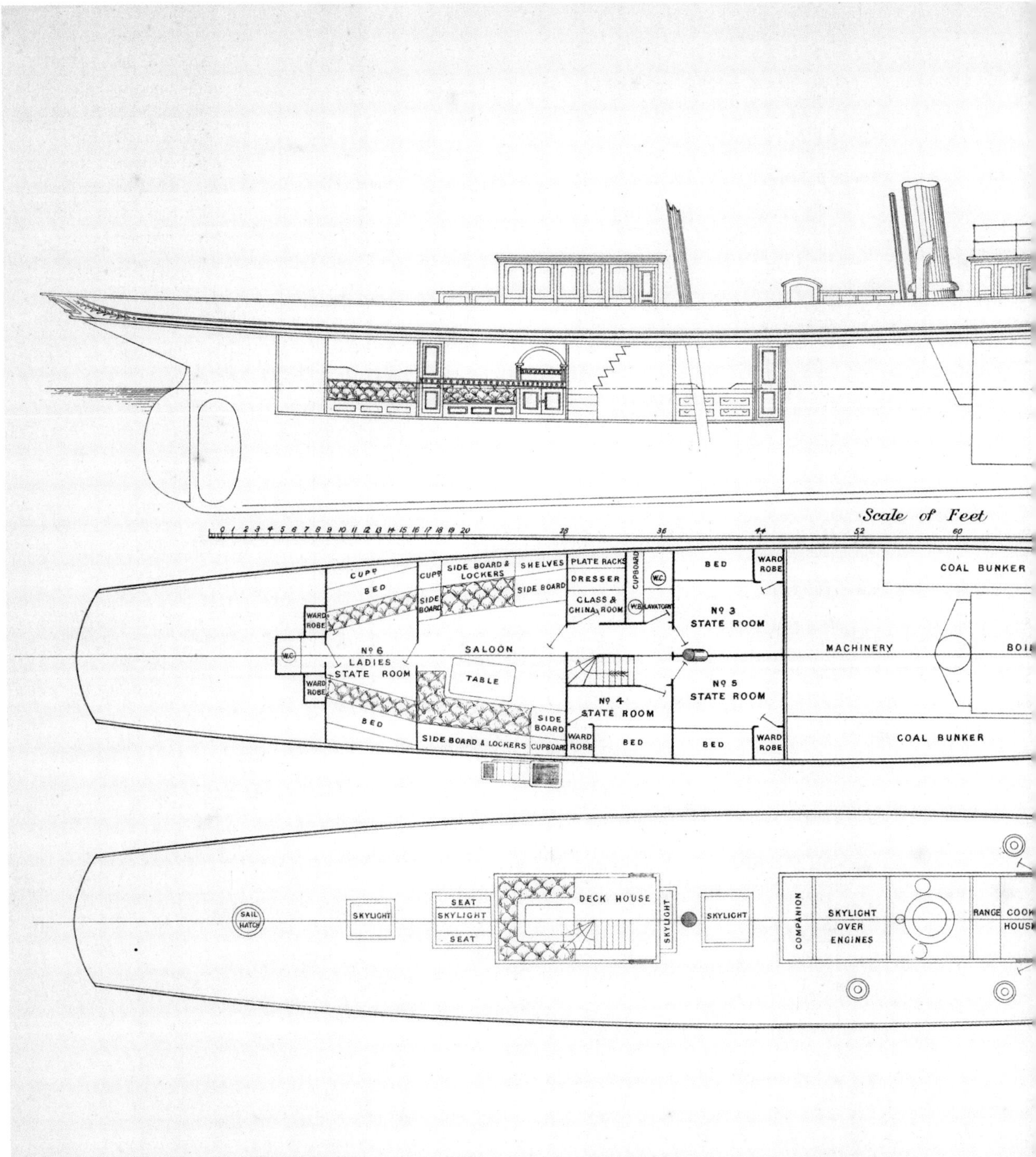
Scale of Feet
0 1 2 3 4 5 6 7 8 9 10 11 12 13 14 15 16 17 18 19 20
28
36
44
52
60
CUPD
BED
CUPD
SIDE BOARD & LOCKERS
SHELVES
SIDE BOARD
PLATE RACKS
DRESSER
CUPBOARD
W.C.
GLASS & CHINA ROOM
W.C.
LAVATORY
BED
WARD ROBE
Nº 3 STATE ROOM
COAL BUNKER
WARD ROBE
SIDE BOARD
W.C.
Nº 6 LADIES STATE ROOM
SALOON
TABLE
MACHINERY
BOI
WARD ROBE
Nº 4 STATE ROOM
Nº 5 STATE ROOM
BED
SIDE BOARD
SIDE BOARD & LOCKERS
CUPBOARD
WARD ROBE
BED
BED
WARD ROBE
COAL BUNKER
SAIL HATCH
SKYLIGHT
SEAT
SKYLIGHT
SEAT
DECK HOUSE
SKYLIGHT
SKYLIGHT
COMPANION
SKYLIGHT OVER ENGINES
RANGE
COOK HOUSE

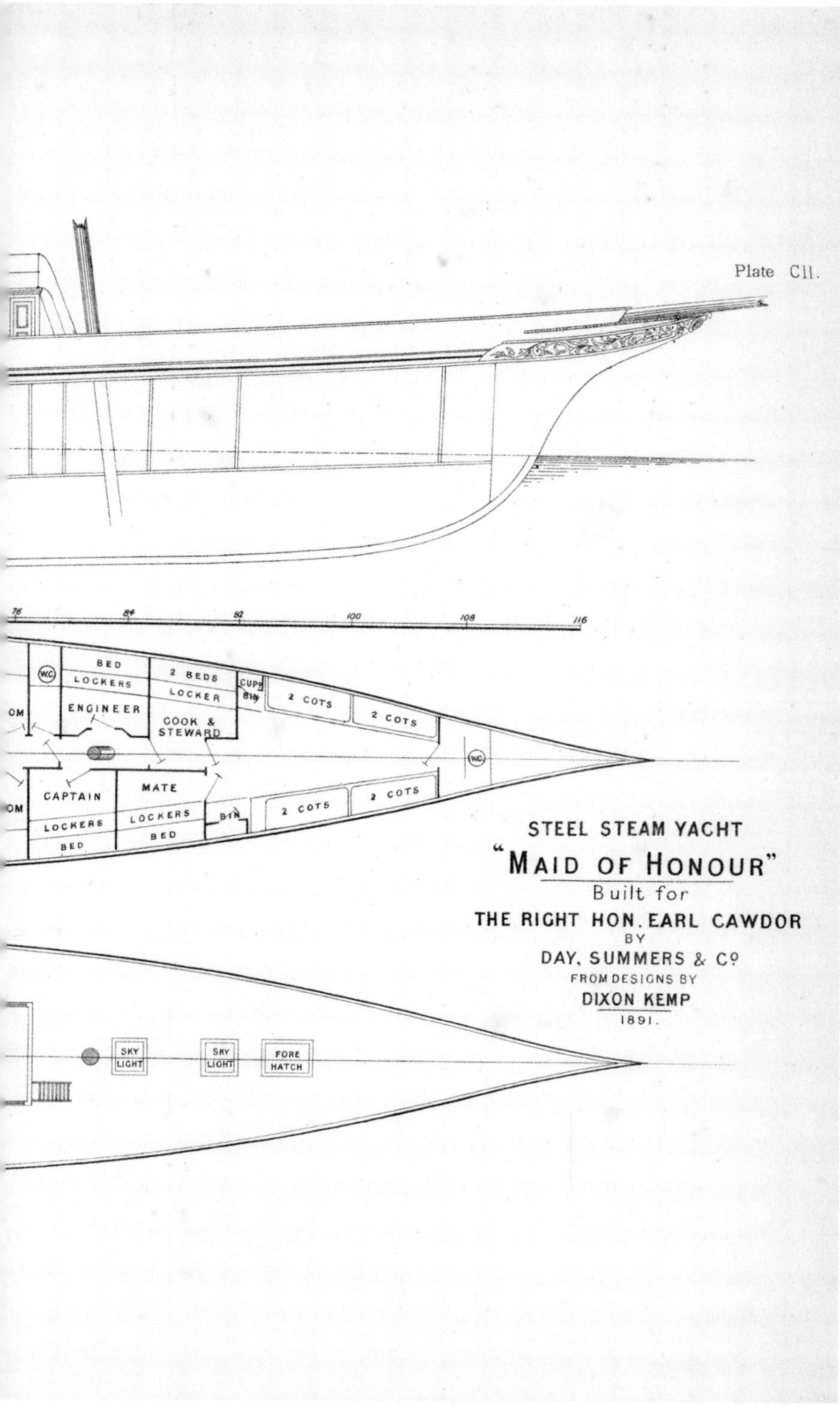

Designed by Dixon Kemp and built by Day Summers and Co., *Maid of Honour* (1891) was commissioned by John Campbell, 2nd Earl Cawdor and quondam MP for Pembrokeshire. His son Frederick was briefly First Lord of the Admiralty in 1905. Note the clear division between crew and passengers' quarters, with the ladies' cabin aft, a prime position usually occupied by the owner and wife. *(Author's collection)*

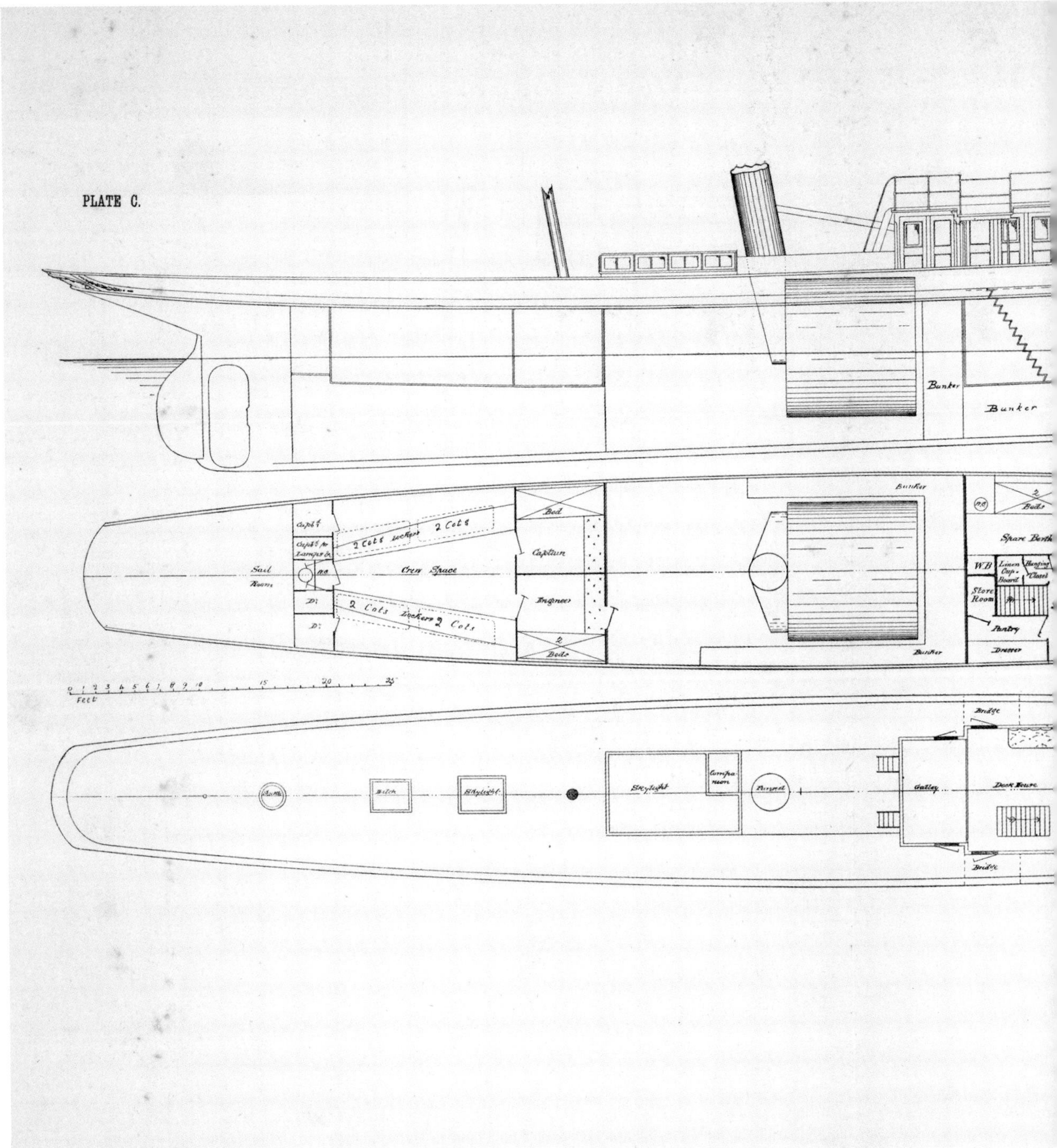

SY *Speedy* (140 tons TM) was designed by Dixon Kemp for 'Baron Barreto' and launched by Ramage & Feguson in 1895. Barreto is probably Henry Edward Ernest Victor (Barreto), 4th Baron de Barreto (a Portuguese title), of Quarry Court, Marlow. In this design, the owner's quarters are to the bow. *(Author's collection)*

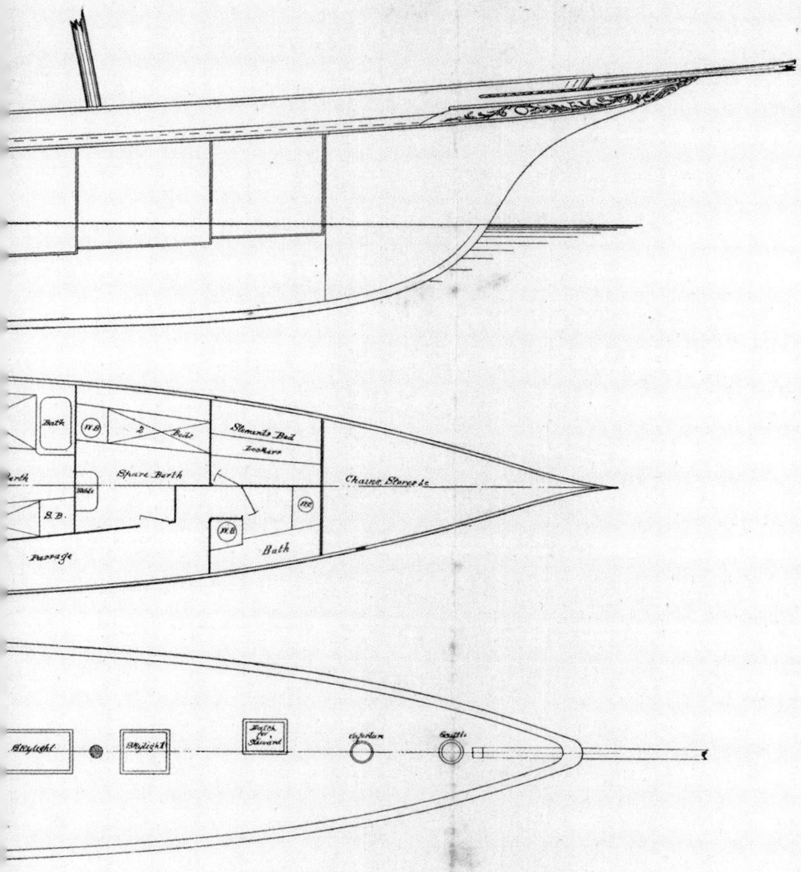

S.Y. SPEEDY

(140 TONS),

BUILT FOR THE BARON BARRETO

BY MESSRS. RAMAGE AND FERGUSON,

FROM DESIGNS

BY DIXON KEMP, 1895.

DIMENSIONS, &C.

Length over all	134ft. 6in.
Length on L.W.L.	108ft.
Length for tonnage on deck	117ft. 10in.
Breadth	16ft. 2in.
Depth, top of beams to top of floors	10ft. 4in.
Draught of water aft	9ft. 6in.
Tonnage, Lloyd's Y.M.	141 tons.
Area of L.W.L.	1250 sq. ft.
Area of mid-section	96·2 sq. ft.
Displacement on trial, tanks full and bunkers half full	178 tons.
Displacement per inch of immersion at L.W.L.	3 tons.
Diameters of cylinders	12in., 19in., and 30in
Stroke of pistons	21in.
Length of boiler	9ft.
Diameter of boiler	10ft. 6in.
Diameter of furnaces (two)	3ft. 2in.
Grate area (total)	36 sq. ft.
Heating surface (total)	1003 sq. ft.
Working pressure	180lb.
Screw propeller, diameter	7ft. 9in.
,, ,, pitch mean	10ft. 10in.
Surface of all the blades (four)	16 sq. ft.
Revolutions on measured mile	138
Indicated horse power	395
Speed (mean) in knots, natural draught	13·05
Speed (mean) with forced draught	13·5 knots
Slip per cent. of propeller	11
Total weight of machinery, steam up	59 tons.

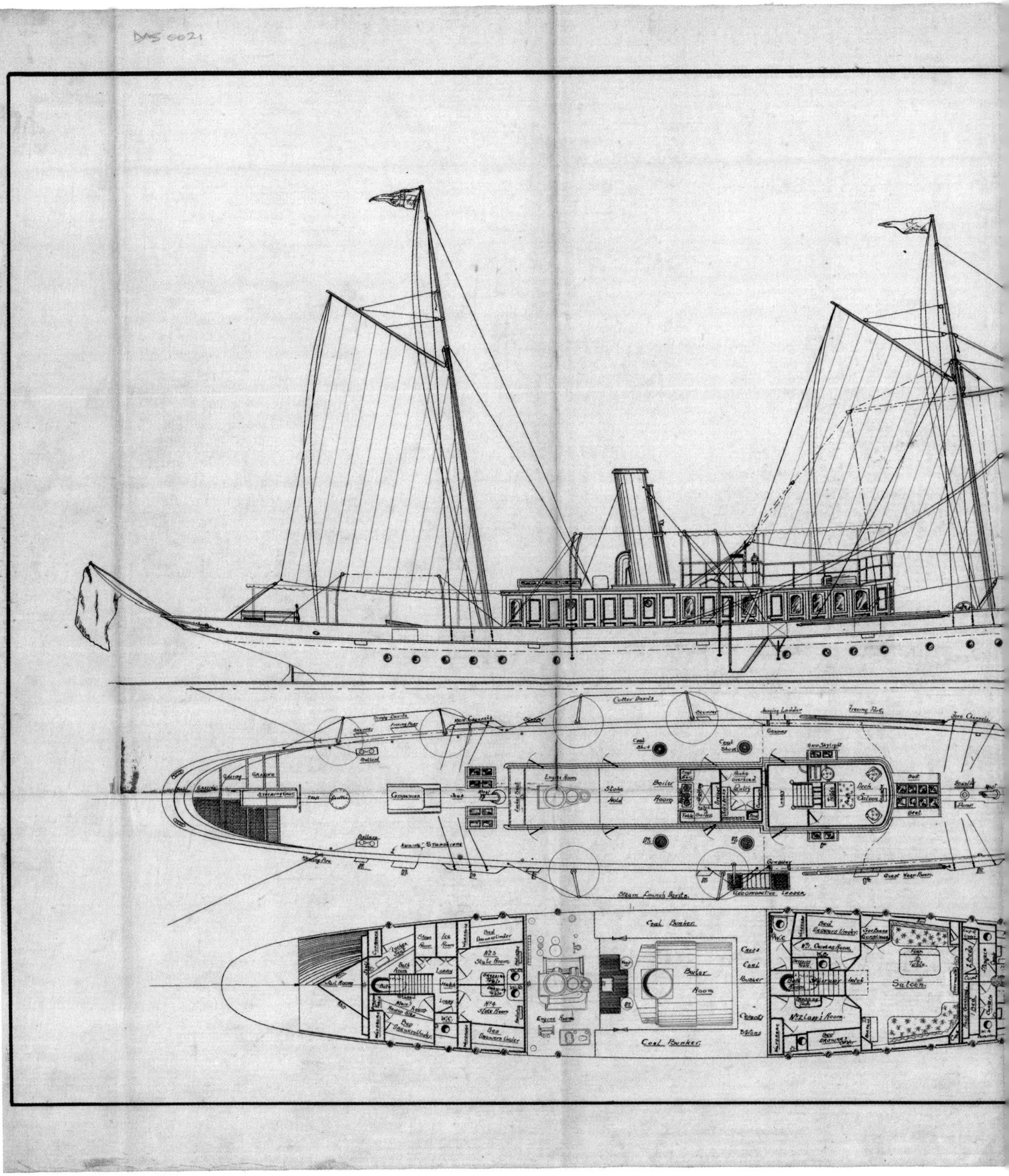
Cutter Davits
Steam Launch Davits
Companion
Engine Room
Boiler Room
Coal Bunker
Saloon
Coal Bunker

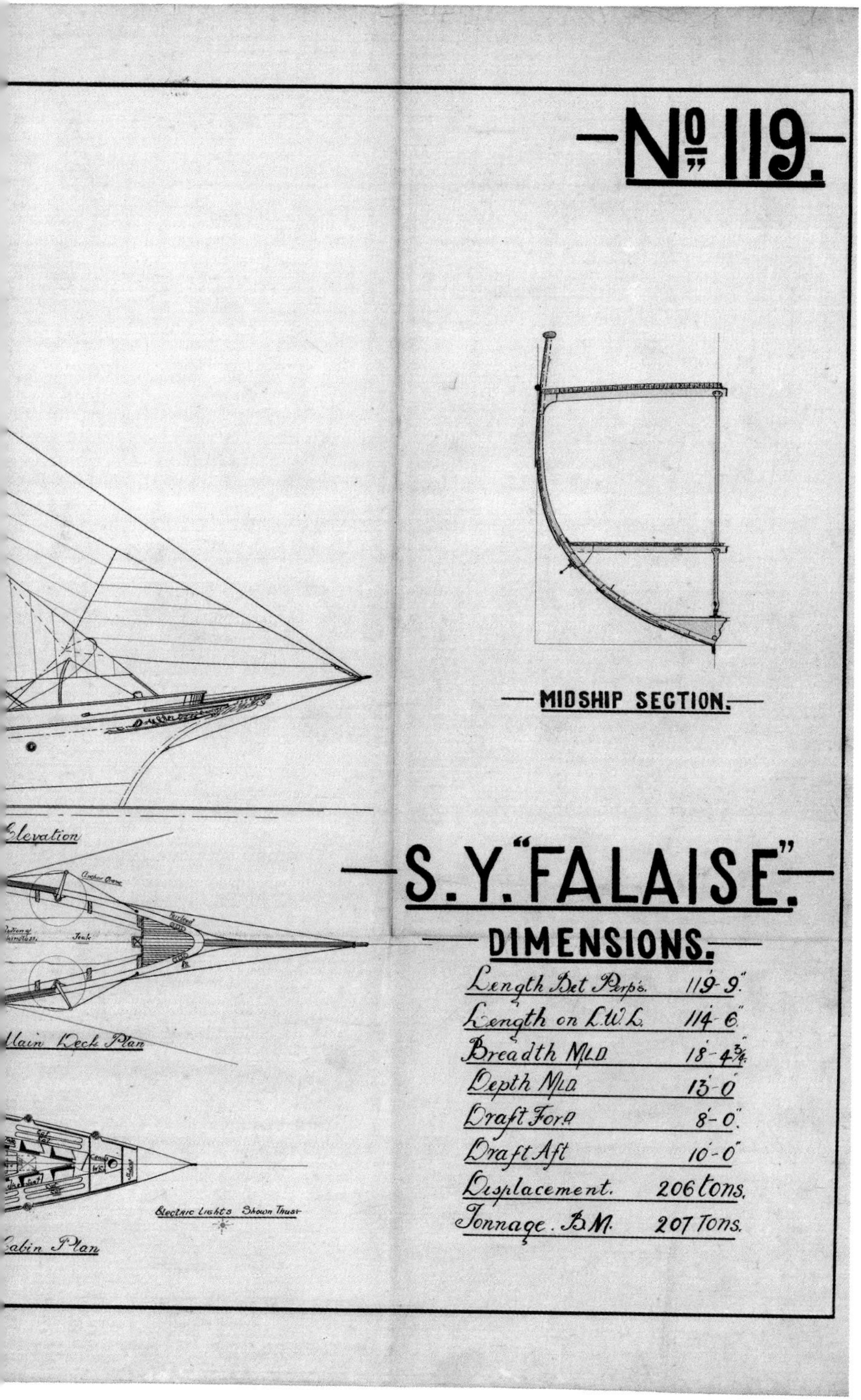

The plan of the steam yacht *Falaise* (1899) built by Day Summers and Co. of Southampton for Forrester Britten JP. *(© National Maritime Museum M1665)*

— No 221. —
— S.Y. "VENETIA". —
SCALE 1/16 IN = ONE FOOT
SAIL ROOM
OFFICERS ACCOMMODATION
DRAWING ROOM
ENGINE CASING
ENGINE ROOM
SHAFT TUNNEL
BOILER
CUTTER
DINGY
LAUNCH
GIG
FUNNEL
CASING
TABLE
DRAWING ROOM
ENGINE ROOM
COAL BUNKER
BOILER ROOM
PASSAGE
PANTRY

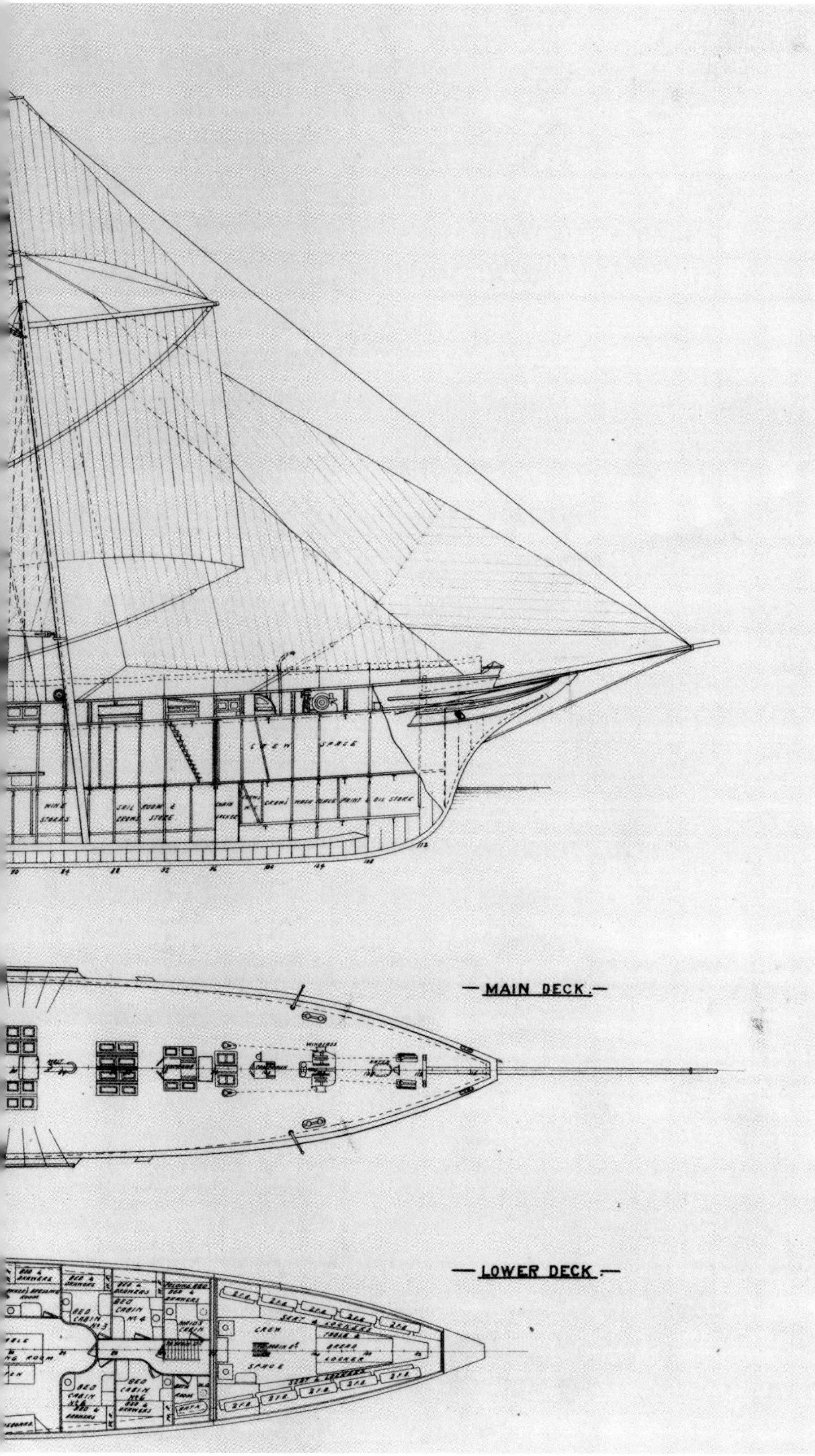

Designed by W C Storey and constructed by proto-Vickers, *Venetia* (1893) was renamed *North Star II* in 1902 and served under that name in the war. Here we see the inboard profile and decks. *(© National Maritime Museum M4057)*

No 423
CENERAL ARRANCEMEN
STEEL SCREW YACHT
SCALE 1/4" = 1 FT
DIMENSIONS
LENGTH W.L. 108'-0"
BREADTH MLD 18'-6"
DEPTH MLD 11'-3"
DRAFT FORD 7'-9"
" AFT 9'-3"
TONNAGE Y.M. 137·935
" B.M. 147·493
20-0' CUTTER
SAIL ROOM
COCKPIT
SALOON
W.C.
STATE ROOM
ENGINE ROOM
ENGINE ROOM SKYLIGHT
COAL BUNKER
PASSAGE
STORE

Branwen was a Thornycroft-built steam yacht of 131grt, launched in 1905 for Royal Yacht Squadron member Lord Howard de Walden, noted in Chapter 3. It was the first vessel built at Thornycroft's new Woolston yard. She was taken up by the Admiralty at the beginning of 1915 and described as a 'special service vessel', which usually meant Q-ship. Armed with two 6pdrs, she was based at Oban until the end of 1916 but was paid off in March the following year, and then purchased by another RYS member, Arthur Salvin Bowlby of Gilston Park, Essex, who served as High Sheriff of Hertfordshire in 1908. 'His interests were music, playing the organ and piano, country life, namely hunting, shooting, fishing and farming, and yachts,' according to the De Laszlo Archive Trust. *Branwen*'s profile and deck plans are seen here. *(© National Maritime Museum M4058)*

SOURCES

The following abbreviations will be used for brevity.

Collections

IWM Imperial War Museum, London
TNA National Archives, Kew
CAC Churchill Archive, Churchill College, Cambridge
BL British Library, London
LC Liddell Collection, Special Collections Unit, University of Leeds
NMI Nottage Maritime Institute

It is the convention that page numbers be given for citations. This is not always possible in the modern world. Some digitised documents lack page numbering and some archives hold unnumbered single or multiple sheets in bundles under one reference or none at all. Thus, page numbers will be given where possible but the reader will understand that they are not always available or, indeed necessary.

Chapter 1

1. McGreevy, *Great Hatred*, p.263
2. Dalton, *British Royal Yachts*, p.134
3. QV Journal, 15 July 1845, p.18
4. *Spectator*, 10 August 1889
5. Penrose-Fitzgerald, *From Sail to Steam*, p.172
6. The author is grateful to Peter Jones, *Spectator*, 21 May 2022, for the information
7. Hofman, *The Steam Yachts*, p.3
8. Ibid.
9. Sennett, Oram, *The Marine Steam Engine*, Ch. 1
10. Ibid.
11. *New York Times*, 28 April 1900
12. *San Francisco Call*, 24 June 1900
13. Ibid.
14. *New York Times*, 26 August 1893
15. *Sheffield and Rotherham Independent*, 20 November 1896
16. Hofman, *The Steam Yachts*, p.4
17. *The Marine Engineer*, 1 May 1886
18. Couling, *Steam Yachts*, p.9
19. Hofman, *The Steam Yachts*, p.7
20. *The Scotsman*, 23 April 1902
21. *Time*, 19 April 1926
22. Ibid.
23. Ibid.

Chapter 2

1. O'Toole, *The Spanish War*, p.44
2. Pedisich, *Congress Buys a Navy*, pp.114–115
3. Roosevelt, *An Autobiography*, pp.220–221
4. Silverstone, *US Warships*, p.169ff
5. O'Toole, *The Spanish War*, p.200
6. Hofman, *The Steam Yachts*, p.67
7. Quoted in Goldman, *American Yachts*, p.83

Chapter 3

1. O'Toole, *The Spanish War*, p.378
2. Bacon, *The Dover Patrol*, vol. 1, p.74
3. Info; author and *The Times*, 11 July 1914
4. CHAR 13/46/77-78, CAC
5. CHAR 13/46/48, CAC
6. Docs 12189, IWM
7. Keble Chatterton, *Auxiliary Patrol*, pp.23–24
8. *British Journal of Nursing*, 21 November 1914, p.404
9. *Hansard*, Volume 109: 5 August 1918
10. CHAR 13/51/53-53, CAC
11. CHAR 13/51/52-53, CAC
12. CHAR 13/51/23-28, CAC
13. Keble Chatterton, *The Auxiliary Patrol*, p.24
14. *Yachting Monthly*, March 1916
15. Docs 1364, IWM
16. Keble Chatterton, *The Auxiliary Patrol*, p.24
17. Ibid., p.63
18. Author's estimates for November 1918 based on Dittmar and Colledge, *British Warships*, p.149ff
19. Keble Chatterton, *The Auxiliary Patrol*, p.24
20. Hubbard, *On the Coast of France*, Ch. 4

Chapter 4

1. Scott, *Fifty Years in the Royal Navy*, p.286
2. Ibid., p.287
3. *London Gazette*, 29668, 14 July 1916

4. ADM 240/52/231, TNA
5. *The Engineer*, 7 November 1913
6. ADM 337/119/164, TNA
7. Bacon, *The Dover Patrol*, Vol. 2, p.430
8. *London Gazette*, 30833, 6 August 1918
9. *London Gazette*, 32169, 21 December 1920
10. ADM 137/2637, TNA
11. *The Sphere*, 23 July 1910
12. Ibid.
13. Docs 19003, IWM
14. WO 95/5302, TNA
15. ADM 53-69170, TNA

Chapter 5

1. ADM 196/39/510, TNA
2. *Suffolk Gazette*, 13 March 1917
3. *London Gazette*, 11 January 1916, Admiral Bacon's despatch of 3 December 1915
4. *Southport Visitor*, 30 September 1915
5. LIDDLE/RNMN/1983
6. Bacon, *The Dover Patrol*, Vol. 1, p.127
7. *Suffolk Gazette*, 13 March 1917
8. *London Gazette*, 28906, 18 September 1914
9. 29 Sept 1914, docs 7907, IWM
10. Ibid., 2 Oct 1914
11. Ibid., 6 Oct 1914
12. Ibid.
13. Ibid., 2 Oct 1914
14. Ibid., 13 Oct 1914
15. Chatterton, *Auxiliary Patrol*, p.54
16. *London Gazette*, 30111, I June 1917
17. Jellicoe, *The Crisis of the Naval War*, p.190
18. Hepper, *British Warship Losses*, p.56
19. https://southamptoncenotaph.com/william-henry-john-chaplow
20. Jones, *A Naval Life*, p.221
21. Ibid., p.227
22. *New York Times*, 14 December 1912
23. Jones, *A Naval Life*, pp.228–9
24. *The Times*, 23 September 1916
25. Ibid.
26. docs 11440, p.5, IWM
27. Ibid., pp.5–6
28. CHAR 13/62/15, CAC
29. Docs 11440, p.7, IWM
30. Ibid., p.8
31. Ibid., p.5
32. ADM 337/119/112, TNA
33. Supplement to the *London Gazette*, 11 June 1919
34. Docs 12189, p.29, p.40, IWM
35. Ibid., p.33
36. ADM 337/121/350, TNA
37. Ibid.
38. ADM 337/121/379, TNA
39. ADM 337/119/701, TNA
40. LIDDLE/WW1/RNMN/REC/015
41. Ibid.
42. Ibid.
43. Roskill, *Earl Beatty*, p.279

Chapter 6

1. ADM 1/8427/194, ADM 1/8427/206, TNA
2. ADM 137/3131, TNA
3. *Aberdeen Daily Journal*, 3 May 1916
4. Jellicoe, *The Crisis of the Naval War*, p.191
5. *Hansard*, HC Deb 24 January 1918 Vol. 101 cc1148–9
6. ADM 196/137/129, TNA
7. Ibid.
8. Ibid.
9. ADM 137/3808, TNA
10. *The Argus*, Melbourne, 20 December 1886
11. ADM 156/112, TNA
12. *Die Jungfrau von Orleans*, Act II, Scene 4
13. ADM 240/15/199, TNA
14. ADM 116/1869, TNA
15. Hepper, *British Warship Losses*, p.147
16. *Hansard*, HC Deb 12 March 1919 Vol. 113 c12601260
17. ADM 53-62866, TNA
18. Ibid.

Chapter 7

1. Jellicoe, *Crisis*, p.153
2. Nutting, *Cinderellas of the Fleet*, p.57
3. Sims, *The Victory at Sea*, pp.38–39
4. Jellicoe, *Crisis*, p.155
5. *International Marine Engineering*, Vol. 22, July 1917, p.286
6. Quoted in Goldman, *American Yachts*, p.86
7. Sims, *The Victory at Sea*, p.301
8. Daniels to Sims, 15 December 1917, Box 23, Sims Papers, Manuscript Division, Library of Congress, Washington, DC
9. Quoted in Havern, *Ensuring the Lifeline to Victory*, p.42
10. Sims, *The Victory at Sea*, p.301
11. Havern, *Ensuring the Lifeline to Victory*, p.44
12. Blazich, *United States Navy and World War I*, p.21
13. Sims, *The Victory at Sea*, p.301

14. Quoted in Rose, *America's Sailors*, p.58
15. US History and Heritage Command 'Aloha'

Chapter 8

1. Rose, *America's Sailors*, p.63
2. Husband, *On the Coast of France*, Ch. 4
3. *The Washington Herald*, 4 January 1918
4. *New York Sun*, 4 January 1918
5. Husband, *On the Coast of France*, Ch. 4
6. *The Pensacola Journal*, Thursday, 17 January 1918
7. *New York Tribune*, 19 May 1918
8. Sims, *Victory at Sea*, p.128
9. Ibid.
10. Medal of Honor [*sic*], 1861–1949, The Navy, p.125
11. Naval History and Heritage Command, Christabel SP-162
12. Hall of Valor [*sic*] Project
13. https://valor.militarytimes.com/hero/9172
14. Wilson, *An Account of the Operations of the American Navy in France During the War With Germany*, US Naval History and Heritage Command

Chapter 9

1. Woodrow Wilson, Message to 63rd Congress, Senate Doc No. 566, 1914, pp.3–4
2. Hadley, Sarty, *Tin Pots and Pirate Ships*, pp.119–122
3. Fayle, *Seaborne Trade*, Vol. III, p.465
4. Tennyson, Sarty, *Sydney, Nova Scotia and the U-Boat War*, 1918, p.1
5. Ibid.
6. Australian National Maritime Museum
7. Australian Naval Historical Review, March 2015
8. Docs 12189, IWM

Chapter 10

1. Letter 16 February 1915, NMI/Wivenhoe History
2. Letter to brother Noel, 2 April 1915, ibid.
3. Letter to brother Noel, 12 October 1915, ibid.
4. Letter 21 December 1915, ibid
5. NMI/Wivenhoe History
6. ADM53/34372, TNA
7. Docs 12189, p.42, IWM
8. LIDDLE/WW1/RNMN/REC/015
9. Ibid.
10. Husband, *On the Coast of France*, Ch. 4
11. Ibid.
12. Ibid.
13. Docs 12189, p.43, IWM
14. Ibid, p.35
15. Ibid.
16. Ibid, p.40
17. All log citations from ADM 53/34373, TNA
18. 6 October 1917, docs 19003, IWM
19. Quoted in Rose, *American Sailors*, p.184
20. NMI/Wivenhoe History
21. *Weston-Super-Mare Gazette*, 8 June 1929
22. *Spectator*, 14 September 1918
23. Wilson, *Account of the Operations of the American Navy in France During the War With Germany*, p.170
24. Ibid
25. Ibid, pp.172–3
26. Rose, *American Sailors*, p.67
27. Wheatley, *The Time Has Come*, p.152
28. Lewis-Stempel, *Six Weeks*, p.254
29. WO 32/11404, NA
30. Hansard, HC Deb 15 April 1919 Vol. 114 cc2728-30W
31. Ibid.
32. Ibid.
33. Hansard, HC Deb 06 June 1919 Vol. 116 cc2413-42413
34. Ibid.

Chapter 11

1. Vigo, *Naval Strategy and Operations in Narrow Seas*, p.187
2. Hansard, HL Deb 29 October 1917 Vol. 26 cc801-34
3. Offer, *An Agrarian Interpretation*, p.93
4. Ibid., p.114
5. Lewis-Stempel, *Six Weeks*, p.34
6. Winter, *Death's Men*, pp.98–9
7. Mary Countess of Wemyss, *A Family Record*, p.235
8. Cannadine, *Decline and Fall of the British Aristocracy*, p.81
9. Ibid., p.87
10. Hansard, HC Deb 25 February 1919 Vol. 112 cc1592–3
11. Hansard, HC Deb 30 July 1919 Vol. 118 c2122W

Envoi

1. Quoted in Rose, *American Sailors*, p.38
2. Docs 19003, IWM
3. Hughes-Hallett, *The Pike*, p.97
4. Crawford, *Fallen Glory*, p.84
5. Friedman, *British Naval Weapons of WW2*, Vol. II, p.10

BIBLIOGRAPHY

The following resources have been cited in the text.

Primary Sources

Various files as referenced in the ADM and WO series, The National Archives, Kew

Various files as referenced in the CHAR 13 series, Churchill Archive, Churchill College, Cambridge

Private Papers of Admiral A Paget, Documents 7907, Imperial War Museum, London

Private Papers of Commander F F Tower, Documents 11440, Imperial War Museum

Private Papers of Lieutenant Commander C E Evans, Documents 12189, Imperial War Museum

Private Papers of J G Sadd, Documents 19003, Imperial War Museum

Private Papers of J E Attrill, Documents 1364, Imperial War Museum

Oral history, Harry Chadwick-Smith, LIDDLE/WW1/RNMN/REC/015, Liddle Collection, Brotherton Library, University of Leeds

Memorials of Sub Lieutenant Norman Middleton, LIDDLE/RNMN/1983, Liddle Collection

Documents held by the US Naval History and Heritage Command, as referenced

Letters of Captain Ernest Brady, Nottage Maritime Institute/Wivenhoe History

Personal Log of Commander Leonard Cockrell, Nottage Maritime Institute/Wivenhoe History

Sims Papers, Manuscript Division, Library of Congress, Washington DC

Secondary sources

Books

The place of publishing is London, unless otherwise stated.

Bacon R, *The Dover Patrol*, two volumes, George H Doran and Co. (New York, 1919)

Cannadine D, *The Decline and Fall of the British Aristocracy*, Papermac (1996)

Chatterton E, *The Auxiliary Patrol*, Sidgwick and Jackson (1923)

Chaneles S, *The New Civility*, Grossman (USA, 1973)

Couling D, *Steam Yachts*, B T Batsford Ltd (1980)

Crawford J, *Fallen Glory*, Old St Publishing (2016)

Dalton T, *British Royal Yachts*, Halsgrove (Tiverton, 2002)

Ditmar F, Colledge J, *British Warships 1914–1919*, Ian Allan (1972)

Fayle C, *Seaborne Trade*, Vol. III, Naval and Military Press (Sussex, undated)

Friedman N, *British Naval Weapons of World War 2*, Vol. II, Seaforth Publishing (Barnsley, 2019)

Goldman K, *American Yachts in Naval Service*, McFarland and Co. (Jefferson, NC, 2021)

Havern (Snr) C, *Ensuring the Lifeline to Victory*, Naval History and Heritage Command (Department of the Navy, Washington, DC, 2020)

Hepper, *British Warship Losses in the Ironclad Era,* Chatham Publishing (2006)

Hofman E, *The Steam Yachts*, Nautical Publishing Company (Lymington, 1970)

Hughes-Hallett L, *The Pike*, Fourth Estate (2013)

Husband J, *On the Coast of France*, A C McClurg and Co. (Chicago, 1919)

Jellicoe J, *The Crisis of the Naval War*, George H Doran Company (New York, 1920)

Jones M, *A Naval Life*, Persona Press (Dulverton, 2007)

Lewis-Stempel J, *Six Weeks*, Weidenfeld and Nicholson (2010)

McGreevy R, *The Great Hatred*, Faber and Faber (2022)

Mooney J, *Dictionary of American Naval Fighting Ships*, Navy Dept., Office of the Chief of Naval Operations, Naval History Division (Washington 1959–1981)

Nutting W, *The Cinderellas of the Fleet*, Standard Motor Construction Co. (Jersey City, 1920)

Offer A, *The First World War: An Agrarian Interpretation*, Clarendon Press (Oxford, 1991)
O'Toole G, *The Spanish War*, WW Norton and Co. (New York, 1984)
Pedisich P, *Congress Buys a Navy*, Naval Institute Press (Annapolis, 2016)
Penrose-Fitzgerald C, *From Sail to Steam*, Edward Arnold (1916)
Ring J, *Erskine Childers*, John Murray (1997)
Roberts A, *The Chief*, Simon & Schuster (2022)
Rose L, *America's Sailors in the Great War*, University of Missouri Press (Columbia, 2017)
Roskill S, *Earl Beatty*, William Collins, Sons and Co. (1980)
Roosevelt T, *An Autobiography,* The MacMillan Company (New York, 1913)
Sennett R, Oram H, *The Marine Steam Engine*, Longmans Green and Co. (1899)
Scott P, *50 Years in the Royal Navy*, John Murray (1919)
Silverstone P, *US Warships of World War 1*, Ian Allen (1970)
Sims W, *Victory at Sea*, John Murray (1920)
Sullivan E *et al*, *The Rich Man's Sport*, Badminton Library of Sports and Pastimes (1894)
Vigo M, *Naval Strategy and Operations in Narrow Seas*, Frank Cass (1999)
Wemyss M, *A Family Record*, The Curwen Press (1932)
Wheatley D, *The Time Has Come; Officer and Temporary Gentleman*, Hutchinson (1978)
Winter D, *Death's Men*, Allen Lane (1978)

Newspapers and Magazines

British Journal of Nursing
Daily Telegraph
International Marine Engineering
London Gazette
Naval Historical Review, Australia
New York Sun
New York Times
New York Tribune
Pensacola Journal
San Francisco Call
Sheffield and Rotherham Independent
Southport Visitor
Suffolk Gazette
The Engineer
The Marine Engineer
The Scotsman
The Spectator
The Sphere
The Times
Time Magazine
Washington Herald
Weston-Super-Mare Gazette
Yachting Monthly

Online resources

Queen Victoria's Journal, Royal Archives, online
https://southamptoncenotaph.com/william-henry-john-chaplow
Blazich (Jnr) F, *United States Navy and World War 1 1914–1922* (online at US Naval History and Heritage Command)
Woodrow Wilson's Message to the 63rd Congress
Gunfleet.net
Wivenhoehistory.org.uk

Other

Australian Maritime Museum
British Vessels Lost at Sea 1914–1918 and 1939–1945, Patrick Stephens (1988)
De Laszlo Archive Trust
Hansard
Lloyd's Register of Yachts, various years
Medal of Honor [*sic*], 1861–1949, The Navy
Schiller F, *Die Jungfrau von Orleans* (The Maid of Orleans) (1801), Act II, Scene 4
Tennyson B, Sarty R, *Sydney, Nova Scotia and the U-Boat War, 1918*, (Canadian Military History 7, 1,1998)
Wilson H, *An Account of the Operations of the American Navy in France During the War With Germany*, US Naval History and Heritage Command

INDEX